Pushing the Envelope

Dennis J. Lyons

This book is dedicated to my father, The Old Bean.

CONTENTS

Forward

This compilation of stories was written to give a perspective of some of the inner workings, or a behind the scenes look at the United States Postal Service and its workers, the rank and file employees and executives alike. During my time of employment with the Postal Service, which spanned more than 30 years, I always felt a great sense of pride working for the company. Over the years, I would get strange looks from people when I referred to the Postal Service as a company or spoke of it as being on par with other businesses. That's just what it is, a large company. A business that employs hundreds of thousands of employees to push the envelope, the package or whatever piece of mail has been entrusted to it.

I felt that pride when I was a carrier, delivering mail daily to my group of customers. Some of those customers looked forward to their delivery time as their favorite time of the day. That usually had nothing to do with me personally, but it was the anticipation of what would arrive each day. I also felt a great sense of pride and accomplishment in having made it to almost the highest grade of Executive and Administrative Schedule employees (EAS).

Though I did fall short of reaching the Executive level within the Postal Service, reaching EAS 25 with EAS 26 being the top numbered grade, my accomplishment of rising to the rank that I did was noteworthy. I successfully competed against individuals with Bachelors, Masters and Doctorate degrees, while never having obtained any college degree.

A few of the chapters within this book are quite long due to the amount of subject matter that is covered.

The following email address can be used by anyone who wishes to contact me for any reason.

pushing_theenvelope@yahoo.com

DISCLAIMER: This compilation of stories is based on personal experiences I had during my years as an employee of the United States Postal Service. They reflect processes and regulations that were in place during the time of my employment. I am unaware of any subsequent changes that may have occurred since my retirement.

CHAPTER ONE: HIRING AND CAREER ADVANCEMENT

I applied for my first position as a letter carrier one month after my 18th birthday. I had only attended one year of high school, with too many of my younger years spent pursuing the wrong things. My father was retired from our local Police Department, and he decided to accompany a friend of mine and me to apply and take the test as well. My father and my friend did not score well on the test, but I achieved a high enough score to warrant consideration by a few different Post Offices in my area, including the office that delivered mail to my father's house, where I was living at that time.

I can't pretend to know how the hiring process worked way back then, but I wanted that job and I began to aggressively pursue it. I started to make phone calls to a Supervisor named Jim at my local office. Once I had made a contact with him, I would call and ask for him every week or two. I would call and repeatedly ask if any jobs had opened. I'm sure that Jim was irritated by my continual calling, but I wanted a job with the Postal Service. After weeks of calling him, Jim finally told me to come in for a job. I do know that it would not be possible today to get hired for a job by simply calling and bothering someone at a Post Office today.

I spent a little more than 3 years working for my local Post Office. I reached the point where I had my own regular delivery route, then began to get bored with the job. I was young and admittedly foolish. I was still living at my father's house at that time with younger siblings. I made the decision to resign from my carrier job, to give up all the benefits and job security that I had no real appreciation for at that time. I had tested for and received my GED in lieu of graduating from high school. I enrolled in classes at my local Community College, with the intent of pursuing a career in Computer Programming. After just a few Quarters of classes, I decided that I was not really interested in the commitment to detail required in that field.

At the time that I had resigned from the Postal Service, it was during the month of July, halfway through the year. I was earning 4 weeks of annual leave (AL) at that time, and I had taken vacation time during the month of April off to go on a road trip with friends. Full Time Regular Postal employees were advanced the leave that they were entitled to for the year at the beginning of each new year. Because I had resigned halfway through the year, I had only earned 2 of the 4 weeks of AL for which I received pay. I was sent a few bills attempting to collect the 2 weeks of pay after I resigned. I didn't have any income or money saved at the time, so I ignored the notices and they stopped coming after a while. I did keep in touch with a few of the carriers that I had worked with when I was employed at that local Post Office.

A few years after I had resigned, one of my carrier friends told me that the Postal Service was sending out checks for the incremental hours that carriers had been working past their 8-hour day. I don't recall if that was due to a lawsuit being filed or a union grievance that had been won, or what exactly prompted the payouts. I was told that it had gone back over the time that I had been working, and that I should be getting a check as well. I received a notice in the mail telling me how much money I would be receiving, and it was more than a few thousand dollars. I was looking forward to the check arriving because I needed it. When the check did arrive, it showed a deduction for the 2 weeks of vacation time I owed when I resigned. Just like an elephant, the Postal Service never forgets.

I spent the next few years working menial jobs. I met my wife and we had our first child while I was working one of those menial jobs where there weren't any real benefits. The Health Insurance that I had provided very lame coverage, and we were struggling to get by. I finally woke up and decided that it was time for this prodigal son to try to return home to the Postal Service. I sent out letters to several offices seeking a reinstatement, and finally was able to find an office not too far from our home that took me back in as a Part Time Flexible (PTF) Carrier, starting over.

When I had resigned a few years earlier, I had cashed out my retirement fund. I would regret that many years later, when I finally did retire. If I wanted to have the 3 and a half years that I worked before I resigned applied to my years of service, I would have to buy them back. It would have resulted in a greater amount of pension money I would receive, but I opted not to pay back the amount that was required to get those years back. A smaller pension, but still a nice one.

We purchased our first home, and I was painting houses on the side when the weather permitted. I considered going back to school while working my carrier job, to pursue a degree that might open other doors for me to provide for my family. I signed up for a few classes, but it didn't take long for me to deduce that this path would be a long one, with no assurance that I would be able to achieve the desired outcome or, more specifically, the desired increased income. I decided that my best course of action would be to pursue advancement within the Postal Service. That turned out to be a good choice.

My initial interest was to attempt to secure a job with the United States Postal Inspection Service. As I investigated it, I found that one of the requirements of being hired for a job with that branch was to have a minimum of a bachelor's degree and to be under the age of 35. I did not have any type of college degree, not even an associate degree. I could do the math to realize that at my age, 32 at that time, I would not be able to achieve a bachelor's degree before turning 35. Working full time as a carrier, and at this point having two small children at home, I knew that this endeavor would be too much for me to achieve. I instead opted to pursue a career in operations management within the Postal Service organization.

I approached my immediate Supervisor to let him know I was interested in becoming an Acting Supervisor. The Postal Service refers to craft workers (carriers, clerks, mail handlers, custodians) who served as Acting Supervisors as 204B's. That title had been in place for years, in the longstanding tradition of using acronyms and numbers to define Postal things and even workers. 204B's were almost always in shortage, and someone needed to do the job of filling in for the titled Supervisors when they went on vacation, out on a detail at another location, when they were sick or there was just a vacancy. One of the main reasons there was a shortage of willing 204B's was the fact that you could be working with your fellow employees as a peer one day, and in the position of giving them instructions the next day. That could often result in animosity against the 204B, especially among the union officials in an office and the management haters in general. It was often not a very popular place to be, but I wasn't in it for the friends. I was in it for the career advancement and the money that came with it.

I received on the job supervisory training from the two titled Supervisors at my office. Tim was one of the titled Supervisors at that Post Office. He did not have very good customer service skills with the employees there. In my role as a carrier, I thought that he was much too intense with the carriers in the office. On many occasions, carriers would be doing their jobs, talking with each other and joking around as they were working. He would often pipe up and say, in a serious tone, "There's too much jocularity going on in here." Tim was very excited when he was notified that he was being promoted to a higher-level position in another Post Office. From what I heard over the years that followed, his career didn't go exactly as he had planned it. When he left, I didn't have further contact with him until years later. My immediate Supervisor at that office, Andy, was much more attentive and helpful to me as I worked towards advancing my career.

There were a variety of forms that had to be completed daily, in addition to assuring that all the mail in the carrier unit was delivered as efficiently as possible and the collections were completed in a timely manner. I began to send applications out and received interviews for vacant Supervisor jobs. The process in place for Postal Service employees to apply for internal positions has improved immensely over the years. At that point in my career, the application process was using a typewriter to fill in a paper application that was several pages long for each position. Yes, this was back in the Stone Age. And to add to my woes, I did not have a typewriter at that time. I would leave my carrier job at the end of my workday to go to the local library, hoping that the typewriters they had for use by their members were not all being used.

I distinctly recall my first interview for a vacant Supervisor position. The Review Board of 3 who took turns asking me questions was headed by a Postmaster of a neighboring office. His name was George, and he was a very intense and intimidating man in his demeanor and in his questioning. I left the interview in a literal sweat. I bought a mini cassette recorder after that, recording a list of all the numbered forms and terms related to the Supervisor job. I would listen to the recording on my way to interviews, until I was finally promoted to my first job as a Supervisor after several interviews.

The job was in a neighboring Post Office, where I would eventually become the Postmaster. I took no small sense of pride in my career accomplishments. I eventually passed up the Supervisors who had trained me as a 204B, and the Postmaster, George, who had given me the sweats in that first interview with his intense, intimidating demeanor. I shared the story with George at a meeting years later, when I became a level 24 Postmaster and he was a level 22 Postmaster. He didn't specifically recall the situation, but it was good for a laugh when I gave him my perspective of that interview and his intensity.

One of the things that I loved about working for the Postal

Service was all the many possibilities for career advancement. As a career employee working in any craft, there were always new opportunities that were posted, or available to be viewed online for entry level management positions. Typically, an entry level management position meant a front-line Supervisor job over a group of employees. Most often, applications for those jobs were restricted to career employees within a certain geographic area. Occasionally, those entry level management jobs were made available to employees within a much wider geographic area. That would generally occur if there were a limited number of qualified individuals for a specific vacancy within proximity to the job location. I recall seeing a nationwide posting for Supervisor jobs in Alaska years ago. The salary range was posted and included a 10% cost of living increase for a move to the area. Tempting… Over the years, I was intrigued by the variety of positions I would see available in Hawaii, Puerto Rico and other United States territories. The main thing that kept me from going for any of those vacancies was the distance from family back in the states.

When I interviewed for the Supervisor job that I ultimately received, I was surprised that the interviewing Manager at that office had the President of the office's carrier union sit in. The union leader even asked me a few questions during the interview. It did make me wonder who the ultimate decision makers were at that office. Would I have gotten that job if the union leader at that office didn't like me? Beyond the hiring of Supervisors involvement, it made me wonder just how much power this local union branch had within that office. I would be shocked to find out, in due time, just how much power had been given over to the local unions from the managers within the office.

Following my interview with the Delivery Manager and the union President, I was brought to the Operations Manager of that Post Office to speak with him. He asked me some questions after introductions were made. He was friendly during our banter, but I was nervous because of the high level that he held at that office. Eventually, he asked me if I knew what a specific manual number was. I do not remember that manual number now, though I did ultimately learn it and its contents well. I told him I did not know. He reached over to the corner of his desk and picked up the contract between the Postal Service and the carrier union. He held it up and said, "You'd better get to know what this is, if you get the job." That did make me sweat wondering if I would get the job, but I did receive a phone call within a week advising me that the job was mine.

My first responsibility I was given when I started my job at that office was as the Supervisor of the Routers. I had never heard of Routers prior to this, so I trained for a few days with the 204B who had been covering that assignment until it could be officially filled by the successful applicant, me. Routers were carriers who were assigned to sort mail on routes in the late afternoons and into the evening. Each Router had a group of routes they were assigned to work on each day. They sorted the bulk mail, or Standard Mail that was either left behind by the regular carrier who delivered the mail or was sorted to each carrier route for the next day's delivery while the carriers were out delivering mail. The Router program was put into place to assist regular carrier routes that were overburdened, requiring more than 8 hours of work each day to sort and deliver the total volume of the regular carrier's mail for their route. The Router program was designed to provide assistance to carriers until anticipated technology improvements would reduce the carrier workload through automation.

I spent my first several months at that job supervising the Router crew. I let my Manager know that it was my desire to move into a position of supervising the regular carriers who actually delivered the mail. That would not only enable me to learn the more traditional aspects of delivery and collections, but it would also enable me to work a day shift instead of evenings with the Routers. There were four Delivery Supervisors at the office at that time. Each Supervisor was assigned to the group of carriers who delivered mail to a specific Zip Code, or Unit, within that city. Those Supervisors each had Sunday and a different weekday assigned as their non-scheduled workdays (NS days, in Postal Service vernacular). I began to fill in for the different Unit Supervisors on their weekly NS days. No Supervisors were assigned to work on Sundays at that time.

I was able to be assigned to a Unit of my own when the assigned Supervisor left to take a position at a different Post Office. There was typically a high turnover of Supervisors at busy, larger Post Offices such as this one. The Supervisors workload was high, and the job was fast-paced and demanding. There was constant pressure to achieve and exceed a variety of goals each day. The Postal Service has always been a very numbers-driven organization, and that pressure would often compel Supervisors to seek transfers to smaller, less demanding Post Offices if they were unable to get promoted to higher positions they may have been seeking. Personally, I enjoyed that fast paced environment. I considered my job to be a good training ground that would enable me to learn everything I could about the Postal Service, assisting me in my desired move upwards in the organization.

During my Supervisor tenure at that Post Office, I worked for the Postmaster who was a very gruff individual. Ken was a Vietnam War Veteran and he ran a tight ship at that office. He was a very heavy smoker, and it was difficult on him when it was announced that all Postal facilities were going to be smoke-free environments. It was just as difficult on those of us in his staff. I remember spending time on hot, humid days and on freezing cold days having to accompany Ken outside the building for meetings. That enabled him to light up while talking to me individually, or to a group of us. I was at least thankful that there was a roof over our heads, as we would meet in the wide-open garage where the Postal carrier vehicles were parked.

Ken's intensity was exemplified one morning when he called all his staff into his office for a meeting. He informed us that one of our Rural Route carriers was out delivering mail until 10 p.m. the night before. When she came back to the office, it was all locked up and nobody was there. The Supervisor who was responsible for closing operations for the day apparently did not realize that there was still one carrier who had not reported back in from delivery. That carrier was a Rural Carrier who had been delivering the mail in her own vehicle, which was a common occurrence at that time. When she returned and found the building locked up, she went home, taking the outgoing mail that she had collected throughout the day and accountable mail that she had in her vehicle with her. That meant the outgoing mail she had was delayed from being processed. He stood up at his desk as he railed at all of us, throwing his keys very hard onto the top of the desk. His face was red, and he was literally yelling at us, threatening that someone would be losing their job if something like this happened again before telling us to leave the office. Years later, when I sat at that same desk as the Postmaster, I remembered that event as I looked at the dent that was still there caused by his keys.

Ken could occasionally surprise me with an unpredictable response to a situation. One such situation occurred when I was dealing with a PTF Carrier we had hired who was near the end of his probationary term. I had been reviewing this carrier's performance records as he neared the end of his probation, and I decided that his work performance level was not up to par with what would be considered minimally acceptable. I brought him into an office for a private meeting to let him know that his employment was going to be terminated. His response to that news was unnerving to me. This carrier was a middle-aged man who was a Vietnam War Veteran, just like Ken. He sat in a chair

15

across the desk from me. His head was hanging down, slowly moving back and forth, and he was muttering about the bad experiences he had been going through in his life. He referred to the time he had spent in Vietnam, then lifted his head up to fixate his eyes on mine. "It looks like I've been killing the wrong people all these years" was what he said to me, with a sneer.

He was sitting between me and the door, and my first thought was that I should not have made the mistake of letting him sit between me and the exit. I slowly picked up the phone and dialed Ken's office number. He answered and I told him that I had a situation in progress that was going to need his attention. The carrier just sat in his chair glaring at me while I talked to Ken. I didn't want to tell Ken exactly what the carrier said to me while this carrier was sitting right across from me. I simply told Ken that this carrier was very upset about being terminated, and he needed to talk to someone other than me. Ken told me to bring the carrier to his office. I had the carrier wait outside Ken's office while I went in, closed the door and told Ken exactly what had been said to me. Ken invited the carrier into his office, and I left to go about my other business in the Post Office.

I had immersed myself into reviewing the performance numbers for the previous day's operations, and I was snapped out of it when I received a page over the intercom from Ken telling me to come to his office. I wasn't sure of what to expect as I walked to his office, but I was initially relieved to see that the carrier was gone. Ken told me to come in and shut the door behind me. I sat in a chair across from him and he told me to keep the carrier on the schedule to work. He said that we were going to keep the carrier on our employment rolls. He told me that the carrier had been going through a lot of rough times since returning from Vietnam, and he wanted to give him the opportunity to improve his life by keeping his job. I knew better than to try to argue with Ken based on the probation review criteria.

I left Ken's office feeling like the bus he had thrown me under was doing a slow roll over me. I felt that I had been physically threatened by this carrier, and by keeping him past his probationary term we were now going to have a much more difficult time dealing with him if his work performance level did not improve to acceptable levels. Considering how he had acted when I was talking to him, and the comment he had made about killing people, I felt that he was not in a good frame of mind. Then there was the probable impact to my credibility and my authority when news of this would ultimately end up being discussed by the other carriers. He was terminated several months later due to poor attendance, and fortunately there were no problems when his employment ended.

There was a competitive atmosphere between the Supervisors at that Post Office. There were 8 of us assigned to different positions of responsibility. Some just did the minimum to get by, and others wanted to excel, to move up the ladder to higher positions. And speaking of Excel, the newly released Microsoft Office products had not yet been made available to us at that time. There was a greater amount of competition between one of my peers and myself. I walked by his office one day and he was not in it. I was amazed by what I saw on his computer screen. Up to that point in time, I had grown accustomed to using ancient Lotus spreadsheets for tracking a variety of information. WordPerfect was the program that we used for letter writing. Perhaps I was living in a cave at the time, but I don't think I had even heard of these newfangled Microsoft programs or Windows. In the basement of my cave at my home, I had an old Commodore 64 computer that I played games on with my kids. I knew that I was looking at something new and exciting on that Supervisor's computer screen, and I wanted it.

I tracked down the Supervisor and asked him what he had on his computer. He told me all about the Microsoft Office products.

He told me that our District's Information Technology (IT) Department had sent him the disks to download on to his computer. I asked him for the disks, and he told me he had already returned them to the District. He had one of the newest computers in our Post Office, and he told me that my old computer probably didn't have enough space to download the programs onto it. Not a good answer. I contacted the District IT folks and asked them to send the disks out to me. They did, and I went through my computer deleting everything I possibly could to get the available space that my computer would need. I downloaded the software, with not a lot of room to spare. My work life was made a whole lot easier after that. Years later, I would be frustrated when I would work on a Microsoft Word document at home on my laptop, then email it or take it to work on a drive to use the document at work. The Postal Service's Microsoft Office programs were an older version and I could not open the documents created on my newer version at work. I had to save them as documents in the older format to be able to open them there.

I remember sitting in on several Labor/Management meetings during my time there. The Postmaster would be in attendance with several of his staff members, myself included. The letter carrier's union would have their local President in attendance along with several of their stewards. I found myself leaving those meetings frustrated over what my Postmaster would give away in concessions to the carrier's union. And how could he sit there and take the demeaning, sarcastic banter and sometimes abusive language that they threw at him during the meetings? It was beyond me. Those memories came back to me years later, when I found myself sitting in that same Postmaster's chair meeting with a younger, leaner and meaner group of local union leaders in my office. I had matured enough to know that I had to look at the big picture.

While I was still a Supervisor at that office, the Postal Service instituted a restructuring of jobs within Post Offices. That resulted in the elimination of two mid-level Management positions in my office, and the Supervisor grades were raised from EAS-15 to EAS-16. Under the new structure, that particular Post Office dropped from a level 24 to a level 22. The level 22 Manager, Customer Services position there was eliminated, along with the level 17 Manager of Delivery Services position. Because of the impact that this nationwide restructure was going to have on individuals in positions that were going to be eliminated, the Postal Service offered bonuses to affected individuals to get them off the employment rolls. There simply were not going to be enough jobs available to place the affected employees whose jobs were being eliminated. The level 22 Manager, Customer Services at that office ended up retiring and received 6 months of his salary as an incentive to do so with Voluntary Early Retirement (VER). The level 17 Manager, Delivery Services was too young to fall within the age and length of time in service within the company to take the VER offer. He ended up downgrading and filling a vacancy as a Delivery Supervisor, EAS-16 at a neighboring office.

The now level 22 Post Office where I worked was not impacted much beyond the loss of two mid-level management positions. Only a few of the craft employees who were near retirement took advantage of the VER and retired. That was going to put a lot of strain on Ken. As Postmaster, he was now expected to manage all the operations within his Post Office with the operations Supervisors reporting directly to him. That was a heavy workload, and he was not going to idly accept it. Even though the mid-level management positions were eliminated, Ken decided to build in some assistance in managing the operations rather than handling the workload himself. Since Delivery Operations was his largest operation, with five Supervisors and over 125 employees, he targeted that operation to make an internal change.

Ken had a few smoky meetings out in the garage with Bob, one of my peer Supervisors at that office. He then let all of us who reported to him know that Bob was going to be the "Lead" Delivery Supervisor at our office. Bob would direct the other four of us Delivery Supervisors in our day to day operations. He was at the same EAS-16 level as those of us who reported to him, and there was no way for Ken to give him any additional pay for his added responsibilities and authority. Bob knew that taking on this assignment would at least give him some positive narratives to add to his applications for future promotions.

After a short period of time in his new role of Lead Supervisor, Bob was getting a lot of pressure put on him from Ken. Delivery Operations performance numbers were not moving in the right direction fast enough, and the smoky garage meetings with Ken took a toll on Bob. He told Ken that he did not want to be the Lead Supervisor any longer, what I considered to be a bad career move on Bob's part. Ken then approached me with the offer of being assigned as the Lead Delivery Supervisor. I did have high career aspirations, and I readily accepted that offer. Bob returned to his role of supervising one of the Delivery Units in our office, and I moved into the office that he had briefly occupied.

There was a female Supervisor working there at that time who was well known to be a major pain in the butt. Extremely anal. She would argue with anyone about anything that she could during her workday. She would rigidly follow rules and regulations to the point of absurdity, letting everyone know if anyone was in violation of a rule. As the designated Lead Supervisor, when I would give her an instruction to do anything, she would most often look at me and say "You're the same level I am. I don't have to listen to you." She was, of course, technically correct. I would then have to call "dad", Postmaster Ken, for him to personally give her the instruction.

As the Lead Delivery Supervisor, my responsibilities now included overseeing all the Delivery and Collection Operations in my office and certain personnel actions as well. As I mentioned earlier, new employees went through a probationary period. It was important that detailed tracking of each employee's progress, or lack thereof, was accurately tracked on the appropriate forms. The Supervisors were often guilty of not accurately filling out the associated forms. They would be busy doing the other functions of their jobs each day, and they would lose track of the evaluation tracking dates of the new employees. Meetings were supposed to take place between a probationary employee and his or her Supervisor at the 30, 60- and 80-day marks after they have been hired. Additional training and counseling were provided to those employees who were lacking in certain areas. At each of those meetings, the responsible Supervisor was supposed to have a form filled out that highlights several relevant factors based on data relating to the employee. "Supposed to" are the operative words.

Even if they did complete the forms in a timely manner, they would frequently "rubber stamp" the list of skills that each new employee was held accountable to learning with increasing, measurable accuracy throughout the term of their probation. Too often, the Supervisor responsible for an employee's probationary period indicated on the tracking forms that they were demonstrating enough progress in their assigned duties throughout their probation. They would then sometimes come to me when the 90th day was rapidly approaching and say they did not want to keep that employee. I would wave the forms at them where they had indicated acceptable performance and tell them they already bought that employee.

Recognizing that we were picking up employees who were not able to adequately do their jobs, I put a calendar into place that I dedicated to the tracking of new employees. On it, the dates were tracked for each new employee, indicating the due dates for their steps in the probationary process. I would review their performance as each step of the 90-day process approached, then meet with the appropriate Supervisor to discuss their performance. I did not allow the Supervisors to meet with their probationary employees until they met with me first, and I had to challenge them about what they considered to be adequacy and what my interpretation was. After finally getting the Supervisors to accurately fill out the necessary forms in a timely manner, the probation process worked much more smoothly. Employees who learned the job well were retained. Employees who did not show that they could adapt to the demands of the job were let go.

Performing the duties of a Manager, without having the title, level or extra pay that accompanied the work I was doing began to frustrate me. I knew that the experience I was gaining was giving me the material necessary to enhance my job applications, and it was time to look for a promotion. There were many jobs that were being posted throughout the country for Remote Encoding Centers (RECs). These were new jobs in facilities that were typically leased. The work that was performed at them involved processing letter mail with addresses that the computers in Mail Processing Centers could not read. I didn't know much about this technology, but I assumed that not a lot of other people did either. The operational work associated with RECs will be covered in much more detail in the Operations and Automation chapter later in this book.

I sent in applications for several of these jobs, and I received a notice to report to a city about 4 hours away from me for an interview for one of them. To prepare for the interview, I contacted a higher-level Manager I knew and asked him to give me whatever information he could about this technology and these new jobs. I went to his office and he had a stack of paper about a foot tall for me. I studied through the documentation as best I could in the days leading up to my interview, and I had a lot to learn. I focused a lot of my attention on the terms and vernacular relative to REC operations, hoping to sound as intelligent as I could in my interview.

I met Ben, the Manager who was doing all the interviewing and hiring of the management staff that would be working at his new facility. Ben had already been the Manager of a REC that was opened in a different Area in the country. He applied for the Manager position at the new REC that was being scheduled to open in the Area where I was working at that time. The Executives at my Area office knew that they were getting an individual on board to open their first REC who had the experience in REC operations that few people had. The move to that new position enabled Ben to get a promotion and relocate to the location where he grew up and started his career, closer to family. The interview went well, and I received a phone call within a week from him, telling me that he was selecting me.

The promotion I received for my selection to that REC Operations Manager position moved me from my EAS 16 level to EAS 20. Moving up more than a level or two is not always a good career path. At that point in time, promotions typically meant an 8% increase in pay. Each level has a pay range built in, with a minimum and maximum salary range defined. Because of the number of levels I was moving up and their associated pay ranges, I was started at the minimum salary for the EAS 20 position. Greater increases in salary can be achieved through promotions to smaller incremental increases in levels, but I was thrilled to take what I was given. When the news of my promotion and my impending move circulated throughout the Post Office where I was serving as "Lead" Supervisor, I received a lot of congratulatory reactions from my coworkers and other employees there. My nemesis, the Supervisor who had kept those Microsoft Office products to himself, had been going out on local details to work his way up to a promotion. He had been a Supervisor for one year longer than I had at that Post Office. Admittedly, I did feel a bit of elation when I saw his surprised reaction to the news of my promotion and the level I was reaching.

Ben, the Manager of the REC who had hired me, told me that he was selecting me for the Tour 1 Operations Manager position. Within the Postal Service's operation windows, that meant I would be working at night into the early hours of the morning. There were two Operations Managers positions authorized for the new REC. Ben selected Max, a Supervisor who had worked at a Mail Processing Center to fill the Tour 3 position (3 p.m. to 11 p.m.). That promotion began a summer of change for me. I was starting my first relocation for the Postal Service and I had a lot to learn. Max was also going to need to relocate for his new position, and he had never previously gone through that process. Fortunately for us, Ben had relocated a few times during his career, and he helped us both through the process.

Ben gave Max and I a copy of the Postal Service's Relocation Policy Handbook. The benefits that were available to employees varied based on the level of the employee. Max and I were both relieved to find that our levels were high enough to cover the real estate portions of our moves. If we had been just a level or two lower, that would not have been the case. I encountered difficulties attempting to sell the house that I had lived in prior to relocating. While that house was being shown and handled by our real estate agent at our old location, my family and I were living in a furnished temporary home at our new location. It had been less than two years since we had purchased our house, and there were many new houses being placed on the market in our old location that were similarly priced. I was able to secure a buyout through the Postal Service, enabling me to move forward with purchasing a new house at our new location.

The buyout process involved averaging out the prices of similar houses sold in that location. The Postal Service provided me with the agreed upon, averaged out funds. I'm uncertain of the process that would then ensue for them to get those funds back through the sale of my old house. The buyout did not give me the amount of money I had hoped to secure through a sale to a buyer, but it was necessary to free up the funds I needed to put down on a house at my new location. Real estate benefits through the relocation process did cover a lot of the expenses involved in the selling and buying of houses, including the packing and moving of all the furniture and property from one location to another.

My wife was at our old house when the moving truck arrived to load up all our furniture. When the truck arrived at our new house, the moving crew placed boxes of items that they had packed up in the various designated rooms of the house. Each item was thoroughly wrapped up in paper, to prevent items from being broken or damaged in transit. I was amused as we opened boxes to unpack as we settled into our new house. Even plastic items were thoroughly wrapped up in paper. My youngest daughter had a play kitchen set, and each little plastic cup and saucer were wrapped up in paper. I assumed that the movers were paid by the hour, or perhaps by the item by the Postal Service.

All the funds that I received through the relocation process were added to my income for the year. It was a significant amount of money, including the real estate funds, temporary housing for my family and several weeks of per diem for myself and the members of my family. My 3 children soon got tired of going out to eat at restaurants. That was something we only did occasionally. But since the Postal Service was reimbursing me for those receipts, it seemed like the best thing to do. I was initially concerned about how this was going to affect my income taxes for the year, but the Postal Service took care of that concern through a routine part of the relocation process.

I have always been more than a bit of a numbers geek, a characteristic that helped me immensely through my rise in ranks through the numbers-driven Postal Service organization. I was doing my customary scrutinizing of one of the bi-weekly paystubs I received when the year-to-date Federal Income Tax Withheld number caught my attention. It had jumped up a noticeable amount, so I talked to Ben and he gave me the answers. To compensate employees for the tax impact they will face when relocation benefits are added to their income, the Postal Service pays out a calculated amount into that employee's Federal Income Tax Withheld. The amount that was paid on my behalf was more than enough to cover me for that year's income taxes.

After my move to my new location, it took a few months for those of us on the new REC staff to interview and hire the employees that would be needed. During that time, our new facility was in the process of being renovated and furnished with all the equipment necessary for operations. When the construction within our facility was finished and all the processing equipment was installed, we began the training process for our Data Conversion Operators (DCOs). Within a few weeks, we were ready to begin processing mail and I moved from working days to my night shift spot. I was glad that our operating window had our operations ending at 5:00 a.m. Operations needed to end to enable our Electronic Technicians (ETs, gotta have an acronym) to perform the necessary backups and maintenance on our equipment. Ben allowed me to set my own schedule, and I opted to work from 8:00 p.m. to 4:30 a.m., with a half hour lunch. Those hours enabled me to drive home, get into bed and fall asleep before others in my house woke up. That was the best I could do with working a crazy night schedule.

After approximately a year on that job, our facility was upgraded due to the increased amount of work we were doing. Ben was moved up from level EAS 23 to EAS 25. Max and I were both moved up from EAS 20 to EAS 22. That was an uncommon increase of levels within such a short period of time for an employee. We had started out processing mail for four major Processing and Distribution Centers, and within a year we picked up four additional sites. The locations of the sites that we supported were spread out over a few different time zones.

That required us, at the REC, to have clocks set up in various rooms indicating what time it was at the different locations. We had regular teleconferences and there were deadlines associated with the processing support we provided to each site. These things required us to continually focus on each site's clock.

Under Ben's tutelage, I was able to learn what I needed to know about mail processing and the operations under my control were very successful. Each of us on the staff at the REC received multiple awards during my time there due to the consistent successes we had in our operations. During my time working as a Supervisor in my first Management job with the Postal Service, I did not have much exposure to the awards process. I received only a few small monetary awards from my Postmaster, and he approved a few that I recommended for employees working in our office. It wasn't until I was promoted to my Operations Manager position at the REC that I became aware of how the awards programs really worked. Unlike the Post Office budgets that were prepared under the scrutiny of the District Managers, the REC budgets for awards was much higher. The RECs were staffed with a 70% non-career workforce. The Postal Service wanted to make sure that these employees were incentivized to stay in their jobs, beyond the hourly amount they were paid. Non-career employees did not enjoy the same benefits that the career employees had, in terms of earned vacation leave, sick leave, higher pay and job security. All our employees were needed to work as many hours as they were needed, especially during the heavy volume Christmas period.

Ben put an award program into place for the employees during the Christmas period. He utilized that program for several years, seeding the mail, until budget constraints finally forced him to stop. This is how the seeding process worked. Ben had his secretary prepare a lot of different letters that were sent to the Mail Processing facilities we supported. He coordinated with the Managers at those facilities to drop specific letters into the mail being processed at their facilities, knowing that the images of these mail pieces would be viewed by our workers on their computer screens for processing. These letters were to be deposited at specific times on specific days to assure that the awards were spread out for employees working on different shifts and different days during the Christmas period to have an opportunity to win something.

There were several big prizes, such as $250 and smaller gift certificates to the local mall. There were many medium sized prizes and loads of smaller prizes, such as video store gift certificates and fast food restaurant gift certificates. The Supervisors worked many hours during those heavy volume days, and all our 400+ consoles were manned, with employees waiting to fill the seats when clerks took their ergonomic breaks every hour. A clerk would be keying the information needed to put a barcode on each letter back at the Mail Processing Centers. They would suddenly be looking at an image that said "Congratulations! You won a $50 gift certificate for the mall!" That clerk would raise their hands up and call a Supervisor over to verify the image. Hooting and hollering would generally ensue for a few minutes before everyone went back to business. We had no problem keeping our employees wanting to work the long hours needed.

When we ended one of our first Christmas periods at the REC, the Mail Processing Centers were very appreciative of how our employees had helped them to achieve success in their operations. They were especially grateful that the few heaviest volume days during the period, which can often be problematic in meeting processing deadlines, were successful due to those long hours our employees worked to assist them. The Manager of the largest Processing Center we supported, which was located about 4 hours away from our facility, made a trip to visit our facility with some members of his staff. He brought along with them a dozen leather jackets with logos of the NBA Team from his city emblazoned on the backs. A drawing was held on the different shifts to give everyone an equal opportunity to win one.

As is customarily the case when anyone has a new boss, the Supervisors who reported to me needed to learn about my expectations of them. One of the major lessons that they needed to learn involved attendance. My Supervisors had worked at the local Mail Processing Center in various positions before starting their jobs at the REC. It was obvious to me that their backgrounds had not had much of a focus on attendance and discipline. The low expectations of the staff concerning attendance at the many facilities where I worked throughout my career never ceased to amaze me. It has always been my firm belief that being regular in attendance was a reasonable expectation of any employer. I routinely reviewed the attendance of employees at every location where I served, and my Supervisors soon learned that I expected them to take disciplinary action against employees when it was needed.

Those expectations included regularity of break times and adherence to acceptable, measured performance standards by my employees. It was necessary for me to provide my Supervisors with templates to use for the levels of discipline that would be issued to employees who had infractions. I contacted the Labor Department within the District where our REC was located to make sure we were using the discipline templates that would be most effective. Because of my Delivery Operations background, I had a greater familiarity with the carrier union contracts. I did not want any justified discipline that was being issued to our REC employees to be overturned in the grievance process due to incorrect language.

When I reached the point where I knew that my Supervisors and my employees were consistently functioning well, I knew it was time to start thinking about my next career step. We began to hear news about REC facilities that were already starting to shut down, and I started to feel a sense of urgency about finding another job. I knew that the Postal Service would have other work available for me when the decision was made to close my facility, but I didn't know where that might be or what kind of job it might be. I wanted to be the master of my own destiny. I had not, up to that point, had the opportunity to serve as an Acting Postmaster, referred to as an Officer-in-Charge (OIC). I knew that a detail as an OIC was a good steppingstone to competing for and receiving an official Postmaster job. That would mean a day job, too!

I reached out to local District contacts I had made, asking about detail opportunities that might be available. I was not shy about putting out requests for opportunities to get a detail (temporary assignment) that would help me to gain more knowledge along my career path. I had contacted a few of the Managers, Post Office Operations (MPOOs) within the District where my REC was located seeking opportunities. My Manager, Ben had allowed me to schedule myself for a Postmaster training class that was being held in the District where we were located. The class was going to be a week long, requiring me to book a room at a hotel to stay at during the training. Ironically, I ended up having to cancel out of the training and hotel stay when I received a call from one of the District MPOOs, telling me that he was going to detail me as OIC into one of the level 21 Post Offices he managed.

George was the Manager who gave me the detail opportunity. He allowed me the use of his company car during my detail, since my family only had one vehicle at that time. The Post Office where I was detailed as OIC was a relatively small one, and the city where it was located was about 5 hours away from my home. I checked into a Super 8 motel, staying there during the week. I worked long hours at that office during the week, absorbing everything I could about the day to day responsibilities of the job, and I went home each weekend. I moved into a furnished two-bedroom apartment after a few months, when my kids were out of school for the summer. That enabled my family to stay with me while I completed my detail.

George and I developed a good working relationship. We spoke on the phone often, especially since this was all new to me. The expectations, the multitude of reports required and the reporting structure itself all took some time for me to soak in. The Post Office had a small number of City Routes and Rural Routes. That gave me the experience of dealing with both of those crafts and their union leadership from the Postmaster level, a step up from the Supervisor experience I previously had at a Post Office. The titled Postmaster of that Post Office was out on a detail to the District, and she met with me at the office to help me get acclimated to the processes in place when I initially arrived there. I had absolutely no experience dealing with Retail Window Operations, and she provided me with the information I needed to verify and validate financial information daily.

When that OIC detail ended, I returned to my home and my job at the REC. I had achieved my objective of having an OIC detail to add to the list of experiences on my application. I soon embarked on a season of interviews. I applied for a variety of positions that were posted all over the country. Because of the respectable level that I had within the company at that time, I was interviewed for many of the jobs where I submitted applications. The rules that were in place at that time, prior to the process being moved to online, required that anyone applying for a job gave their immediate manager a copy of their application they submitted. After Ben had received more than a dozen applications from me, he asked me to stop giving him copies.

I went on 15 – 20 different interviews during that period. Many of them were long shots. I did not have any performance record to support some of the jobs I applied for, but my paper (application) and my level got me in the door for that interview. At one point, out of curiosity, I asked Ben how many calls he had received about me. I wondered how many of these people who were paying my travel expenses to come for an interview were calling Ben to ask about what kind of Manager I was. He told me that he hadn't received any calls. I was very surprised to hear that, and it later influenced me to take the responsibility to make and take those calls seriously when I was on various promotion Review Boards and as a Selecting Official.

Ben was certainly aware by that time that I was intent on moving ahead in my career. He was contacted by Skip, his Manager at our Area office. Improvements in automation had already begun to facilitate the closing of a few RECs within our Area. There were 5 RECs that were serving Mail Processing Centers within my Area, and the Managers of each of those RECs reported to Skip at our Area office. Skip informed Ben that Headquarters had scheduled another REC in our Area to be shut down. It was a small REC that only processed mail for a few cities in our Area, and it was unique because the REC was physically located in a neighboring Area. That was unusual. Although RECs were designed to be self-sustaining, independently handling the processing of their own employee's personnel actions, they did occasionally need assistance from their Area office and its staff. Fortunately, the staff of the Area where this REC was geographically located willingly helped that REC when it was needed.

The individual who was the titled Manager at this REC was selected for an Operations Manager position at another REC that was not being considered for closure at that time. Skip needed someone to fill in as the Acting Manager of the facility as it moved towards its closure date. He asked Ben if he had anyone who would be willing and able to fill in, and Ben recommended me. I was grateful to Ben for giving me this opportunity, and he told me that I needed to call Skip for a conference before travelling to the REC. I called Skip at the scheduled time, and it was a very surprisingly short conversation.

Skip didn't ask me many operations questions, as I was nervously waiting to hear. The main point that he wanted to get across to me was that the REC I was going to manage would be closing after the upcoming Christmas season. Ben had been made aware of this, but this was the first that I was hearing of it from Skip. He told me that I was not to share the closure information with anyone. None of the staff or employees at that REC were aware of this, and the news of it could not leak out to them or anyone else at that location. Skip told me that I was not to tell anyone at my home location about the upcoming closure either. He told me not to tell any of my friends, my family or even my wife about it. I got the point. The only other thing that Skip said to me during our brief conversation was "Just don't screw anything up."

The Postal Service did not want employees at that location to start fleeing, in search of other employment prior to or during the upcoming heavy volume Christmas mail processing. The closure would be announced soon after Christmas, to avoid the potential of employees fleeing. I suspect that there may have been negative consequences at other locations that had been scheduled to close due to closure news coming out too quickly. There was not too much concern about the career employees fleeing. The Postal Service had contractual obligations to provide work at other locations for career employees in the event of a closure. The concern was more associated with the casual employees. As I shared earlier, they made up about 70% of the workforce at RECs, and they had minimal benefits and virtually no job protection in the event of a closure.

The first time that I met Skip in person was when he travelled to meet me at the REC where I would be detailed. He introduced me to the Manager I would be replacing and gave me additional information about the facilities that the REC supported. After he left and the Manager I was replacing left to go to his new job location, I settled into the new facility and my new temporary job. I had to learn how to put on a good poker face. Throughout the time that I was at that location, I would continually have staff and other employees ask me that same question. "Have you heard anything yet?" They were referring to any news about an upcoming closure. I would put that poker face on, look them in the eye and say "No. I haven't heard anything."

Did it bother me to blatantly lie to them? Of course it did. I knew that each of the employee's lives were going to be affected when that facility shut down, some more drastically than others. My employer gave me a job to do, and I was going to do it as instructed. Although I was tasked with not telling anyone about the imminent closure that was being planned, every employee who worked at a REC anywhere in the country knew that their facility would be shutting down at some point. It was, after all, the nature of the RECs. As technology improved, enabling the electronic readers at Mail Processing Centers to read the addresses on mail items, the need for DCOs declined.

The REC was an approximate 8-hour drive from my home, and Skip allowed me the use of his company car while I was detailed there, just as George had done during my previous detail. I once again was practically living at the REC during the week. I would leave around noon on Fridays to drive home to be with my family. On Monday mornings, I would leave at 4 a.m. to start the drive back to the REC. I had to be on a teleconference every Monday at noon, so there was no room for additional travel time on Mondays.

I left late one Monday morning due to not moving quickly enough to get out the door. I knew I was going to have to make up that time while I was driving. Fortunately, the route I took was almost exclusively expressway driving. The speed limit in the states that I drove through was 65 mph, and it was 70 mph in the REC's home stretch state. I was averaging 90 mph on the day that I was late, trying to make up for that lost time. I would slow down when I observed a police car that was parked looking for speeders. During one stretch on the trip, I took notice of a car that came up on me from behind. The driver came up very close, then backed off. At first, I was concerned that it was an unmarked police car. I slowed down but resumed my speed when I determined that it was not a police car. The driver then started pulling up on my left to pass me, or so I thought. The man who pulled up alongside my vehicle matched my speed. He held up a piece of paper for me to view that he had written my license plate number on.

Vehicles that were owned by the Postal Service had government license plates on them. They started with a capital P. The driver of the vehicle next to me gave me enough facial expressions and gesturing with his hands to understand that he was indicating that he was going to report me for the way I was driving. I had made up enough time by that point to begin to drive at my customary 4 mph over the speed limit. I started to sweat it out, worried that at some point I was going to be contacted by Skip about how I was driving his vehicle. Fortunately for me, I made it back to the REC on time for the teleconference, and I never did hear anything about that event.

Skip approved travel requests that I submitted to visit the Managers of the Mail Processing Centers that the REC supported. I wanted to visit them and meet the staff prior to the Christmas period that would soon be upon us. If the Managers that I met were aware of the impending closure of the REC, their poker faces were as good as mine. That subject did not come up. We had discussions about the expectations they had of the REC on the different tours during the upcoming Christmas period. I had prepared slides highlighting our staffing that was being scheduled to accommodate their needs, with the customary focus for such planning placed on the anticipated heaviest volume days of the period. We casually talked about our facilities and our careers, but the elephant in the room, closure of the REC, was not brought up.

I returned to the REC after those visits, and I had my wife bring my kids to my temporary location during their Thanksgiving break from school. We once again managed to figure out the sleeping arrangements for the five of us in the furnished two-bedroom apartment where I was staying. I did have a full kitchen with customary cookware, dinnerware and appliances, but I decided that we would go out somewhere for our traditional Thanksgiving dinner. My kids did not like that at all. They wanted their mom to cook dinner, like she always did. I had asked around at the REC about locations where traditional Thanksgiving dinners were served. I was told that a specific restaurant that specialized in barbecued ribs always had a good turkey spread on Thanksgiving.

I called the rib restaurant and made a reservation for the five of us for Thanksgiving Day. My grumpy faced kids got into the car and we drove to the restaurant at the appointed time. Their faces grew even grumpier when we arrived at the rib restaurant. We walked in, gave them our name, and were told that they ran out of turkey. They invited us to wait around for an hour or so while they switched over to their rib meals. We left that location and I began to drive around looking for another restaurant. After checking out a few places that were open, I finally found a restaurant that was serving turkey dinners. We ate at that location. I thought the food was good, but there was no satisfying my kids at that point. With Christmas coming up soon, I learned my lesson about making sure I went home for that day. The kids would be out of school again for a while after Christmas, and I planned on having my family come down again to my location after Christmas Day.

Some time prior to Christmas, I sent a letter to the owner of the rib restaurant. I shared the disappointment that my family and I felt over what had occurred when I took my family there for our Thanksgiving reservation. A few days later, I received a letter of apology with 5 coupons for free rib dinners. When my family arrived after Christmas, we went there with our coupons and the ribs were excellent.

Meanwhile, back at the REC... The processing volume began to pick up. I had worked with the Supervisor who handled our scheduling to do some fine tuning. Idle Time was unproductive time that occurred during the Christmas period at the RECs. Idle Time was spent when excessive workers were scheduled to capture console down time during DCO hourly breaks. DCOs who did not have a console available for them to sit and work would wait in the wings for another DCO who would get up to take an ergonomic break or lunch. We had to keep those consoles running to keep the mail flowing at maximum processing levels. Ultimately, the tweaking that I did to the schedules enabled us to save close to $100,000 over the cost of idle time during the previous year's Christmas period.

I would stop the employee's work on each shift daily for just a few minutes, gathering them together for a talk. I would convey how our operations had done during the previous day and share other pertinent information with them. I always ended those sessions by giving the employees an opportunity to ask any questions, or share any comments, within a reasonable amount of time. I was surprised one evening when a literally little old lady raised her hand for my attention at the end of one of my talks. "Yes?", I asked her. "I just want to say how nice it is to not be getting hit anymore" she told me. I noticed the murmurs of agreement among the older employees in the group. I was certainly curious about that comment, but I thanked her and dismissed the group to go back to work.

After the employees had gone back to work, I asked the Operations Manager what that was all about. She told me that prior to the Postal Service taking over the facility, they had contracted the work out to a private company. I was unaware that remote encoding work had been contracted out at

37

locations that were called Remote Encoding Sites (RES) before the Postal Service took them over as RECs. For the sake of this situation, I was told that one of the non-Postal Supervisors at this RES had a protocol that she used when she found an employee who was falling asleep while working. She carried a ruler around with her, and she would smack the sleeping employee on the arm or shoulder with it to wake them up. I was surprised that there weren't any assault charges filed by employees over this treatment. Actions like that would certainly not be tolerated within the Postal Service.

There were award funds available in that REC's budget, just as they were for every REC, but apparently not much had been done to use them previously. I decided to implement the seeding program I had been a part of at my home REC. As stated earlier, this facility was much smaller than my home REC. There were less employees and an appropriately smaller budget for awards. I worked with my staff and the Mail Processing Centers we supported to shamelessly steal the idea that Ben used for our REC employees. The process was put into place, and the employees were thrilled to be receiving prizes as they worked through the Christmas period.

I was able to find a few other ways to cut costs during my time at that facility. I was developing a habit of wading through the variety of reports that are available on different internal systems for each facility and each operation within the Postal Service. Working at that facility provided a good training ground for me that would help me along on my career path. By the end of my detail, when I prepared a narrative for Skip that highlighted the successes I had and the costs reduced during my time there, he was duly impressed. I had far exceeded his expectation that I would "not screw anything up." He rewarded me with a cash bonus after the detail ended and I returned to my home REC.

I had a few memorable interview experiences during my quest

to move up the corporate ladder. The first one was for a REC Manager position that was the same level that I had detailed into. The Manager over this facility was domiciled in the Area office that the facility reported to, several hundred miles away from the facility. I was surprised to learn that my interview was being held at the REC. Previous interviews had me reporting to the Area Office, not even knowing what the REC locations looked like. I reported for my interview before the scheduled time. It became obvious to me very early on after the interview started that there was an agenda in place. The higher-level manager who I would be reporting to was alone with me in an office at the facility interviewing me. As I answered the questions that he read to me from his list, he did not take notes or write down anything that I was answering. Perhaps he had a recording device set up that I was unaware of, to review my responses compared to the other interviewee responses, but I doubt it. He knew who he was selecting, and it was not me, regardless of what I said in response to his questions.

A similar experience occurred when I applied for a level 22 Postmaster job. I reported to my interview with an Executive Postmaster of a large city in his office. It was late on a Friday afternoon, and he was more focused on leaving his office for the weekend than he was on me and my answers. He would ask me a question, and while I was responding he was looking through papers and packing things in a briefcase he had on his desk. He barely even looked at me during the interview process, and he took no notes when I answered his questions. He paused long enough to say goodbye to me, telling me that he would be in touch. I received my Dear John letter from him within a few weeks.

On the other end of the spectrum, while working at my REC I received a notice to interview for an Operations Manager position at another REC where I had applied. I booked a flight to the city where the REC was located, and the Manager had his secretary pick me up at the airport mid-morning. The REC

Manager wanted to minimize the expenses of the interviewing, so he let me know in advance that I should plan to fly in and out the same day. When I entered his office, he introduced himself and welcomed me in. He told me to take my jacket off, my tie and my shoes also if I wanted to, because I was going to be there for a while. That interview was the longest one I ever experienced, lasting close to three and a half hours long.

Over that amount of time, a multitude of topics were covered. Most of the topics were business related, but he wanted to learn what he could about me on a personal, family level as well. He took copious notes throughout the interview, and he was not intimidating in the least. He made me feel very much at home, though I did leave my shoes on. His secretary barely got me back to the airport in time to catch my return flight. I found out a few weeks later that I was not the successful applicant. I did, however, replace him when he retired as I was promoted to his Manager position several years later.

I spent a lot of time sitting in airports waiting for flights. I also spent a lot of time in hotel rooms when travelling for interviews, meetings and many training events. My Postal Service laptop was always a companion on my trips. Blackberries had not yet been put into use by the Postal Service, so I needed the laptop to keep up with the email messages that never stopped. When going on interviews, I always wanted to have the most up to date information I could get from our intranet reporting systems. I always carried a disk or two for my A: drive. Remember those? I would spend some of my idle time typing up notes that I planned on referencing later when I wrote this book. I did not want to save those notes on my Postal Service laptop. My work in progress (this book) was paused for a few years while work and life events took over. When I finally felt the inkling to resume this work, I was concerned as I realized that the A: drive had become a thing of the past. Fortunately for me and the notes that I had on a few different disks, I was able to buy an A: drive that plugged into my laptop's USB port.

My summer of interviews did not yield any results. I had been out on a few details, but I was still working nights and concerned about what the future held for me career-wise. Then I got an unexpected phone call that changed everything. Skip, the manager who I had worked for while on detail keeping quiet about the REC closure, was now in a District Manager position. The responsibility in his job was over a large group of Post Offices of all sizes within a defined geographic area, and the 3 Mail Processing Centers within that area as well. He called and told me that his District was having a hard time finding good Managers to serve in Acting Postmaster (OIC) positions. He asked me if I would be interested in a detail and I said yes.

Skip told me that he had a level 21 Post Office where he wanted me to serve as OIC. The office that was available was very close to the city where I had been promoted to my first Supervisor position. I had a lot of family in that area and there were a lot of Post Offices in that area. I knew that accepting this detail could potentially lead to a selection into a vacant Postmaster job, a change in my career that would open the door for further advancement. I could tell when I met the Acting MPOO, Tim, who I would be reporting to during this OIC detail, was not very happy that Sam had brought me in from outside of his group. There were always people looking for opportunities to serve in an OIC position, to help further their own careers, and most Managers are understandably loyal to the workers within their group. This increased the challenge that I had of proving myself to the Tim. He was in a position of furthering my career and I needed to earn his confidence.

During my detail to the level 21 office, I was able to achieve positive results for my Tim. His resentment faded away and we became friends. I brought a fresh, new perspective to his group and I was achieving positive results at the Post Office where I was assigned. As my detail neared an end, another level 21 Postmaster position became vacant in Tim's group. I knew that

41

if I were to get that job, I would drop from my current level 22 to a level 21. I would also be moving back to a higher cost of living area. On the positive side, I would be back to working days, there was room for advancement to higher level jobs in the area and my salary would not go down with my level. Because of my rapid increase in levels in a short period of time, I was at the low end of the pay scale for my level 22 job. My current salary would have me at about the middle of the pay range for a level 21. I applied for the vacant Postmaster job and Tim selected me from the 3 individuals he interviewed.

I had my family move into temporary housing with me and we began the process of relocation to the area of my new Postmaster job. This was my second relocation experience. As I had previously experienced, the Postal Service provided good benefits when management employees relocated. Along with paying for many of the costs associated with selling my old house and buying a new one, travelling from my old duty station to the new one for myself and my family members, food and many other expenses were covered with the appropriate documentation. There was also that $2,500 miscellaneous expense payment received by EAS employees. Relocating Executives received a $25,000 miscellaneous expense payment, but that's another story. A Google search may still yield some stories about Postal Service Executives relocation scandals if you are interested.

I sought an audience with Skip, the District Manager who had facilitated my introduction to Tim and my new career path. I shared with Skip the negatives that were involved with my new position and relocation. There was no pay increase, I was moving back to a higher cost of living area and I would be losing the 9%-night differential I received working at my REC job. I asked him if it would be possible to receive a $5,000 miscellaneous expense payment instead of the typical $2500. He told me that it wouldn't be a problem and he signed off on the requisition for that.

All relocation matters were handled at an office in San Diego, and my form was sent there. After a few weeks, I started getting concerned when I had not received any funds or any contact. I knew from my previous relocation that those funds arrived quickly. I called the office in San Diego that handled relocations to inquire about why there was a hold up. The individual who I spoke with told me that anything over the customary $2,500 had to be approved by an Executive at Headquarters. I went to talk about this with Skip, but he was not in. The District Finance Manager was filling in for him. I told him what had happened, and he said that I should just forget about it. He didn't verbalize it, but I knew that nobody was interested in sticking their neck out and calling Headquarters. He signed the paperwork to get my $2,500 and I did receive that within a week.

When I was selected and appointed to that first official Postmaster job, I was responsible for the delivery and retail unit for a medium sized town. I also had responsibility over the Centralized Forwarding System (CFS) Unit for our geographic area. The Post Office was in the same facility as a Mail Processing Center and the District offices. It could be a bit intimidating at times, since I never knew when a higher up District official would walk through my doors to check on things. They certainly didn't have far to walk. My management staff and employees knew that I wanted to be notified as soon as possible when unexpected visitors would show up in my Post Office. They were usually pretty good about giving me warning.

Late one morning, after all my carriers were out on their routes delivering mail, one of my clerks poked his head into my office and said, "We have visitors." I exited my office and walked towards the doors that separated my Carrier Unit from the Mail Processing Center. The Area Vice President had moved Skip back to a position at the Area office, and she appointed a new District Manager to that executive position. I found Sam, the

Mail Processing Center Manager and our newly appointed District Manager, my District's top two Executives, looking at Priority Mail packages in a hamper by the door. As I approached them, Sam asked me why these Priority Mail pieces had not gone out for delivery. I told the two of them that the hamper was pushed in from the Mail Processing Center after the carriers had left the building. There was no placard on the hamper identifying the mail type and when it had been dispatched from the Plant, as is the customary process, and I told them that this was a common occurrence. Sam informed me that he would direct his staff to make sure that placards were put on items that were brought in, and that we would be notified when this occurred, rather than just wheeling them through the door.

Things calmed down a bit after this exchange, and Sam took the opportunity to introduce me to Corey, my new District Manager. Corey was an African American man who had just recently been appointed to his District Manager position from an Executive Postmaster position. I paused to see if he would recognize me. He had interviewed me for that level 22 Postmaster position just a few months earlier. He was the selecting official who had been busy packing his briefcase while he asked me questions, barely looked at me and took no notes. Corey did not recognize me, and I did not let on that we had previously met. I was told that when he had his first meeting with the managers who reported directly to him, he looked around the room and asked, "Where are all the brothers?" I knew that he had selected an African American manager for the Postmaster position I had received no obvious attention for, so I wasn't surprised to hear how vocal he was about his Affirmative Action leanings.

Corey was a tough, demanding District Manager. He wanted to impress the Area Vice President who had selected him, and everyone I spoke with had no doubt that he had high aspirations to move further up the corporate ladder in the executive ranks. I could respect that. Corey expected positive results from the

Postmasters in his District, and he leaned hard on the MPOOs who managed those Post Offices. He restructured the MPOO groups and ended almost all the details that were in effect in the District. My Acting MPOO, Tim applied for an open MPOO position in the District, but he was not selected. He returned to his titled position as Postmaster of a Post Office close to mine, and he was replaced.

My Post Office was assigned to one of the MPOOs, Stan, who had been in his position for several years in my District. I talked to a few of the Postmasters in my new group who knew Stan, wanting to learn what I could about my new boss. I was told that he was a tough, but fair boss. His office was located on the second floor of the building where my Post Office was located, just down the hall from where Tim's office had been located. As I got to know Stan, I could sense that he respected the job that I was doing and the contributions I was making to his group of Postmasters. I was regularly meeting the budgetary and performance goals I was given for my Post Office, and I was making positive, noticeable changes within the CFS Unit under my management.

Stan showed me how much confidence he had in me when he signed me up to attend a unique training class called the Advanced Leadership Program. I will go into that program more in depth in the upcoming TRAINING chapter of this book. One of the requirements necessary for graduating from the Advanced Leadership program was to receive a certain number of credits for taking business related classes at a college. Since I did not have a degree of any kind, it was not hard for me to complete this requirement at a local Community College. My classes had to be approved in advance by Corey, the executive District Manager over my level 21 Post Office. I would then be reimbursed for my expenses after successfully completing each class.

I requested and received approval for a Business class and a

Speech class. A Sign Language class that I requested was disapproved by Corey. I requested an audience with him to discuss this. He told me that he would not approve the class because it was not business related. I told him that I had worked with and managed hearing-impaired employees in every facility where I had been domiciled. Unlike most Postmasters, I was also very aggressive about seeking opportunities to speak at Chamber of Commerce and other business organization meetings. On occasion, there would be a hearing-impaired individual in the audience. I felt that being able to better communicate with hearing impaired individuals, whether they were employees or potential new customers, would be of benefit to the Postal Service. The fact that I was aggressive in the pursuit of new business was well known throughout my District. He still declined to approve the class. Executives know best seemed to be the recurring lesson I learned.

While serving in that first official Postmaster position, a job vacancy was posted for the Postmaster position in the city next to the location where I was living at that time. Even though it would not be a promotion, because it was the same level as the current job that I held, I applied for it to reduce the amount of time and money that I spent driving each day. It wasn't necessarily a good career move, but the dollars, cents and time do add up.

I was always very detailed and meticulous when filling out applications for jobs. I spent a lot of time making sure that I addressed each of the qualifications for a job by highlighting my most recent accomplishments applicable to the requirement topic. I also took the time and made the effort to make sure that I left very little to no blank space on each page where I had to address qualifications. I would delete older experiences to replace them with newer ones on my applications that I saved for future use. I was so anal about this process that I would occasionally reduce font sizes to make my narratives fit to fill the page. I was once told by a Manager that he used my application when giving training on career advancement to Postal Service employees. He told his students that my application was the way that applications should be filled out. I felt confident that I had the "paper" portion of job seeking down as well as I could.

I received a letter from the Review Board that was handling the Postmaster job I applied for, advising me when and where to report for an interview with them. I felt at the time that the interview went well, so I was surprised when I found out that I didn't make the final list for the Selecting Official's consideration. I happened to know Mike, the Chairman of the Review Board that interviewed me, so I gave him a call. He was also a Postmaster, one level higher than my EAS 21. I showed him all due respect, as I always did when communicating with someone who was a higher level than myself. I asked Mike if he could tell me why I did not make the final list for the Postmaster job. He told me that it was because I did not do a thorough enough job of selling myself during the interview. I shared with him that I thought my application did a thorough job of explaining my accomplishments. He said that it did, but I should have been as thorough during my interview as well. I was not happy, but I accepted Mike's answer. What else could I do?

As I considered what had happened concerning my interaction with the Review Board, I began to have questions about what had taken place in the process. I visited the Personnel Manager of my District, whose office was a walk down the hall from my own office and voiced my concerns to him. I asked him if it was normal for 2 of the 3 Review Board members to be a lower level than the person that they were interviewing (me, a level 21). Along with Mike, a level 22 Postmaster, there was a level 20 Postmaster and a level 19 District employee on the Review Board. He said that it was a good question and he would have to talk to his boss, the Human Resource Manager of the District.

I received a call from the Personnel Manager a few days later.

He advised me that the Postmaster position I had unsuccessfully interviewed for was going to be reposted. He encouraged me to reapply for it. I received the real answer to my question when an email and an accompanying official notice was sent out to all the District's management employees by the District Human Resource Manager. It basically stated that no member of a Review Board could be a lower level than the applicants being considered for a position. I did not reapply, deciding that I would only apply for positions that would give me an increase in level and pay, but I did speculate that the District Human Resource Manager may have been concerned that I might take some action over how my Review Board had been comprised.

The Postmaster, Mike who had been the Chairman of the Review Board I had contacted about my interview eventually transferred to another Post Office in another state. It was notable that the state where he transferred to had a much warmer climate, conducive to a much longer season for playing golf. When he left his office, I was eventually the successful applicant who took his place as the level 22 Postmaster. Two of the Supervisors who worked at his old office told me how they would golf with their former Postmaster a lot. He was also a golf buddy of the District Manager who had lived close by, but he had been reassigned to the District Manager position close to the office where their former Postmaster was being transferred.

Before too long, I was advised that one of those two Supervisors was being transferred to his former Postmaster's new office, several states away. I had learned quite a lot about the relocation process, and I knew that there typically were not a lot of relocation benefits given to lower level Supervisors. I do not know if there were any exceptions made for that Supervisor in the area of relocation benefits, but at least the golf buds were back together again.

Because I worked in the same facility as Stan, back at my EAS 21 job, he would call on me to fill in for him at times. My Post

Office was on the first floor of the building, and he was in the District Offices on the second floor of the building. Sometimes I would fill in for just a few hours while he took personal time off. At other times it would be for a day or two while he was on leave or had to officially travel elsewhere. I know that there was some resentment on the part of other Postmasters in my MPOO group. I was a mere level 21 Postmaster, and Stan had several level 22 Postmasters and even a few level 24 Postmasters who reported to him. Some of them were vocal about asking why he was picking me to fill in for him when they should be getting that opportunity. I know that Stan trusted me and appreciated my work ethic. It was also very convenient having me in the same building, ready to fill in at the drop of a hat. I would still usually have to make sure that my Post Office was running smoothly while I filled in for him. His secretary would call me at my office or refer calls to me. I would also just go upstairs when needed to sign off on reports, respond to email messages on his computer and meet with people as necessary there.

I learned quite a bit about him during my meetings with him in his office. Looking around his office, I saw that he had his Doctorate degree framed on his wall. I was somewhat surprised by that, since I never heard him referred to as Doctor. I had never heard that he had such an advanced education, and I learned that he was humble about his many accomplishments as I got to know him more. On one occasion he told me that he needed me to fill in because he had to go for his Learjet flying lesson. I asked him about that, and he told me that he needed to fly a few states away and return with his instructor.

Another time when I was sitting in his office with him, I asked him about the piano music that was playing in the background there. He told me that it was a duet that was recorded of he and his wife. He shared with me that they performed together at a variety of events in the nearby city. The music was beautiful, and my admiration for my boss grew on multiple levels. I felt honored that he was taking such an interest in my career and providing me with the opportunity to regularly fill in for him. There were occasions, however, when I would have preferred someone else other than me sitting at his desk.

Stan had me come to his office one Friday afternoon, to give me a heads up about the things I would be dealing with when he would be going on vacation the following week. There were a few meetings I would have to attend in his absence, along with the usual reports due, handling of email and regular mail that came in daily and one unpleasant situation that was in progress. The situation involved one of his level 24 Postmasters who had fallen under the crosshairs of our District Manager, Corey. As the saying goes, shit rolls downhill and this level 24 Postmaster was the recipient at the tail end of this particular roll.

The roll was taking place due to that Postmaster's level 24 Post Office ending up at the top of a nationwide bad performance list. An executive at Headquarters rolled that excrement ball downhill to an executive at our Area office. From there, it was rolled down to our executive District Manager, Corey. Corey told Stan that he expected some serious action to take place, and I'm sure the recommended action was probably Corey's idea. Stan told me that he had notified his level 24 Postmaster that he was to report to a level 22 office within Stan's group of Post Offices, to assume the duties of a front-line level 16 Supervisor. He would perform those duties for some undefined period, until he proved that he had mastered those duties effectively. From there, this Postmaster would be placed in a Branch Manager position or a lower level Postmaster position, working his way up to resuming his titled position at his level 24 Post Office. I knew this Postmaster. I had attended many meetings with him and my perception of him was that he was a very knowledgeable, experienced and tough Postmaster. He was a go-to kind of guy and I had personally gone to him for help and answers to questions I had in the past. I knew that he was probably not going to take this action without putting up a fight.

Soon after I reported to Stan's office on that following Monday morning, to assume his duties as Acting MPOO, I received a call from that Postmaster. He advised me that he was not going to report to work in that front-line Supervisor position because he was going to file a claim for an on the job injury. He told me that his physician would be faxing me documentation to substantiate that he had been injured on the job. The injury was stress caused by work. I received the notification from his physician and, as is customary in these cases, there was no end date in sight at that time as to how long he would be affected by this stress. I had dealt with employees in the past who had filed for an on the job injury caused by stress. Those claims were often not deemed as valid by the Department of Labor, but there was a process that had to be followed, nevertheless. It was difficult for an employee to prove that such a condition was exclusively caused by their work environment. I was not looking forward to the things that needed to be done.

There is a lot of paperwork that needs to be filled out when a reported accident occurs. The accident form needs to be accurate, and it needs to be signed by the individual filling out the report with a concurrence by their immediate manager. In this case, since I was filling in for Stan, Corey would have to sign off as the concurring official. Intimidated by the hard ass nature of Corey, I needed to be certain that I presented a flawless report to him for his signature. I consulted with my District's Injury Compensation and Safety Managers, both of whom were domiciled in the same facility with me. They were the experts, and they were both sympathetic to my need to have this document filled out right. Any errors would ultimately end up causing them more work down the road. After more than a fair amount of deliberation, the three of us finally agreed that I had an acceptable, accurately completed document. Now I just had to bring it to Corey.

I called Corey, whose office was just a few doors down from Stan's office, and told him that I needed to speak with him. He told me that I could come to his office and I did, bringing the accident report with me. I informed him about what was happening with the level 24 Postmaster and he looked through the document, asking me a question or two along the way. I was able to answer the questions that he had, but I could easily see the look of anger on his face as he read. When he got to the bottom of the report, to the spot where he was required to sign as the concurring official, he told me that he wasn't going to sign it. I nervously stood in front of him, unsure of how to react to this. I pressed him about it, telling him that it needed to be signed by him.

Corey called the Safety Manager and put her on speaker while I stood there waiting. He told her what he had told me, that he was not going to sign off on the accident report. He said that he did not agree with it and wouldn't sign his name on it. The Safety Manager reported directly to Corey, so she presumably had been through many different situations with him in the past. They went back and forth about him signing for a bit, and then she finally said to him "Now, Corey. Just because you sign it doesn't mean you agree with it. It's just part of the process for that document. As the higher level official, we need your signature on it to move forward. We can argue the merits of this case as we move along in the process." Corey reluctantly picked up his pen and signed the appropriate spot as the concurring official. Under his signature he printed: "I do not agree with this." He gave the document back to me, smiled at me and asked, "How do you like filling in for Stan so far?" I answered that it certainly wasn't a boring job so far, wishing I was on the first floor at my Post Office.

That level 24 Postmaster never did return to his job. He ultimately filed for a Disability Retirement and received it. He was one of several employees under Corey who either retired or were forced out of their positions while he was the District

Manager. As I have intimated earlier, Corey was a very tough Manager to work for, and if you didn't produce the desired results, he knew how to make your life miserable. My MPOO Stan and his peer level 25 MPOO in our District both ended up retiring sooner than they would have liked to under the pressure from Corey. Stan's wife worked for a major airline company as an executive and they relocated to California. He took a job with that same company working in their training department. I was happy that he moved along to start a new career where I was certain he would be much more appreciated.

While I was still in my level 21 Postmaster position, one of the jobs I applied for was a level 22 Postmaster job that was a few states away from where I lived at that time. I received a notice that I would be interviewing with Mark, the Selecting Official for that job. Since there was no Review Board involved, it meant that there were only a few applications received for the job. I did my customary research on that office in preparation for the interview. Since the Postmaster job was currently vacant, there had to be an OIC assigned there. The performance numbers that I accessed for that Post Office looked good, better than the Same Period Last Year (SPLY) numbers. The OIC was obviously doing a good job handling the office. I made a few calls to find out if the OIC was one of the people being interviewed for the job and found that to be the case. Since the OIC was doing a good job, and was probably a local to that area, I knew that I would have to deliver my best during my interview. Relocation expenses would be incurred by Mark if I was selected, in addition to the interview expenses he would already be incurring, and it would make sense to avoid those costs if a qualified individual was already at that location and effectively doing the job.

I arranged my travel plans to get me to the interview area. There were no flights that could get me close enough to where the interview was without having to rent a car. I found a less expensive flight to a major city a bit further away from my ultimate destination. From there, I rented a car to get to the exact interview location. It was about a 4-hour drive from the airport. I reserved a room for the night close to the interview location. My plan was to go to the Main Post Office that I was interviewing for before going to the hotel. It's always a good idea to visit the office in advance, whenever possible before an interview. It was about 10 p.m. when I finally arrived at the Post Office. I walked around the facility knocking on doors, and I was fortunate to find a custodian who was the only person in the building. He let me in after I showed him my official Postal Service documentation, and I made notes of several things that I observed that would be good talking points to use for my interview.

I was concerned as I drove into the city on my way to the Post Office. I passed more than a few strip joints, advertising naked dancers. I also noted many seedy looking areas I drove through, with shabby looking buildings and the roads looking like they had needed repair for quite some time. The Post Office was in an industrial part of the city. As I looked the office over, I noted that the dock area where the trucks pulled in and out to drop off and pick up mail was quite large. I looked at containers that were staged on the dock and saw the names of several Post Offices listed. When I asked about this, the custodian advised me that this Post Office also processed mail for several offices up and down the river from its location. I was also told that there were other facilities within the city that were under the responsibility of that office. It looked like quite a large workload and responsibility for the Postmaster, a lot more responsibility than I currently had, and it was only one level higher than my office.

I made my way to my hotel and headed to my interview early the next morning. I met Mark and during our conversation he informed me early on that he was an ex-Marine. He was very firm and business-like towards me, but I felt that the interview went well. I asked him if there was a possibility of the office being upgraded to a higher level, which would mean an increase in level and pay for the Postmaster. This occurred when an office had enough growth in the number of deliveries and/or an increase in the amount of revenue, or business being handled in the office over a sustained period. Mark told me that there was no possibility of that happening.

When I returned home from my interview trip, I talked with my wife about the experience. We had children that were in grade school at the time, and we agreed that it didn't seem like the kind of place where we would like to relocate with our kids. I would also be taking on a lot more responsibility, with all the accountability headaches that come along with it, for not much of an increase in pay. Also, because it was in a secluded area, there wouldn't be much of a chance of higher-level details without me having to leave home for extended periods. I felt confident that the OIC would probably end up getting the job, until I received a phone call at work a few days later.

Mark called me at my office and said "Congratulations. I am selecting you for the Postmaster position." I was shocked. I told him that I was in the middle of something at work and asked him if I could call him back. He said yes. I had never heard of anyone turning down a selection for a promotion before, but I did not want the job. I wondered if the expenses I had incurred going there for the interview would be approved by him if I turned it down. I called him back within an hour and told him that I had talked it over with my wife, shared information about the area with her, and we decided it would not be a good move for our family. He said "Okay." Pause. "Well, it was nice meeting you." That ended our call. I turned in my expense report soon after for his approval and breathed a sigh of relief when Mark approved it.

At one point in my career I applied for the position of Postmaster of the Key West, Florida Post Office. It isn't a very large office, but the location had a lot of appeal to me. I received notification that I was to call in for a telephone interview for the job. I did all the research on the Key West Post Office that I would typically do in preparation for an interview. When the date and time came, I called in for my interview. The Review Board that I called was at a location in Miami. I was introduced to the 3 higher level members of the Review Board, given the usual banter about the process we would be going through in the interview and asked if I had any questions. I said that I did have one question. I told them that I was unaccustomed to doing a telephone interview and asked why this interview was being handled in this way. I was informed that they had received over 50 applications from all over the country for the Key West Postmaster position, and that this was the most economical way that they could handle it. Ultimately, I was not selected for the job.

As I have shared, I interviewed for dozens of management positions throughout the country. If a position was posted for applications and there were just a few applicants, the selecting official would interview those applicants and select the individual he or she wanted. If there were more than a few applicants, a hiring Review Board, typically consisting of three managers, would work together to select the number of applicants that the Selecting Official requested to personally interview. I worked on several Review Boards during my career. There were usually somewhere between 6 and 12 or more applicants and the Selecting Official would typically want the Review Board to narrow it down to 3 qualified individuals.

The members of the Review Board would meet to look over the qualifications that were addressed by each applicant on their applications. This was not always easy to schedule, as we each had our own responsibilities that we still had to handle in our own operations. Portions of the review process were often handled through telephone conferencing with the Review Board members, especially if the Review Board members who were chosen by the Selecting Official had a great distance between them.

I can recall being the Chairman of a Review Board for a vacant Postmaster position of a medium size Post Office, a level 20 with about 50 employees. The application process had moved from paper applications being mailed in by applicants to an online process. The applications would be submitted online, and the Review Board would print them out to review them. The three Review Board members had to agree throughout the process and there was documentation required to substantiate why we made our decisions about the applicants along the way through the process. The steps involved in the processes used to fill vacancies had several documentation requirements built in to avoid potential discrimination complaints being filed against the Postal Service.

In this situation, we received 26 applications. We weeded out several of them due to the applicants never having served in even an Acting Supervisor capacity, a great lack of experience. We then looked at the current positions of the remaining applicants, considering such things as details where they may have temporarily served at a higher responsibility level, the duration of those details, how long it had been since their last detail and how well they documented their accomplishments while in those details on their applications. We also contacted their current manager and a manager they worked for while on a detail for character and leadership assessments.

I contacted the MPOO, who would ultimately interview the applicants we recommended for further consideration prior to selecting a new Postmaster for the vacant position. I told her that there were six individuals who were qualified that we would like to recommend for her consideration. As I mentioned earlier, Selecting Officials typically wanted only three or four applicants passed along to them as finalists. She understood that with such a high number of interested applicants, there would be several that had the right stuff for the job. She agreed that it would be appropriate to send her six finalists for her consideration under the circumstances.

I was surprised when I was contacted by a few of the applicants who had received "Dear John" letters from me, as the Chairman of the Review Board. I knew the individuals, having had business contact with them on unrelated matters during my tenure in that District. I was not surprised by their contact, inquiring as to why they had not been selected as finalists. It was the unprofessional way a few of them approached me that bothered me. They had an arrogance to their demeanor, angered by the fact that they had been considered unworthy to advance to the finalist status. I explained the criteria that was used to seek the finalists, encouraging them to pursue details that would provide them with the work experience they needed to move them ahead in their careers. I added that in the course of pursuing career advancement it was, in my opinion, never a good idea to approach a Review Board official in such a contentious manner.

The other members of the Review Board and I did interview some of the applicants to get to the six that we would send forward. One of those applicants brought along three copies of a portfolio he had assembled, highlighting his career accomplishments and other non-work personal accomplishments. He was not happy during his interview when I told him that we did not have time to look through his portfolio. I told him that his application, our research and his answers to our questions would serve to give us what we needed to make our decisions. I gave his 3 portfolio copies back to him, and we each asked him our interview questions.

He did not make it as a finalist based on his answers and his work history, and I did not hear from him about his interview or his lack of moving forward for that position. He did get promoted a few months later to a different Manager position, for one that I did not serve on the Review Board. During the time that I had spent with this individual in his interview process, he struck me as someone who was an ass kisser. Individuals who attempted to work their way up the organizational food chain by kissing ass, endlessly complimenting higher ups, always turned me off. That was never my way of doing business, and I considered those who did conduct themselves in that manner to be insincere phonies who were not to be trusted.

I will mention that this ass kisser was African American. I am not sure whether that factored in to how he behaved in certain situations, but I was amused by what occurred at a meeting he attended held by our African American District Manager, Corey. The meeting took place inside a large auditorium at a local Community College. There were approximately 80 Postmasters and Managers in attendance. It always amused me to see where different individuals would sit at these meetings. I could predict who would be sitting obscurely in the very back of the auditorium, those who would be nestled safely in the middle and the more adventurous, attentive ones who would sit towards the front. I was in the sit closer to the front group, and I'm sure that others had their critical thoughts about me as well. This was the first meeting of its kind that the African American Manager was attending, and he made a point of sitting in the very first row.

That was a predictable spot for an ass kisser with high career aspirations to sit. The front row was typically only occupied by the few other speakers who would be addressing the group during the meeting. Corey started his speech to the group, pontificating about how the District was performing in several operations compared to other Districts within our Area and in the country. He opened and closed these meetings, and in between we would hear more pointed information, typically from the Managers of Delivery Operations, Mail Processing, Finance and Marketing. There would also be a lunch catered by the students of the college who were taking food prep courses. Although I could not see his face, it was obvious what was happening when Corey veered from his talking points after about a half hour into his speech. The new Manager who had taken a seat in the front row twitched when Corey commented loudly, clapping his hands, about how some people must be bored with what he was saying because it was obviously putting them to sleep. He said that people who were not interested in hearing what he had to say should not sit in the front row. There was audible laughter from those in the rear of the arena.

While serving in my final Postmaster position, I was fortunate to have been selected to that job in the same office where I had started out in my first supervisory job for the Postal Service. I had first applied for the Postmaster position of a level 24 office that was in a neighboring city. There weren't a lot of applicants, so I had my interview directly with the Selecting Official, the MPOO who managed that Post Office. My research showed that the OIC in place at that office was doing a good job, especially notable for a large Post Office, so I was cautiously optimistic as I went into my interview. I was working in a neighboring District at the time as a level 22 Postmaster, an outsider competing against an insider. Loyalty to insiders from Selecting Officials was not uncommon. The interview went very well, and I was excited when I received a phone call at home from the Selecting Official early one evening after my interview. A phone call, as opposed to a letter, almost always meant that the job was yours. That turned out not to be the case. He told me that he was calling to let me know that I was not going to receive the job. He went on to tell me, which I think was the reason for a call instead of a letter, that I should keep an eye on the postings because the neighboring office's same level Postmaster job would be posted soon.

I kept an eye on the job postings, and the Postmaster position that the Selecting Official referred to was posted two weeks later. The level 24 Post Office that I had not been selected on and the newly posted level 24 Post Office were located next to each other. If I were successful, I would be promoted from a level 22 to a level 24 Postmaster job. The daily drive that I had from my home to my level 22 Postmaster job at that time was over 80 miles total each day. I had been at that office for 3 years, and the drive during the winter would sometimes take 2 – 3 hours one way if the weather was bad. The prospect of being promoted, receiving a pay increase and reducing my drive time to only 20 miles round trip was quite appealing. There was also a great appeal to me at the thought of returning as Postmaster to the office where I had first started out as a Supervisor.

I applied for the job and I received a notice advising me of when and where to report for my interview. The notice was signed by the Chairman of the Review Board, which told me that there were more than a few applicants for this job. That did not surprise me. Although they were the same level, the office that I had not been selected for and the office that I was encouraged to apply for were much different. The city where the Post Office that I was now seeking a promotion to lead was much more affluent than the neighboring city. It was often cited on lists of "Best Places to Live" in the country. Through my inquiries I found out that there were 14 applicants for the job. What surprised me was that the Chairman of the Review Board was my old buddy who had served with me as a Supervisor at that Post Office. The guy who had those Microsoft products on his computer who did not share them with me. He had gone on to become the Postmaster at that office and had recently been promoted to a level 25 position at the District office. The fact that he was the Chairman added a new dynamic of apprehension to how I felt leading up to the interview.

I did my usual preparation for the interview. I looked over all the data I could get my hands on for the past several months, seeking improvement points that I could elaborate on during the interview. I went to visit the office and saw many familiar faces from my Supervisor days at the facility. My interview with the Review Board was only a few days away, and there were other applicants who were being interviewed who were there visiting at the same time I was visiting. The other applicants had a variety of different levels and accomplishments in terms of on the job successes and scholastic degrees. I found out that one of the people being interviewed was already a level 24 Postmaster from another state. My confidence was not at an all-time high, but I went in with as much information as I could and exuded the necessary confidence and assuredness during my interview with the Review Board.

Within a few days I received a notice advising me that I was a finalist, telling me when and where I should report for my interview with the Selecting Official. I continued to study up on every bit of data I could find on the office in preparation for this final interview. I also had conversations with different management staff working at the facility, finding inside information on strengths and weaknesses that I could use for my interview. I finally had my interview, and I left the Selecting Official's office feeling as confident as I could. I received that phone call about a week later, and this time it was the Selecting Official advising me that this job was mine.

I had to contact the Sales Manager at a neighboring District where I had been interviewed for a Sales position. The position I had interviewed for was a level 23 Sales Specialist, and I was glad that I was selected for the level 24 Postmaster position prior to being contacted about the Sales position. While I did have a passion for sales, I was concerned that I might get a bit bored doing nothing but sales. As a Postmaster, I could focus on several things at the same time, including sales. There was no chance of getting bored at that job. As it turned out, I was contacted by that Sales Manager of the neighboring District, advising me that the job was withdrawn. I had apparently been interviewed for a job that did not exist. The District was in a very large city and they did not have an adequate number of individuals to handle the potential sales within their District. As is often the case within the Postal Service, things change. The new level 23 position that was pending final approval for that District was disapproved. I was already in my new position when I received a letter advising me that the Sales Specialist job was withdrawn.

When I reported to my new office to begin my new job as the EAS 24 Postmaster, I needed a bit of time to get acclimated to the office, the staff, the union officials and the facilities under my responsibility. The telephone system, for example, was a system that I had not previously worked with. Telephone systems varied from office to office. There were several different telephone numbers assigned to the office, including my own private line, and I had to get accustomed to how the intercom system worked as well. I was just a few days into my new job when my telephone rang in my office. I answered with "Hello." I thought that it was an internal call coming in from one of my staff members. I was caught very much off guard when I heard my new boss' voice asking, "Is that how you answer the phone there?" I apologized and explained that I thought it was an internal call coming in.

There were times during my career when the Postal Service would allow bonuses, or awards to be given to employees for performance that was typically above and beyond their normal job duties. One of the most common awards was called a Spot Award. Those awards were given out in varying increments in the form of a check, with taxes withheld as appropriate. The maximum amounts allowable have increased over the years, and I can only imagine the sizes of bonuses and awards paid out to executives.

When I was promoted to the level 24 Postmaster job, I had to deal with a lot of practices that were put into place by my predecessor. One of those practices that he had in place was what was referred to as his Supervisor Retention Program. We were a few months away from Christmas, and one of my Supervisors filled me in on the staff's expectations. Muhammad told me that the former Postmaster would take the staff out to a local restaurant for lunch, and they would each receive a $1,000 check as a bonus award. The former Postmaster reasoned that he needed to give his staff something to keep them happy and to keep them from applying for jobs elsewhere. I called Gary, the MPOO who had selected me for my job, to discuss this with him. He asked me what I thought about it. I told him that since the office had not achieved anything notable in the fiscal year that was ending, I didn't think there should be any awards given out. He agreed with me and it was decided.

When Christmas was approaching, I made a reservation for my staff and I at the restaurant where they were accustomed to going. There were about 12 of us. We had our appetizers, and as we were nearing the completion of having lunch, I made them lose their appetites. At least I let them eat first. I told them all that they were going to have to apply themselves more diligently at their jobs and that we needed to start seeing results. I advised them that there would be no awards given out for the past year because awards had not been earned. All of them were disappointed, and there was noticeable disgust and hostility on a few of their faces. There were no awards given out for the next few years.

Jim, a Supervisor working for me at my level 24 Post Office applied for a job at a Post Office in Hawaii. This was one of those situations where they did not have enough good, qualified local applicants to fill some vacant entry level Supervisor jobs that they needed to have filled. They posted the available jobs nationwide. Jim was a single young man with a few years of experience working as a front-line supervisor. He had an eye for the young ladies, and I'm sure that he thought Hawaii would be a good place to spread his wings on a personal level.

Because of the large number of applications that were received in Hawaii for the available jobs, and the expense that would be involved with flying applicants in for face to face interviews, the interviews were conducted over the telephone. Jim had his interview and was awaiting notification of whether he was one of the selected applicants. He received a call that he informed me about, seeking guidance from me. He was told that he needed to be more descriptive about his experience in dealing with different matters in his on the job experience.

I reminded him of certain situations that he had been involved with in our office, and how he had contributed to positive results that were measurable. I was surprised that Jim was given this information about how he should bone up on his responses. Apparently, they had not received applications that yielded enough possibilities for them following the interviews. They reposted the Vacancy Notice nationwide once again, and Jim applied once again. He had another telephone interview and again he was not selected, but the positions were filled by other applicants.

As a Postmaster and a Manager with the Postal Service, the lackadaisical attitude that many of my subordinates had when it came to achieving and exceeding goals always amazed me. First, there was the matter of performing their jobs to their utmost capabilities for the Postal Service, a reasonable expectation. That is what all Managers and Supervisors are paid to do, and they received good pay and benefits to do so. In addition to that, the structure that was in place to determine what kind of an annual pay increase for each year's performance was based on several goals each Post Office was given at the beginning of the year. There were a built-in range for those individual goals, and the increases in pay that would be received were based on a composite score for the combined goals. The percentage of salary increases was larger if the staff was able to reach higher defined increments of the goals.

When I held regular staff meetings with my staff at various

locations, I would always have information ready to share with them about how we were performing as an office. That information would include those items that were going to impact our pay. I would include printouts that showed where we currently stood in relation to our goals. There would be discussion about how improvements could be made within our operations, and each of my staff members would leave those meetings knowing what they needed to do to be successful. As my Supervisors would leave the room, I knew which ones I could depend on to tighten up the operations under their control. I also knew which ones would need more specific, directed attention from me to do their jobs.

Before too long, I was dealing with my new MPOO, Dick. The MPOO who had hired me, Gary moved on to another position. The first few years in that office had been rough for me. I had problems with my management staff, which are chronicled elsewhere in this book. Ineffective Managers and Supervisors directly impact the performance of the craft employees, and when craft employees aren't performing well the heat comes down from on high. When I had put an end to the Supervisor Retention Program, holding my management staff accountable for measurable results within each of their areas of responsibility, a few of them applied for jobs in other offices. I had no problem with that. I also had no problem disciplining staff who were in violation of Postal Service regulations or failing to follow my instructions, a few of them resigning while their discipline was pending. I was able to eventually hire the replacement staff that I needed to achieve positive results.

As my level 24 Post Office continued to finally show good results in many areas, we were recognized by our District Manager. He came out to my Post Office on a few occasions, bringing in breakfast or other goodies for the employees. The most notable area where we were excelling was in sales. The carriers, with my prompting through many service talks, were turning in more leads to our Sales Department than any other Post Office.

The District Manager took those opportunities to speak to all the employees in a group while he was visiting. On one such visit, he was questioned by one of my Part Time Regular (PTF) carriers about when they would be turning over PTFs to regular carrier positions. I was caught off guard, and I could tell the District Manager was not pleased by this.

We had just recently had increases in the amount of automated mail that my carriers were receiving. Whenever that occurred, the expectation was that carrier routes would be adjusted, to assure that they had enough work for an 8- hour day on their routes. With less mail to sort, they needed additional deliveries to carry to keep in line with the reduction in office time. A lot of calculations went into those expected reduction in hours on the routes, and the Districts, Areas and Headquarters were unforgiving if their expectations were not met. The calculations showed that my office had more carriers than were needed to handle the reduced workload. When a situation such as that exists, carriers are expected to be excessed out of a Post Office. The number of carriers that would need to be excessed, according to the numbers, was more than 10. Excessing meant that those individuals would be sent to offices that needed carriers. Full Time Regular carriers were the pool that was tapped for excessing, according to our contracts with the union. PTFs were safe from excessing.

After the District Manager left my office, having pretty much blown off the question from that PTF, I had her come to my office for a talk. She was one of our top seniority PTFs at that point in time. I asked her if she liked working at my Post Office. She said that she did, and I knew that was the case. I explained that if she were turned over to a Full Time Regular position, she would be excessed to a location that she might not like. That did calm her down. As it turned out, the fancy calculations that were being used to show how many carriers needed to be excessed were incorrect. The amount of mail that was being projected to be automated did not turn out to happen. When I showed my superiors, based on my own internal tracking, how far off they were on the automation, they backed down and I kept my carriers.

After 5 years in my position as Postmaster at that level 24 office, I felt that I had accomplished everything that I had set out to do, and the measurable numbers validated those accomplishments. It was time for me to start seriously looking for a new position. I applied for a few level 26 Postmaster jobs in other Areas. I travelled to those Areas to interview for those jobs, but I was not selected. I had interviews scheduled for 2 other level 25 jobs. One was for a Manager position over several Post Office Branches in a nearby large city. The other interview was for a REC Manager position several states away from my current office.

By that point in time, there were only two RECs that remained open. I abandoned my former opinion about RECs closing and not wanting to be stuck in one that was being scheduled to close. Through contact that I kept with staff at my former REC, I knew that they had finally shut down recently. My former REC lasted far beyond their expected duration, and most of the staff had been transferred to other jobs in that area that they wanted. My old manager, Ben had taken the place of the Postmaster that retired in the city where he lived. The Post Office that he took over was only a level 20 office, but because his previous position had been eliminated, he retained his topped-out level 25 salary. His responsibilities were now greatly diminished, and that was a position I was determined not to be in if I was selected for this job.

To prepare for the REC Manager interview, I contacted Ben to get up to speed on the changes that had taken place since I had last worked in the REC operations environment. When I had left the REC that Ben had managed, we were supporting Mail Processing Centers in 8 different cities in our Area. Ben's REC continued to pick up additional Processing Centers, extending beyond his Area, as other RECs were closed. His REC had finally closed, lasting much longer than any of us thought it would. The workload of Ben's REC and a few other RECs that were shut down was split up and awarded to the final two remaining RECs.

It was difficult for me to reach Ben at his Post Office. He was now the Postmaster at a lower level Post Office with a very small staff. The first few times I tried calling him, I was told that he was out delivering Express Mail. Because of the importance of Express Mail being delivered on time to avoid payouts, Express Mail could be delivered by management or any other employee without being grieved by the carrier unions. This was certainly a change for Ben. When we finally were able to connect, Ben informed me about all the changes that had taken place in the REC environment. Where they had once started out with a dedication to automating letter mail, as the letter mail volume reduced overall and technology improved to the point of being able to read and print barcodes at the Mail Processing Centers, the REC work had expanded to flats, Priority Mail and forwarded mail. He shared enough operational details with me that I felt comfortably prepared for my interview.

The Executive, Al, who interviewed me for the REC Manager position was located several states away from me. I received an email message advising me that the interview would be conducted over the telephone. I did not feel comfortable about being interviewed over the telephone. It made me question the sincerity of an interview when the travel expenses necessary for a face to face interview were not put out. When Al called me for my interview, we spent about 45 minutes on the phone. I was surprised that he barely asked any questions at all about REC operations. In fact, I was a little disappointed since I had spent a lot of time studying up on the latest REC issues. He did tell me that he had recently lived in the city where I was Postmaster, when he had an Executive position in my Area. He knew that the city where I was Postmaster was very affluent, and he was impressed by the performance numbers I was achieving.

At the end of our conversation, he told me that he had one more interview to conduct over the telephone before he would look at his data and reach a decision. I felt good about how things had gone. I had connected with Al, and my feelings panned out when he called me a few days later to tell me he was selecting me. I contacted the neighboring city's Post Office to let them know that I was cancelling the interview and withdrawing my name from consideration for their Manager position. My MPOO, Dick seemed to be legitimately happy for me. The members of my staff were all happy for me as well, though they were apprehensive about who would be coming in to replace me when I left.

Dick called me to inform me that George, the level 22 Postmaster who had given me my first interview at the start of my career, was going to be coming in to replace me. George had just finished a detail working in a position at our District office. Paul, the District Manager, wanted Dick to place George in the detail as the OIC at my office when I left. Even though he may not have been Dick's first choice to replace me at his most important office, Paul was the king of the District castle and he got what he wanted. I decided with Al, who had selected me for my new REC Manager job, to stay at my old office for a week to work with George.

I had two thumb drives that I used to copy all the Excel spreadsheets, Word documents and other data that I used, as necessary, to assist me in my Postmaster job. I gave one copy to George, and a second one to my Customer Service Manager, Tom. I spent the week working with George, showing him the day to day things that I did to review operations and hold craft workers and staff accountable. I had notified the Chamber of Commerce of that city that George would be taking over my membership at that organization. I familiarized George with the many processes that I had in place to identify new opportunities to increase sales. I even had him accompany me on a visit to a few of the businesses in the city that were using our competitors for their shipping. That was foreign to George, as it was to most Postmasters I knew. A Postmaster actually going out to a business to try to convince them to switch to the Postal Service for their shipping was unheard of. I sensed that George would not be interested in pursuing sales anywhere close to the degree that I had done so. I hoped, for the sake of our financially challenged company, that he would. I spoke to Tom a few times after I left that Post Office and was told that he largely abandoned many of the processes that I had put into place. I wasn't surprised, but that Post Office was no longer my concern.

Prior to leaving that Postmaster job, I gave Customer Service Manager Tom the information he needed to continue the safety program I had put into place. That program is outlined with greater detail in the DISCIPLINE chapter of this book. I gave him the passwords to the two accounts that were in place to accumulate fuel purchase reward points. Those points were used to earn gas or merchandise cards for employees. A few weeks after starting my new assignment, I logged into the fuel awards account and saw that there were enough points accumulated to redeem a few $50 gas cards. I emailed Tom and advised him to change those passwords and move those points to the safe account I had opened. He replied that he would do that, and I stopped checking at that point in time. Years later, I found that the program had stopped. More on that later.

I sent a message to the District Manager and the Senior Plant Manager at my District detailing what I had done to put this incentive award plan together. I offered the suggestion that they disseminate the outlined plan to the MPOOs or the Postmasters in the District. Since award programs had been stopped, due to budgetary constraints, I made the naïve presumption that the Executives above me would have an interest in a no cost way of rewarding employees for good behavior. I knew that the fuel company had the gas stations that participated in the points program throughout most of the District. I never received a response from either of them.

I once again started the relocation process, travelling to the REC's location a few states away. When I arrived at the REC, I was happy to find out that the Acting Manager would be staying for a few days to help me get acclimated to my new job. Mary was the Acting Manager who had been assigned to cover the job through the posting and selection process. She was one of the Operations Managers at the other REC that remained open. The competition. That theme would remain constant throughout my time at that REC. Mary and I talked openly about which REC would ultimately be the last one standing. I found that very refreshing. Her openness and accessibility continued after she returned to her home facility.

At this point in my life, my kids were all grown, and I was separated from my wife with a divorce pending. I was alone in my new location, and with 3 tours of operations at my REC I knew what I had to do. I spent most of my days at the facility, often including weekend visits on the 24/7 operations. I would also regularly show up during the night operations, much to the chagrin of the staff working nights. They were not accustomed to this kind of attention from a Manager. The employees, however, loved it. Some of my visits were scheduled. At other times, I would just pop in to see what was happening unannounced.

I had packed up all my personal files and belongings that I had in my old Postmaster office before leaving there. Those items filled up two cages, items that are used to transport mail between the Post Offices and the Mail Processing Centers. I was surprised by how much I had accumulated over the course of my career. I placed placards on the outside of the containers to have the cages shipped to my new location. It took me several hours to get those cages unpacked and settle into my new home office. When I finally had those files put away, the framed pictures I had from my old office hanging on the walls, my mini-refrigerator by my desk and my coffee maker ready to go, it was time to dig into the work that needed to be done.

I learned that my predecessor was not much of a people person. She did not stray from her 8 – 5 schedule, and many of the workers did not even know who she was, or what she even looked like. That was a definite fact with the night shift workers. They never saw her, but it was also the case with a lot of the day shift workers. Whenever I was in the REC after I arrived there, I made a point of straying from my office to walk around on the work floor. There were approximately 500 computer workstations in place, with a break room on each side of the building. I would walk through each of the break rooms, stopping to talk with employees who wanted my attention while they were taking a break or on their lunch or break times.

I was a bit surprised the first time an employee walked up to me on the work floor to talk to me. She had a big smile on her face and said, "I just want to thank you for caring enough to come out and see us." I heard that common refrain often from employees, especially on the night shift. The smiles I would receive as I walked throughout the facility prompted me to spend more time out on the work floor whenever I was in the facility. My presence was having a positive effect on the morale of the workers, and that was necessary to help positive movements in improving operations. Especially with the challenge of being the last REC standing ever looming in the background.

For the first time in my career, I now had a secretary assigned to me. That was not an easy transition for me to make. I had grown very accustomed to handling things on my own. My secretary would answer the phones and screen calls for me, and that was much appreciated. I was not often in my office, spending my time on the work floor or in other parts of the building. I would try to think of things to give her to do, wanting to make sure she was keeping busy. One of the tasks I assigned her to do was to put all the monthly charges for each of the facility's utility bills on a spreadsheet I set up for her. I had her plug in the costs for the previous 12 months. With a facility as large as ours was, and with the multitude of electronic equipment that was powered daily for processing mail images, those bills were quite high. It was my intent to find ways to decrease those expenses. It also satisfied my nerdy desire to focus on numbers.

As I reviewed the actual bills for our water, I saw that we were being charged for taxes. I knew that this was a problem, because federal facilities are exempt from many taxes. I had my secretary contact the provider, and they admitted that they had made a change to their billing that inadvertently added the tax cost to our bills. This had been occurring for several months. When the correction was made, the credit that we received on our account resulted in no cost for our water use over the next few months.

I knew that many of the employees at the facility were focused on conservation. There wasn't any recycling program in place at the facility. Everything went into the same trash cans. I tasked my secretary with contacting the disposal company to find out about recycling. She was told that we would have to pay an additional amount if we were to have a recycling dumpster added to the current dumpster we had in place. I investigated it further and found that the large dumpster we had in place currently was picked up a few times each week. I had one of my staff monitor it and found that it was not close to being filled prior to being picked up. I spoke with the disposal representative and we decided to go with a smaller garbage container and add a recycling container. The cost ended up being lower than what we had been paying previously, and the employees were happy to see that we were being responsible about our disposal and recycling.

The monthly electric bill at our facility was astronomical. I spoke with my Manager who was responsible for the Electronic Technicians (ETs) and my Industrial Engineer. We worked out a way to have a 10-hour daily lights out in one of the sections of the work floor. To accomplish this, the work that was typically done in that area had to be internally shifted to workstations in the lights on area. It did not result in large savings, but perception is an important consideration. The employees who were most focused on conservation were very happy, and I was always happy to save the Postal Service money anywhere I could.

I always kept up with different programs that the Postal Service would put into place, and it caught my eye when I saw a Conservation Award program announced. I had to fill out paperwork, identifying the areas where we had identified and achieved results that cut costs and reflected responsible changes we had made. I know that there were a few other changes that were added to the list, but I simply cannot recall what they were. We did not ultimately win whatever the top award happened to be, but we did receive an Honorable Mention for our accomplishments in the area of conservation. My goals were accomplished. My employees were happy to hear that we were being recognized as a facility for our efforts, and I wanted the Area Managers who I reported to made aware of every little positive thing that we did. It always came down to which REC would be the last one standing, and we were both situated within the same Area.

I wanted every employee at that facility to feel and know that they were important to me. I started a process of having Quarterly meetings with the employees. To accomplish this, I would have the 3 Operations Managers on each tour review their staffing for the day that these meetings would be taking place. They would give me the times that would maximize the attendance at those meetings. A large room that was typically used for training would be set up to handle the groups that would attend these meetings. The average group would be about 40 employees, and I pushed the Managers to make sure that each of them sat in on one of the meetings during their tour, as well as their Supervisors and the ETs. Some of the groups were quite large, and there would only be standing room at the back. As the room filled with each group, some employees would come right up to the front to sit. Most of them would opt for the obscurity of the safe middle area, or the back of the room. I would stand in the front as the employees filed in, smiling and telling them that there were plenty of seats available in the front.

The first meeting would typically take place at about 7 a.m., and the last meeting would typically take place at about 1 a.m. the next morning. There would sometimes be an hour or more between meetings, but certainly not enough time for me to get much rest. It was well worth it to me to have those meetings, even if it did mean a very long workday. The facial expressions on the different employees ran the gamut of emotions, as I would expect. Even though I would expect that all the employees would have welcomed the break from their routine work, there would be several them that looked like they would rather be anywhere else than in that room. I would focus on the smiling faces to keep me motivated. Most of the employees in the later groups, especially in that 1 a.m. group, were typically happy to see me there. That latest group was the one I had to be most cautious with. They wanted to ask the most questions and keep my attention longer, and I was getting pretty worn out after the full day of meetings. I had to put a limit on the time and the number of questions I would take because they did need to get back to the processing work at hand.

Amidst all the "feel good" events that took place at that REC, I also did my customary review of employee operations productivity, performance and attendance. I ran into the usual resistance from the staff on these matters. What they considered to be "acceptable" attendance, for example, I did not. I was blazing trails with discipline on issues that had not received any attention in the past. The head clerk union steward at the REC geared up for a lot of grievances. That did not surprise me. I did my best to schedule meetings with the union on a regular basis. I wanted them to know, in advance, per our national contract with them, any time a change was going to take place.

I felt fortunate that my Tour 2 Operations Manager had a very strong clerk contract background. She was my go-to person whenever potential troubles would loom over changes I was making. Unfortunately for me, somehow my Manager at the Area office formed the opinion that my Tour 2 Operations Manager was the one at our facility making all the decisions. Apparently, he thought that I was just the figure head, and she ran the ship. I never did find out why it was that he reached this errant conclusion.

Changes had taken place at the Area office since I had become the REC Manager. Al, the executive who had interviewed me over the phone and selected me for the job, had been assigned to a District Manager position a few states away from the Area office. When I tried to contact Al at his new office, he did not respond to me. Writing on the wall, perhaps. When he hired me, he had done so on the behest of the Area Distribution Operations Manager, who he reported to. After Al's departure, I had a few conversations with my real Manager, Bill. Through those conversations, I discovered that he had formed the opinion that I was not making decisions. He came right out and told me that, and he was not interested in hearing anything to the contrary from me.

Reaching an Executive position was the ultimate goal that I had for my career, and I knew that my lack of a formal education would probably be a deterrent. Succession Planning was a process in place that allowed EAS Postmasters and Managers, those of us in the EAS numbered positions, to be selected for grooming for an Executive job. Employees were able to submit a self-nomination when the window was open for Succession Planning, which was approximately every two years at that point. I had done so on two earlier occasions. There was, of course, a fair amount of paperwork that had to be submitted along with the self-nomination. It was necessary to provide as much documentation on measurable results that I had achieved as possible.

The first time that I self-nominated was when I was a level 22 Postmaster. I was, of course, anxious to hear any kind of news at all about what was going to take place after I submitted my paperwork. Corey was the District Manager where I was working at that time. I received a message from Corey's secretary, advising me when to come to his office for a Succession Planning Feedback meeting. I did not know where I stood at that time, but I was happy to be receiving attention of any kind. I reported to Corey's office at the appointed time, and I was not at all prepared for what took place at that meeting.

I sat at a desk across from Corey, and he had paperwork in front of him that referenced the Post Office where I currently worked at that time. He started out by advising me that I was not going to be considered for Succession Planning. I wasn't terribly surprised at that news, but I was caught off guard as he went on to beat me up about all the negative things he could find about my Post Office. I remember thinking that I wished I had brought along paperwork to reference some of the many accomplishments that I had achieved, but I had no idea that this was going to be a beat-up session. Corey had very little, if anything at all, of a positive nature to say to me. I left his office feeling quite demeaned and, in retrospect, I doubt that anything I might have said to refute his negative points would have been considered. After all, Corey was that guy who had interviewed me for a Postmaster position a few years earlier and barely paid any attention to me during that process. I went back to my Post Office, shook it off, and went about my business of doing the best that I could for the Postal Service.

A few years later, soon after I was promoted to the level 24 Postmaster position, the Succession Planning program opened once again. Of course, I applied for it once again. As I settled into my new Postmaster job, I waited with much anticipation to find out what would happen with this latest Succession Planning attempt. I was now in a different District, so a different District Manager would be looking at my application. I thought that now that I had moved up a few more levels, being only a few numbers away from that top level EAS 26 number, I would have a much better opportunity for consideration into the program. I was very disappointed when I was contacted by my new District Manager.

My new District Manager contacted me, telling me that since I was new to his District, he really didn't know much about me. Because of that, he was referring my application to my former District Manager for his consideration. That meant that once again I would be dealing with Corey. I didn't have very high hopes for what that would mean. I talked to a few past contacts I had made in my old District and was told that Corey was on a big detail assignment at Headquarters. I was sure that he had high aspirations to move further up the Executive ladder within the Postal Service. I wasn't too sure about how he was going to handle my Succession Planning request while he was out on his detail. I found out when I received an email from him giving me a date and time that I was to call him at Headquarters regarding my Succession Planning application.

I called him at the appointed time, and I wasn't surprised to hear that I was being turned down again, though his tenor was vastly different from the previous time. He told me that he had talked with my new District Manager, and he had told him that he was getting an excellent Postmaster. Corey complimented me on the job that I had done at my former Post Office since our previous meeting. He told me that he was impressed with the numbers that were being achieved at that Post Office and told me that the new sales that I had accrued were outstanding. But... There was that big but. He told me that although I had proven myself as a level 22 Postmaster, I was just starting out at my level 24 Postmaster job. He wished me luck in proving myself through great accomplishments in my level 24 Postmaster position, telling me that I would then be in a better position to again apply for Succession Planning.

And back to my REC Manager position, Succession Planning was opening once again. As I read through the program information, I noted that this time there was not a self-nomination feature. Candidates had to be nominated by an Executive who was over them. Considering the misgivings that Bill had about who was running my office, I once again did not have very high hopes. I had not met Bill in person up to that point, so I decided that would be a good thing to do. I contacted him and told him that I wanted to request a few vacation days off, and that I was planning on travelling by his area. His office was about a 12-hour drive from my location. I told him that I would like to stop by his office to meet him, and we set up a time for me to do so.

I put a packet together that had printouts that highlighted the successes I had in previous positions. I included the highlights of things that I had achieved while working for him. He was cordial when I entered his office to meet him. We spoke about current things that were happening in the automation environment, as well as some personal non-business items. I handed the packet that I had brought along to Bill, telling him that I knew the Succession Planning program was then currently in place again. Bill looked at me blankly and matter-of-factly stated "There is no self-nomination this time." I told him that I was aware of that, but I didn't feel that he knew enough about me to truly consider me for the program. I told him that I hoped he would look through what I had brought to him and give me serious consideration for the program.

He didn't open the packet while I was there, and I'm doubtful that he did open it up after I left his office. He set it down on his table and the conversation veered back to work at my REC. He once again told me, this time face to face, that he thought my Operations Manager was making the decisions at the REC. I made a vain attempt to convince him that the changes that were taking place were at my direction. My Operations Manager and the rest of the staff did what I told them to do. I could easily sense by his demeanor that he did not believe me. His mind was made up and would not be changed. Before too long, I officially discovered that I was not being considered for Succession Planning. I had to make a few phone calls and do some prodding to find this out.

Out of curiosity, I contacted Mary, the Operations Manager from the competition REC who had been Acting Manager at my REC when I arrived there. We spoke on the phone infrequently about operational issues, and I knew that she was trustworthy. After a bit of friendly bantering, I turned to the subject of Succession Planning. I told her that I would understand if she felt uncomfortable sharing information with me. She encouraged me to ask away. I started out by asking her if she was aware whether her Manager had been spoken to about Succession Planning. She told me that Bill had called her Manager and told her that he would nominate her for the program if she was interested. She had declined, because she did not want to potentially have to go out on details to other locations.

I thanked her for sharing with me, then asked her more pointedly if she had been offered entry into the Succession Planning program. She told me that yes, Bill had offered it to her as well. She turned it down for the same reason. Her husband was having health problems, and she did not want to have to be away from him for any great length of time. I was feeling more than a little demoralized at that point. My peer level 25 Manager from the other REC and her level 22 Operations Manager had both been offered Succession Planning, and I was not receiving consideration. I had no problem going wherever I was sent for any length of time, but my Manager apparently lacked the confidence in my abilities to recommend me.

I was surprised one day when I received a phone call that was quite uncharacteristic from Bill. He stressed that it was a confidential matter, and that I was not to discuss it with anyone. He asked me if I would be interested in a detail to an office as the OIC of a level 26 Post Office. I said yes without hesitation. He told me that there was a Post Office in the Area that was not performing well. I asked him where it was, but he said he could not tell me. He told me that he would be back in touch with me about it within the next week or two. I was excited to hear that news, thinking that perhaps he had looked through the packet I had left him after all.

After several weeks passed without any contact from him about the detail, I emailed Bill to arrange a meeting time to discuss operational issues over the phone. He gave me a time to call him, and I did. I spoke to him about the operational issues, then casually threw a question in about that detail. The answer was short, and not too sweet for me. He told me that the office in question was no longer a problem and ended our conversation. I continued with my work, not letting these personal disappointments affect the aggressive job I was doing at the REC.

More than a few months earlier, I had heard that the Postal Service was gearing up for more structural changes to take place within management. Current Postmasters were being offered $10,000 to resign or take an early retirement offer. Even if I had still been a Postmaster, I would not have considered that offer.

I had ambitions to still move up the career ladder at that point in time. Many Postmasters did take that offer, and I neglected to take advantage of the vacancies that resulted until several months later. Unfortunately, my delay hurt me. I did feel that I would need to aggressively start looking for my next promotion, especially since my Manager was obviously not going to help me along with my career aspirations.

I was a level 25 Manager, with many successes to point back to when I served as a Postmaster. The next progressive position for me to go would be to a level 26 Postmaster job. I started to look at the vacancy announcements for level 26 Postmaster jobs on the Postal Service website. There weren't any vacancies to be found when I started looking. I began to do research to find out which Districts across the country had level 26 Post Offices, since not all of them did. I crafted a letter that I sent to the District Managers where level 26 Post Offices were located, after calling the secretaries at those locations to seek the most acceptable way to approach those District Managers. My letter highlighted my career accomplishments, with a request for consideration to a detail, if a level 26 Post Office became vacant.

I received several contacts back from the District Managers. Some were very complimentary about the successes I had in my past, but none had any opportunities available. I sent an email directly to one of the District Managers whose name I recognized, attaching my detail request letter and the summary of my accomplishments. I tentatively messaged "I'm not sure if you remember me, but I would appreciate it if you would look at the attachments for your consideration." The last time I had spoken to this District Manager was when she was in a MPOO position, sitting next to her District Manager at my Advanced Leadership graduation (covered in depth in the TRAINING chapter).

We ended up talking on the phone, and she said yes, she

remembered me. There were six level 26 Post Offices in her group, but none were available at that time. She told me that if I had contacted her a few months earlier, when Postmasters had taken the $10,000 offer, she could have done something for me. She said that her offices were now stable, and she did not think any vacancies would be opening any time soon. I was grateful for the REC Manager job that I had, and I continued to apply myself towards making any improvements I could while I was there.

The competition continued with REC vs REC, as I tracked what I perceived would be the categories that would be scrutinized to determine which one would remain open and which one would close. I finally received another hush hush call from Bill, being sworn to secrecy. He told me that he was coming to my city, where he would be meeting with me accompanied by the Headquarters liaison who had been overseeing the RECs since their inception. The decision had been made, and my REC would be shutting down.

As with the other positions I held throughout my career with the United States Postal Service, other events that took place during my REC Manager position will be further elaborated on in the appropriate upcoming chapters of this book.

CHAPTER TWO: SALES

While serving as Postmaster in my level 22 Post Office, I began to take more of an interest in growing our business. The Postal Service had internal programs in place to track the outreach activities of craft employees (carriers, clerks, etc.) and management employees. At my previous Post Office, I had just gotten started regularly encouraging my carriers to fill out cards that would provide information about potential new customers to our District Sales Department. I continued this at my new Post Office but ramped it up exponentially. I would draw names for carriers to win gift cards from among those who had turned in lead cards through the Customer Connect program. That was the name of the program that was in effect for carriers to turn in potential sales leads. The carriers would typically turn in the names and addresses of business or residential customers who were using one of our competitors for their business. I later found out that there was an agreement in place with the carrier's union that there should not be any awards given out to carriers for this program.

I could somewhat understand the rationale, from the union's perspective, once I became aware of the agreement. It wasn't fair for carriers who had no businesses on their routes. Carriers on routes that had a fair amount of businesses were in a better position to turn in more leads. I was made aware of this agreement in a rather embarrassing way. I was being interviewed by the MPOO for my next position, touting all the successes I had in growing the business at my Post Office. When I mentioned the gift cards, he looked at me and dryly commented "You're not supposed to give anything out with that program. There's an agreement in effect on that." Fortunately for me, it did not cost me that next promotion.

Not knowing any better prior to that interview, I continued to give out awards to my carriers. That encouraged more of them to turn in leads for our Sales Department. Since no grievances were filed over this practice by the carrier union officials at that office, perhaps they were unaware of this agreement as well. It wasn't long before those leads were turning into sales, and my Post Office was being noticed by our District for all the activity going on. We had staff from the Marketing and Sales Departments coming out to recognize our carriers for their accomplishments. On a few occasions they brought out donuts and coffee for our carriers for the great job they were doing turning in leads. Marketing Department staff had a breakfast brought in for my employees when we achieved the prominence of having turned in the most leads in the District at the end of my last year at that Post Office.

I always appreciated having the ability to purchase items that I needed to help me in the performance of my duties. As a facility head (Postmaster or Manager), I did not have a credit card of my own to make purchases for items I wanted. I had to go to one of my employees who would initiate purchases. It was important to me to always have two employees at facilities who were assigned Postal Service IMPAC (International Merchant Purchase Authorization Card) credit cards to make approved purchases, wherever I happened to be working.

I was a firm believer in having backups in place for every job. It was necessary to cross train employees to assure uninterrupted operations in every area. Life happens, and it was impossible to know when someone who was at work doing their job one day might not be there the next day. Because of the importance of security placed on purchasing, new IMPAC cardholders had to go through several online documented training and ethics classes prior to being issued a credit card. Only a few IMPAC cards were allowed within an office, and I did not want my purchasing power interrupted due to an employee suddenly being absent from work for an extended period.

I made a habit of calling into whichever office I was running while I was driving in to work, and occasionally on my way home. When I was the Postmaster at my level 22 office, the drive from my home to my office took a minimum of one hour. I left early enough to avoid rush hour traffic, but if the weather was bad it would mean a longer travel time. I would usually get to work by 7 a.m. and leave at 5 p.m. The drive home would unavoidably occur during rush hour. I can recall a few times, when the weather was particularly bad, that the drive home took up to 2.5 to 3 hours. What I noticed during my calls to that office was that there was dead silence when I was put on hold. That meant missed opportunity to me.

I crafted a message that would play during the time that individuals were put on hold. I had to contact the company that put the phone system in place at my office for their assistance. I picked one of my female clerks who had a pleasant-sounding voice to record the message. The message covered several topics, including our hours of operation, the availability of Post Office Boxes at 3 different locations in my city and information about Express and Priority Mail. I had my clerk rehearse the message several times before finally recording it and having it placed into our phone system by the company that handled the system. Several months later, I did catch some grief from my District's Marketing Department for making a homemade recording. The Marketing Manager became aware of my message when one of his staff called my office and was put on hold. They replaced my message with a canned message that was being used throughout the company, and that was that. It would have been nice to know that a company canned message was available.

I knew that as a Postmaster I could be doing more, so I decided to take my aggression in sales to a new level. I purchased a portfolio case that was large enough to hold a variety of folded Postal Service Priority Flat Rate boxes. I had driven around the city where my office was located enough to know where the heaviest business areas were located, so I picked a building to start and went to work. After my morning business in my office was finished and my carriers were out delivering the mail on their routes, I hit the road and drove to that building with my portfolio case. I started on the first floor and went door to door to each of the businesses that were in that building. I would enter each office, introduce myself to the first person I would see, and tell them that I would like to speak with whoever was handling their mailing or their shipping of items.

Most of the customers that I met were quite surprised to see the Postmaster visiting their offices. I would pay attention to any items that were waiting to be picked up near the entrance to their offices. If there were Priority Mail or other Postal Service items awaiting pickup, I would thank them for their business. If there were items awaiting pickup from one of our competitors, I would point to those items and tell them that I wanted to talk to them about those items. I would often show customers how they could go to the Postal Service website and sign up for Click-N-Ship. I would show them how to order any of the free supplies that the Postal Service had available for them online, letting them know that those products would be delivered to them at no cost. Customers were able to see the different sizes of Priority and Express Mail Flat Rate packaging that I had with me, and it wasn't long before I started seeing the results of new sales.

My portfolio also contained Stamps by Mail and Stamps by Fax forms for the businesses to use. I did not want customers waiting in line at my Post Office. Mystery Shops were and are regularly conducted at Post Offices. The subject of Mystery Shops is covered more in depth in the DISCIPLINE chapter of this book. The length of time that a Mystery Shopper spent waiting in line was always a concern to Postmasters. If the wait time exceeded five minutes, the grief that would rain down on the Postmaster from up the food chain was something I worked hard to avoid.

There were close to a quarter million residential and business customers in my city, and with only a few Postal Service locations available for customers to conduct their business, keeping that wait time down to an acceptable limit was a challenge. There were occasions when a Mystery Shopper would report waiting in line at one of my locations for up to 20 minutes, or even longer. The grief and attention that fell on me as a result was not at all pleasant.

Advertising the Stamps by Mail program required placing an order to a centralized location within the United States, and there were costs associated with placing orders for this mass mailing. The mail pieces were delivered to every residential and business customer within specific Zip Codes, encouraging them to send the mailer back to their local Post Office with their stamp order. I remember having to justify those expenses to my MPOO when I wanted to place my order. I was able to provide him with documentation showing that the stamp sales that were generated after the Stamps by Mail forms were sent out provided a more than adequate return on that investment.

I tracked down several retail businesses in my city where customers could purchase books of stamps at no additional cost, listing them on handouts that were available at each of my official Retail Units. I had shamelessly stolen the Stamps by Fax idea from another office, and the form used for faxing in orders was one of several items that I regularly mailed out to businesses for their use. Orders could be faxed in and their items were delivered by the carrier with the customer's regular mail delivery. The customer would give the payment to their carrier and it would save them a trip to the Post Office.

There were retail businesses located in the cities where I served who had CPU (Contract Postal Unit) partnerships with the Postal Service. Those businesses were able to provide Postal Service products and services to their customers, receiving payments that were outlined within their agreements based on the sales that they achieved. I looked at geographic locations within the delivery area of the different cities where I served as Postmaster, attempting to provide relief for my Postal Service Retail Units. I visited several businesses in key locations, soliciting them to become a CPU partner with my Post Office. I would attempt to sell them on the idea of having additional customers coming to their locations that could potentially lead to more business for them. Despite the time I took and the efforts I made to sign up new CPUs, I was not able to see any come to fruition. The rules that they had to follow, particularly in the area of having physical alterations done within their business to Postal Service specs, were onerous. The red tape and obstacles involved invariably caused them to drop out at some point before finishing the process.

I would spend time in my Retail lobbies talking to my customers, particularly when I did not have a Supervisor available to do so. If the number of customers waiting in line was beginning to grow, I would ask if anyone had business to conduct with a debit or credit card. I had Automated Postal Centers (APCs) available in my lobbies. That equipment was new at the time, so customers were leery of them, as they often are when new things are introduced. I would take them to an APC, encouraging them by telling them that I would walk them through the entire transaction. As I walked them through the transaction, I would let them know that the APCs were available for use 24/7. It was my hope to convert as many customers as possible to using the APCs.

Like virtually everything else in the Postal Service, APC sales were regularly tracked and reports were put out ranking the standings within each District. If an APC was not producing enough sales, there was an ever-present threat that it would be taken out and placed elsewhere. My APCs were commodities I did not want to lose. My SSAs (Sales and Service Associates, or Window Clerks) did not at all share my opinion on those APCs. They felt that the APC was a threat to their jobs. Many of them preferred that the customers wait in line to be served by them, regardless of how long it took. They found it especially annoying when I would give an instruction to have one of the SSAs leave their post behind the counter to greet customers at the door and steer them to the APC if their business could be handled on that machine.

When I would see a customer bringing in many packages, I would invite them to my office to talk about Click-N-Ship. If they took me up on my offer, I would help them to sign up online and send them off with their first set of packaging supplies from my Post Office. The SSAs were often appreciated by the customers they regularly served. I approached a man one day who had several packages with him, waiting in line to be served. I asked him if he had a debit or credit card with him to handle his mailing, and he said that he did. I asked him if he would like to accompany me to the APC in the outer lobby, and he said he would not. He told me that he was aware of the APC, but he preferred to talk to my employees at the window while he did his business.

At one point during a particularly hot summer day, the air conditioning at my Post Office crashed. It ended up taking a few days to get the necessary repairs made, and I had many unhappy employees throughout the building. I had a few large floor fans on hand to help circulate air on the workroom floor, where there were approximately 200 employees working. I also provided bottled water for them to drink. I had a few smaller fans placed up by the SSAs and in the lobby for the waiting customers. After the first day of the air conditioning being out, I was surprised to see small fans in place at each of the five SSA spots I had at the Retail Unit. I asked the Supervisor where they had come from, and I was told that a customer had brought them in for the SSAs.

Because many APCs were available at Post Offices 24/7, they needed receptacles for their items to be placed during times when the Post Office was closed. Some Post Offices had free standing containers that customers would drop their items into during off hours. Those metal containers were large but limited as to the number of items that could be placed in them. If they became full, or if a package that was dropped in blocked the pull-down door from opening, items could not be placed securely inside of them to await being emptied when the Post Office staff arrived. The drop location in my Main Post Office emptied into a large hamper inside my Post Office work area. The hamper was positioned under the deposit door with a cage around it, and the contents were often spilling over inside the cage when staff arrived on duty to empty it. There were occasions when there were so many packages that the deposit door was blocked, preventing additional packages from being deposited.

My Main Post Office had the distinction of being one of the very few offices in my District that had retail window hours open on Sundays. That made the scheduling of my SSAs difficult, particularly since the Sunday hours were within a 6-hour window, from 11:00 a.m. till 5:00 p.m. I needed to make sure that my full-time employees had measurable work to do during their 8-hour shift. I have no idea what those full time 8-hour employees did with the few hours they were on the clock without the Retail Window being open prior to my arrival as the Postmaster. I made a point of making sure they had work to do. One of the tasks that they were given was to handle the APC drop hamper, emptying it if necessary, or moving the items around to allow additional room. I would occasionally drop in on Sundays, usually in street clothes conducive to the season, rather than in my customary suit and tie. I liked to keep my SSAs off guard, never knowing when I might show up there. Going in on those Sundays gave me the opportunity to get some work done on my computer without the interruptions of employees or phone calls. I also liked to occasionally send my MPOO, Dick an email about a business-related matter, hoping that he noticed that the message was sent on a Sunday from his hard-working Postmaster.

I noticed that some of the return Zip Codes on items that were dropped into my APC receptacle were not within my Post Office jurisdiction. There were Zip Codes from a few of my neighboring cities, and occasionally from an office nowhere near my location. I placed a clipboard by the internal APC Cage for the employees who were emptying it to write down the names and addresses of the individuals from other Zip Codes who were dropping their items into my APC drop box. Those customers were printing their labels and paying for the postage at their homes or offices, and the revenue they paid was appropriated to the Post Office where their Zip Code was located. My office was doing the work of moving their items, but another Post Office was receiving the revenue. Unacceptable.

Many of the items that were being dropped into my APC drop box were items that were being sold through eBay. I presumed that the shippers lived in the cities identified in the return addresses, and probably were on their way to their day job when they made their drops at my Post Office as a matter of convenience. I developed a standard letter that was sent to those customers. It basically said that I appreciated the business that they were giving to the Postal Service, but there were rules that I cited about having the correct return Zip Code when bringing items to a specific Post Office. The letter admonished them to use my APC to purchase the postage and label for their items or there could be a delay in the processing of their mail.

The District Marketing and Sales Department Managers and the employees within those functions were pleased to see the results that I was getting in terms of Business Connect and associated sales. Business Connect was the program in place to track leads and sales initiated primarily by Managers and Postmasters, like the Customer Connect program used by the carriers. I talked to the Marketing Manager at my District about an upcoming Postmaster meeting, requesting a block of time during that meeting to address the Postmasters on the topic of sales. She was happy to oblige me, hopeful that other Postmasters would be encouraged to take a more active role in sales. I took that opportunity to speak to over 100 Postmasters of varying levels about the processes that I was using to increase sales. I could see the looks on the faces of those Postmasters who felt that they had enough to do on their jobs. I knew that my presentation would only impact a small number of them, but it was worth it to me to make that effort for the sake of our struggling company.

I did receive a few phone calls and email messages from Postmasters within my District after my presentation. They wanted additional information from me about pursuing new business for their offices. I was always more than happy to share whatever tips I could to them. I was surprised when I received a call from the Postmaster of a very affluent city nearby. He wanted to visit me to see firsthand what I was doing. When he arrived at my office, I talked to him about some of the practices I had put in place, sharing the flyers and forms that I had developed to increase sales. He had quite a look of surprise when I told him that we were going to go out to visit some businesses.

I took him out with me to visit an office building, with my portfolio of Flat Rate shipping packages and forms in hand. He was obviously nervous and uncomfortable as we started going door to door, cold calling the businesses to solicit sales. I would introduce myself first, then him, asking to speak to the individual who handled their mailing and any shipping. He could not believe the effort that I was putting into capturing new business. I cut the visiting short on that day, sensing that he preferred to perhaps be at his dentist's office rather than cold calling with me. I don't know if he ultimately used any of the tips that I gave him during his visit, but I'm doubtful that he did any cold calling.

When I received my promotion from my level 22 Postmaster position to the level 24 position, I did have to stop giving out those gift cards and other cash value awards to the employees who turned in leads. I did not at all relax my attention on the lead programs or on sales in general. As I mentioned in the previous chapter, my interest in sales had prompted me to apply for a Postal Service job in Sales. Being promoted to a level 24 Postmaster position did not diminish my interest in winning over new customers. I made a habit of regularly including Customer Connect information in the service talks to my employees. I would highlight any leads that had been turned in, checking with the employees to find out if they would mind their names being mentioned for turning in leads. I did not want any of them to be offended or embarrassed by being recognized in public to their peers. Most of them did not mind at all being mentioned. I also included Rural Reach information in the service talks that were given to the Rural Carriers. Rural Reach was the name of the program that was in place for the Rural Carriers to turn in leads for our Sales Department. Recognizing that every employee potentially knew of business possibilities for sales, I additionally included Submit-a-Lead information in service talks to my employees. The Submit-a-Lead program was in place for any employee, other than carriers, to turn in sales leads.

As the leads were coming in from employees within each craft, new sales were being achieved as well. I had developed contacts within the Sales and Marketing Departments at each of the Districts where I served as Postmaster. They knew the nuts and bolts of pricing that I did not know. There were different ways to reduce costs to our customers, all within the existing product price structures that were in place. I would typically make the first contact with customers who were using one or more of our competitors. I found that most of those customers were caught off guard when I would call them to set up an appointment to go to their location and meet with them. This was not typical Postmaster behavior.

There were several unconventional processes that I put into place to facilitate new business and sales while I was serving in my final Postmaster position. The lead programs that were in place were good, but not aggressive enough for my ambitions. In addition to regularly including encouragement to the employees to participate in the lead programs, I wanted any businesses that were being conducted out of my resident's homes. I told my carriers and Post Office Box clerks that I wanted the information on any customers who were receiving statements through their mail from any of our competitors. I also told my carriers that I wanted the addresses of any customers where a competitor was observed picking up packages at their locations. I followed up on many contacts that were given to me through that process, with new sales resulting in several situations.

I had different letters that I crafted for initial contact with perspective customers. In some cases, I would follow up with phone calls if I was able to find a customer's phone number. Through researching our database, I was able to isolate the businesses in each of the four Zip Codes that were served by my Post Office. I included the businesses that were being served through the two different Post Office Box Zip Codes that were at my Post Office. The businesses numbered in the thousands. There were always one or more employees at my Post Office who were unable to perform their normal duties, due to either on the job or off the job injuries. I would utilize those employees to fold letters and stuff envelopes to those businesses, placing labels on them as well. The subject matter of those letters would vary, depending on different planned events that might be scheduled to occur.

I designated a standing day each week during given hours where I encouraged business owners, or their representatives, to come to my office for information sessions that could help them to reduce their shipping costs. I would let my business customers know about these sessions through flyers in my retail lobbies and the occasional mailings I would send out. When I had first arrived at my new level 24 office, I found that I had a desktop computer for my use. I contacted Gary, the MPOO who had promoted me, requesting that I get a laptop. Gary was resistant to that request, and it took no small amount of assurances of sales increases from me to get him to authorize my request. I told him that I was going to give presentations outside of my office to promote sales, and I would also need a projector and screen to accomplish that. Fortunately, after a brief time he acquiesced, and it worked well for me. I ended up receiving a hand me down laptop from someone at our District office who received a new laptop.

I would have the conference room that was attached to my office set up prior to those meetings. I had coffee ready for my visitors, with many handouts and informational flyers set up on the conference table. I could seat up to 12 people comfortably at the conference table, with additional chairs ready for the overflow that would occasionally occur. I found that it was necessary for me to switch connections around in the telephone wiring panel near my office prior to using my laptop in my conference room. There were a limited number of connections in my Post Office, and I couldn't permanently disable any of the connections that were in place for our other operations. I had to switch my office connection within a control panel over to the conference room when I needed internet access there, then switch it back to my office when I was finished. Where was Wi-Fi when I needed it?? The security within the Postal Service network necessitated hard wiring for access.

I gave the same presentation that I would give to my customers to my employees. I had groups of employees come to my conference room, abbreviating their presentation down to 10-15 minutes. Productivity was a constant measurement that was scrutinized up and down the food chain of the Postal Service. I made sure that all the time for each employee who attended my presentation was charged to training. Training time was also heavily scrutinized, because hours that went into training did not count against productivity. The higher ups were suspicious if too many hours were showing up charged to training, ever concerned that cheating was going on to keep productivity numbers high. I was ultimately questioned about the time that was used for my presentations, but my Manager turned the heat down when I explained what I was doing.

I would show the audience a short video about Click-N-Ship from the projector that was set up in my conference room. I would then log into my own Click-N-Ship account on usps.com, explaining how to sign up for an account, build an address book, register credit cards to make payments for postage, print labels and order supplies. I had the same thought process every time I gave a presentation to anyone, whether they were a customer or an employee. If they had business they were conducting that involved shipping, and if they happened to be using a competitor, I wanted them to see the ease of using the Postal Service. If they did already use the Postal Service for their shipping, I wanted to keep their business, but keep them out of the retail lobby. It didn't matter to me whether it was one of my Post Office lobbies or some other Post Office lobby. Waiting time in line was an issue everywhere, and there was a discount given to customers using Click-N-Ship, to incentivize them to do their business online. And if they did not conduct any business themselves, my hope was that they would share this information with their neighbors, friends, families, etc., anyone who they knew that might be involved in any kind of business that involved shipping.

I found that there was a membership that my Post Office had that had lapsed with the local Chamber of Commerce. I paid the necessary fee to rejoin that organization and started to attend the meetings that were held at their office. The Chamber of Commerce in my city was very large, with hundreds of members and many different groups that met each month. The group that I chose to join had about 40 members in it. Meetings were held every two weeks, and the time of day when they occurred worked with my Postmaster schedule. Each member rotated through opportunities to give a presentation to the other members of the group, promoting their business and working to build relationships within the group.

I would attend after-hour events that were held within the city at various locations. I would regularly review the calendar of Chamber events to determine which events would potentially lead to new business connections. There were ribbon cutting events for new businesses that were starting up and events that were held in conjunction with other Chamber of Commerce organizations from nearby cities. I decided to broaden my horizons by attending Business Expositions, Trade Shows and other Trade Events. Those events typically occurred after hours. I did not receive any additional pay for events that I would attend beyond my normal schedule, being a salaried employee. Those events did not typically occur more than once per month, and I felt that they were worth my time for the potential value they would bring to the Postal Service.

Prior to attending those events, I had to make certain that I would have everything I needed to bring with me. Attendance at a Business Expo involved signing up and paying a fee for space that you would need to set up. I always rented the smallest amount of space for my setup. Some of the businesses attending these events would have elaborate setups requiring two or more spaces, with a variety of products and displays that they would bring in with them. There were often restaurants or other food vendors in attendance, and they would often give away their food and drinks. That was usually my dinner when I attended those events.

I had a Postal Service mail tub or two that I would pack my items in to bring to the events. I had a variety of handouts that I would place on the eight-foot folding table I brought with me. I brought along my name plate that I had on the desk at my office. I would have a card stand in place on the table with my business cards in it. I always carried a nice, leather business card holder in my suit jacket pocket, to make as positive an impression as possible when meeting new contacts. On most occasions I had my laptop facing me behind the table, with a separate monitor pointed outward for interested parties to view. Occasionally I would use my projector and bring along a portable screen for viewing. I had a few other props that I would bring along to place on the table, but I needed an official looking cover to place on the tabletop. I had seen Postal blue colored cloth tops with the official Postal Service emblem on them, and I wanted one. Those were not available to me through the usual product catalogues I used to find items. I ended up calling someone I knew who worked at the District Marketing Department, and they were able to find me one to purchase through them.

I needed an electrical outlet to power my laptop and projector I would bring along, and that was usually not a problem. I also needed internet access to hard wire for my presentations. I do recall one event where I did not have the electricity or internet access available that I had requested when signing up. The individuals who were managing the event ended up having to run several extension cords together to get the power I needed to my table location. We also linked several cords together to get me hard wired to the available internet access. By the time I had an actual connection, it was so weak I couldn't end up using it for my online demonstrations, so I did have to improvise.

It always amazed me to see the looks on the faces of some people who came to those Business Expos when they would get to my table. I often heard "What's the Post Office doing here?" I would smile at them and say "I'm in a business that is looking for new customers, just like everyone else here. Can I show you what I have?" I would usually show people how to sign up for

Click-N-Ship. I would log into my own account and show them how easy it was to build an address book and select from a variety of Priority and Express Mail Flat Rate products, if they did not have a scale available. I would often bring a mailing scale along, or a piece or framed art that we sold at my Post Office.

Other businesses at the Expos would give away items during the event, attracting more attendees to their tables, so I thought I would join in on that. I would purchase items internally through my Retail Unit, and have people sign up to win whatever it was that I had at an event. My Post Office was in a very conservative area, and the Ronald Reagan framed art piece that I gave away was always a favorite when I brought it along. There would be much fanfare as one of the event organizers would come to the tables of participants who were giving items away with a microphone. They would reach into my box that had cards filled out by attendees, pull out a card and call that person's name to come and claim their prize.

I was invited by a member of the Rotary Club in my city to speak at a luncheon that was being held. I felt a bit intimidated when I drove to the location where it was being held. The location was at a very expensive Country Club in the city, and the class of vehicles that filled the parking lot left no doubt that the members were very wealthy. The major topic I chose to speak about was the rumors that were circulating about the Postal Service possibly dropping a day of delivery each week. I did not validate those rumors. I told the group that any change as large as cutting a day of delivery would have to go through many obstacles along the way. I informed the group that the Postal Service had the largest fleet of delivery vehicles in the world. Cutting delivery down to 5 days per week would save a lot of money on gas and maintenance for those vehicles. It would also cut a lot of hours out of the Postal Service budget. I could see looks of concern on many faces. I know that a lot of customers do not want to lose a day of delivery, and I had seen those same looks of concern when talking at Chamber of Commerce events and to other groups.

Although this was only talk about what might occur, there was also talk about how Retail Units would be open on that sixth day, and Post Office Boxes would be delivered to on that sixth day. I used that "talk going on" to my advantage. IF the Postal Service did cut a delivery day, and IF they did decide to deliver to Post Office Boxes on that sixth day, it would be advantageous for businesses and individuals to have a Post Office Box. And I did have many of them available to be rented at my Post Office locations. I was not in the least shy about letting customers know that. I had flyers in the lobbies of my Post Office locations, letting customers know that there were Post Office Boxes available to be rented, telling them to take advantage of their availability while it was there, just in case any changes in delivery were made.

As I have shared earlier, my Post Office was in a very affluent area. The city received a fair amount of press as a favorable place to live in a variety of publications. The border of the city that was next to mine was approximately one mile away from my Post Office, and it was a very heavy business area. Although they were comparatively the same size, both with level 24 Post Offices, that neighboring city did not at all share the renown that my city had. Being the sales-focused Postmaster that I was, I wanted to take advantage of that. I reviewed a map of my neighboring city to see which of its Zip Codes were closest to my city. I put a mailing together and sent it to the customers in those Zip Codes. The letter from me was an invitation to them to obtain a Post Office Box in my fair city. They didn't have to be situated within my delivery area to rent a Post Office Box at my Post Office, and I knew that the appeal of my city's name in their return and mailing address would be desirable to many of those customers.

Prior to the removal of vending machines that were in place at

Post Offices, I visited a mall that was located close to my Post Office. The mall was in that same bordering city served by my neighboring Post Office. I spoke to the management at that location about placing one of my vending machines inside their mall. It was my hope to place a vending machine in a highly trafficked area within the mall. At one point in time, the neighboring Post Office had a staffed Retail Unit located inside the mall, but staffing cutbacks and rental expenses caused the Postal Service to decide to end the lease there. I wanted to fill in the gap, bringing that revenue to my Post Office. I didn't consult with my neighboring Postmaster about it. I figured if he didn't have the foresight to try to pick up that revenue, I would. As it turned out, I was told by the manager at the mall who I spoke to that every inch of floor space came at a cost. I tried to appeal to the manager on a "Customer Service" level, and she told me that she would investigate it and get back to me. I never heard back from her, and though I may have requested the funding to place a vending machine there if it was in my city, there was no way I was going to ask for funding to place a vending machine in another city. I did not always allow a city limit to be the obstacle for increasing sales for my Post Office.

Employees from the different crafts (carrier, clerk, mail handler, custodian) can apply for a transfer to different work locations across the country. If that desired location has a vacancy, the applicant would receive consideration from the head of the facility. I received many such requests. Due to the size of my Post Office, I almost always had vacancies to fill. It would be desirable to have an employee come in who knew the job and would require little, or no training before going to work. Most of the requests that I received were from employees working at the large city that was approximately 30 miles away from my office.

I held my employees to high standards, and I would meticulously review the files of employees who wanted to come to my office. If I found that the applicant had discipline on file, or an attendance record that was unacceptable to me, I would reject their request. In some cases, as I reviewed their files, I wondered why they had not yet been fired. I was surprised that I was questioned by my Human Resources Department about why I was turning down specific transfer requests. The HR individuals I spoke with attempted to argue with me that my attendance requirements were too stringent. I stood firm about the criteria I used for selecting transfers, wondering what the attendance records of those HR representatives looked like.

I received a transfer request from an employee, Chang, who worked in a major city on the west coast, located far away from my Post Office. He was a carrier there, and he had an excellent attendance record with no discipline in his file. I accepted Chang for the transfer, and I was curious about what was bringing him to a location so far from home. I presumed that he must have family in my area. He was a young Asian man and he turned out to be one of the best carriers I had working at my Post Office. He turned in some Customer Connect leads on routes where he was temporarily assigned, obviously paying attention to the messaging that I regularly put out about sales. He was a Part Time Flexible (PTF) carrier, and it would probably be a few years before he was able to have the time in to get a route of his own.

I was pleasantly surprised when one of my Supervisors told me that he wanted to talk to me. I had an open-door policy, and I had no problem listening to employees who wanted an audience with me. I invited Chang into my office, asking him how I could help him. He told me that he knew how important sales and new business were to me, and he wanted to tell me about a friend of his who was having problems with the Postal Service. I encouraged him to continue, and he told me about his friend. His friend lived in a smaller, neighboring city and ran a business out of his home. I put the neighboring city part on the back burner in my mind and let him continue. He told me that he had been visiting his friend at his home the previous evening, and his friend was ready to take the business he was giving to the Postal Service to one of our competitors. His friend was busy still taking care of business at his home recently, and his wife loaded up their car with packages they were sending out, along with their two small children, and headed to their local Post Office. When his wife arrived there, a Supervisor told her that it was too close to closing time for her to have her packages processed for acceptance. She had to reload her children and her packages into her vehicle and bring them back home. The packages were already labelled with the postage paid for them.

I asked Chang to call his friend from my office, to see if he would be willing to meet with me. He called his friend and I asked Chang to accompany me to his friend's house. Chang was off the clock at that point, and I told him that I would not be able to pay him to go with me. He said that would not be a problem and we started our drive. Along the way, I asked Chang what had prompted him to request a transfer to my Post Office. He told me that he was married and had two small children of his own. He told me that the area where he had lived was not very safe, and the school system was not what he wanted for his young children. I asked him if he had family in the area and he said no. He had chosen my city because he had been researching online and saw that the city was on a list of desirable, family friendly locations and had an excellent school system.

We arrived at his friend's house. I noted that it was located a few miles outside of my delivery area, in a very nice middle-class subdivision. We were invited into his house and led to his kitchen. Along the way, I saw what appeared to be a living room and a dining room. Both rooms were full of packages. We sat in his friend's kitchen and I was introduced to his wife and his two small children. The friend and his wife did not have a good command of English, and occasionally they spoke in Chinese with Chang to translate to me. The children were running around doing what kids do, playing with their toys in areas somewhat limited due to the packages stacked up. I was offered and accepted a cup of Vietnamese coffee from my host. It was very strong, and I did not end up drinking it all during my visit.

I heard a repetitive mechanical sound that appeared to be coming from the package filled living room. It was distracting as we sat talking in the kitchen, and I finally had to ask him what that sound was. He told me that it was labels being printed out for packages that were going to be shipped the next day. He walked me into his living room, where I saw the labels printing out and stacking up on a table. I was determined to not let my company lose that business.

Chang's friend showed me the different rooms in his house where he had packages stacked up. He then led me down the stairs into his basement. He had shelving units set up in aisles with a variety of products on them from floor to ceiling. He told me that he had a website where he ran his online business selling products. His products were sent to him from a company located in China. He said that his business had been growing a lot and he was having difficulty keeping it in his house. He told me a few times about his frustrations dealing with his local Post Office. They were not very friendly to him or his wife when they would go there, and he was fed up with the hassle of dealing with the Postal Service. He finally led me into his garage. The 2.5 car garage was also full of packages. There was a large section of the garage that had different colored packages than the ones I had previously seen, so I asked him about those. He told me that those packages were waiting to be picked up by one of my competitors. I told him that I was going to help him, that I wanted to keep his business with the Postal Service, and that I was also interested in those packages that were being sent through my competitor.

We returned to his kitchen, and I told him what I was going to do for him. I had a few large trucks with lifts on them, and I knew that his local Post Office did not have those vehicles. I told him that I would be sending a truck over the next day to pick up his packages. The truck would be bringing rolling containers for him to place his packages in, and we would pick up his packages 6 days per week. We would bring him empty containers to fill when we picked up the full containers. I told him that the only thing he would have to do would be to open a Post Office Box at my Post Office. Any returns would come back to the Post Office Box address at my Post Office, where we could deliver them back to him when we came to pick up the following day. Having him use a Post Office Box address for his shipping would also assure that the revenue went to my Post Office. If I was doing the work, I wanted the revenue that came along with it. He was happy to hear that he and his wife would not have to go to their local Post Office again, so he agreed. Before we left his house, I told Chang's friend that he would be contacted by one of our Sales Specialists about those competitor packages.

The next day, I contacted a Sales Specialist who I worked with at my District and told him about the situation. I set up an appointment with Chang's friend and met the Sales Specialist at the house to introduce him. Chang's friend was happy to hear that we were going to be able to provide service at a better rate than he was getting from our competitor. I sat in on the meeting for a brief period, then left them to discuss the fine points about how we could get that competitor business moved to the Postal Service. I had to move a few collection spots around to accommodate this new pickup on an existing collection route. Things became routine in short order, with just a few hiccups along the way that were easily corrected.

I did not speak to anyone at the Post Office where Chang's friend lived, and as far as I knew they were unaware that they had lost this business from their coffers. I was in a situation that I knew could be problematic. There were clearly defined lines between Post Office delivery zones, and I had crossed those lines by having one of my carriers driving a few miles into that neighboring city. I had not yet made my MPOO, Dick aware of the situation, but I knew that I would have to at some point rather than have him find out from someone else. The table was set for a good opportunity to talk to my boss when I found out how much money was being projected for the competitor business we picked up.

I went to Dick's office and sat in a chair across his desk from me. I sheepishly advised him that I had to tell him something before he heard about it from anyone else. He gave me a wary look and asked what it was. I told him that I was sending a truck daily to pick up packages from a neighboring Post Office that was under his jurisdiction. He looked angry and asked me why I hadn't told him about this before I started doing it. I told him that this was business we were going to lose, and I had to act fast to retain it. He calmed down a bit, asking me why their local Post Office wasn't making the pickup. I told him that I had the right truck and the staff to do the job and they did not.

He knew that I had two of the lift bed trucks, so he started down the road talking about reassigning one of my trucks to that Post Office. I told him that I needed both trucks I had, that they were both used for collecting and transporting mail throughout the day. He still wasn't very happy, but he did brighten up when I told him that not only did we retain the business we were already getting, but the additional competitor business we picked up as a result of my visit amounted to $3.5 million annually. I think I saw a smile he was trying to hold back.

Dick admonished me to talk to him first before I did anything like this in the future. I assured him that I would, knowing that I probably would not. I had experienced the slow boat of decisions being made too many times within the Postal Service. Particularly in time crunch situations, I would much rather embrace the adage "It's better to ask forgiveness than permission." I knew that if I had taken the time to bring Chang's friend's problem to Dick, the Postal Service probably would have lost the millions of dollars of business we currently had, and we would not have picked up the additional business.

I did get nervous when I received a call from Chang's friend, letting me know that he was renting a warehouse and moving his business out of his house and to that location. I asked him where the warehouse was located, and he gave me the address that was in the same neighboring city. I knew that if it was further within the city than I was already sending my carrier, it could be trouble for me. My stress was relieved when I mapped it out and saw that it was only .2 miles further than his house was within the neighboring city. I didn't bother telling Dick about this minor shift. Why risk my office losing that business? Chang's friend made the move, and I adjusted the Collection Route to accommodate him. He invited me to come and visit the new warehouse, wanting me to meet his supplier who was visiting from China.

I contacted my Sales Specialist who was handling the business, and we both went to the warehouse for the meeting. I considered it to be mostly just a good PR move, wanting to keep my customer happy. We needed an interpreter to talk to the supplier, who did not know any English. The warehouse was very large, and full of products neatly shelved within it. The Sales Specialist and I were both very happy when we were told that the business was going to be expanding. They told us that sales were going to be expanding into Canada and Mexico, with an anticipated increase of up to $5 million in new revenue for the Postal Service. I shared all this information with the employees back at my Post Office, and Chang was the rock star. I started seeing more leads being turned in by employees, encouraged by the Chang success story. At times, I had the impression that the Sales Specialist assigned to my Post Office felt a bit overwhelmed with the many business leads he was getting from my Post Office.

I visited a few of the major business buildings in my city to talk to the management at those locations. I persuaded a few of them to let me set dates and times to set up a table for the businesses to visit me. I sent out a mailing to the businesses in those buildings and to the neighboring buildings as well. I would bring the same items I used at the Business Expos, setting up my table and talking to the business representatives that would come by. As I shared earlier, Customer Connect was the program in place for carriers to submit sales lead. Business Connect was a program in place for Postmasters and Station Managers to use for reaching out to businesses and achieving sales. I did not like the length of time that it took to input information about the businesses that I made connections with, but Postmasters were given goals to achieve for the number of connections that they made each year. The contact names that I collected from people who stopped at my table at Expo and other events were entered into the Business Connect system.

Business Connect goals for Postmasters were in the low double digits. The contacts that I entered into the system, particularly during my last few years as a Postmaster, were more than 300 annually. I finally had an excellent Manager who was working for me, after a few disasters that are covered elsewhere in this book. Knowing that my operations were being appropriately monitored, covered and running well gave me the freedom to devote more time to the sales end of the business. I took full advantage of that by devoting additional time going after new business for the Postal Service. In addition to the mailings that I sent out to the business customers in my area, I would look through the lists of the thousands of those customers to identify ones that I would give additional attention.

I discovered that there was a company headquartered in my city that sold cards, party and celebration items. They had retail stores nationwide, but all their internet sales were handled through their office in my city. I made a few calls and found out that most of their shipping was through one of our competitors.

The only business that the Postal Service was getting was from items being shipped to Post Office Boxes or to military addresses, because the competitors could not deliver to those addresses. I wanted that business. I called and made an appointment to speak to the manager who handled the shipping at that location.

I wanted to cut to the chase on this visit, so I invited the District Sales Specialist I worked with to attend as well. We met at the business location and talked to the manager for about thirty minutes. He then invited us to take a tour of the facility. The warehouse was huge, with large containers full of packages that were waiting to be picked up by our competitor. The manager was quite proud of his company, and his demeanor suggested that he had a very high opinion of himself in his position with the company. We returned to his office and started talking numbers. The manager was impressed with the numbers he was hearing from the Sales Specialist, and he indicated that he was willing to exclusively switch his business over to the Postal Service. We were given a date certain of about a week out when the switch would be made.

I knew that the trucks that I had at my Post Office would not be enough to pick up the outgoing packages, so I contacted the Mail Processing Center that was located nearby. We were initially going to start out with my largest truck going to the location to make a few pickups daily, prior to getting the transportation set up for the semi-trailer trucks that would be scheduled to make pickups. I was given the dock number where my truck should go to pick up the packages at the warehouse during our ramping up for the new business, and I made the arrangements to have my truck arrive there the next day. Although ultimately the Mail Processing Center would be handling the pickup of packages, the revenue would be coming to my Post Office. We were looking at over $10 million dollars in new revenue, and I wouldn't have to expend the hours doing the pickups once we were fully operational. This was the best-case scenario for me.

I was not happy when I was notified that my truck driver arrived at the warehouse and the only items waiting for pickup were the Post Office Box and military packages. I attempted to call the manager I had met with and I could not reach him. I did not want to overreact, so I left him a nice, calm message asking him to call me back. I waited a few days, and the same thing was happening whenever my truck arrived at that location. I was not receiving a call back from the manager, so I left a more pointed message. I had to assume that he knew I was trying to reach him, since I had by this point left a few messages on his cell phone and with an employee at his office. I never did hear back from him, and we never did pick up that business.

I considered trying to go over his head. He had to have a boss that he reported to, and the numbers we had given to him were obviously better than what the company was paying our competitor. The Postal Service also always had the added advantage of Saturday being a normal delivery day. Our competitors did not have that. I ultimately decided to just let it go. I figured that he may have gone to the competitor who handled the business and worked out some kind of discount, or kickback with them. I could not compete if that was the case. Whatever the reason may have been, the manager would not talk to me, so I could not work anything out.

I also found that there was a nationwide auto parts company that had its internet order filling handled in my city. Their shipping was being handled by one of our competitors. Auto parts can be quite heavy, with odd shapes and sizes, so I knew that this would present some potential difficulties when pricing items against the competitors. I also knew that heavy packages with odd shapes and sizes would be good revenue. As a carrier, I remember seeing and delivering auto tires and other car parts that were sent through the Postal Service. Those larger items had no wrapping around them. They came with a tag attached to them showing the postage that was paid, where they were coming from and the delivery address. Unfortunately, the manager of the auto parts location would not even let me make an appointment to talk with him.

I visited a few prominent hotels in my city, to talk to the proprietors and managers at those properties. Most of them had Business Centers, with computers, printers and other equipment available for use by their customers. I did not receive any objections to wanting to help their customers out with their business while they were staying at the hotels. I left Priority Mail envelopes and Flat Rate packaging at those locations, for the customers to use to ship documents or items during their visits. I also left flyers with instructions for how to create a Click-N-Ship account on the Postal Service website, to pay for their mailing and labels online prior to shipping from those locations. I spoke to the carriers who delivered to the hotels and had them track items that they were picking up for me. They were also tasked with keeping the mailing supplies stocked at those locations. There was not a great increase in the number of items my carriers were picking up, but any increase in business was fine with me.

There were many successful connections that I made along the way. They were not up to the multi-million-dollar level of the most successful sales that were picked up, but they collectively added to the revenue that my office was taking in. Any time I added a new pickup stop for my collection drivers, there would be an increase in hours used. Carrier hours were heavily monitored to make sure they did not exceed the allocated budget amount. Hours that were used for collections did not impact my Post Office's performance numbers, but they would still get attention from the higher ups. I expected to have to defend my use of additional collection hours, and I was prepared to do so. The new revenue that my Post Office was picking up far exceeded the cost of the additional collection hours that were being used to collect that mail. It also gave my local carrier unions and my carriers incentive to turn in sales leads. This was job security at work, and the more collection hours that were added could result in needing to hire additional carriers for that work. Fortunately, I was never challenged about the additional collection hours being used, so I did not have to pass along my tracking spreadsheets to my bosses.

While I did concentrate on ways to increase the revenue for my own Post Office specifically, my company-mindedness extended beyond my own office's coffers. I had an opportunity to take a vacation to Hawaii with my wife, cashing in on frequent flyer miles I had accumulated over the years. The luggage that we took with us was just below the weight that would require paying a surcharge. Of course, we had to purchase souvenir items to bring home for ourselves and our kids. I knew that we were going to be exceeding the weight limits on our return trip, and I did not want to have to pay any surcharges. My solution was to go to the local Post Office and pick up two Priority Mail Flat Rate boxes. I loaded them with our dirty laundry prior to our departure and shipped them to our home. One of our suitcases was still over the acceptable weight at the airport when we left, and we had to shift some items from one suitcase to the other to balance things out to an acceptable level. Our dirty laundry arrived at our home three days later. I shared that story with individuals and groups of people, always looking for ways to bolster the company business.

Revenue protection was an active review process that I focused on as a routine part of my job. Express Mail failures were costly to the company, since refunds had to be paid out if the items did not arrive within their guaranteed time. While reviewing the payouts that were going out due to Express Mail failures, I discovered that these payments were regularly being made to one customer. Through my research, I found that these items were being shipped from a remote location in a western state, and the transportation connections made it impossible for them to arrive within the 24 hours that was guaranteed in our system.

I contacted my District's Marketing Manager and gave him the information that I had gathered. He contacted whoever he needed to change the guaranteed time to a two-day guarantee. The customer, who had been accustomed to coming in and collecting payouts, was not happy when he arrived to collect and was advised that the guarantee time had changed.

Each morning a truck arrived at my Post Office with Express Mail. Most of the items had a guaranteed noon delivery time. Occasionally the truck would arrive late, and Supervisors would be running around trying to catch carriers who were already on their way out of the office to deliver their routes. The only time that a carrier could deviate from their normal route delivery pattern was if they had Express Mail items that were guaranteed by noon. On rare occasions, the truck would not arrive until almost all the carriers were out on their routes. When it did finally arrive, we had to scramble to salvage the noon delivery pieces to avoid the payouts. As I have shared elsewhere, because of the importance of Express Mail with its potential liability due to guaranteed delivery times, the carrier unions were contractually unable to file a grievance if anyone other than a carrier delivered those items in crunch situations.

Postmasters, Managers, Supervisors and employees of any craft were sent out with Express Mail when the situation called for it. There was also a truck that arrived daily at approximately 10:30 a.m. at our local Mail Processing Center that had Express Mail items on it. As I was researching failures that were occurring, I saw that on many days there were items that were scanned in transit at the Mail Processing Center at 10:30 a.m. They were then sent out on a regular trip that arrived at my Post Office at 12:30 p.m. Any of the noon delivery items on those trips were built in failures that would result in payouts. I contacted the staff at the Mail Processing Center to make them aware of the situation. I told them that they could bring those Express Mail pieces down to my Rural Route Unit, which was located at the other end of the same building where they were located. My staff would then do what needed to be done to reduce the failures.

As I continued to monitor the situation, I saw that the failures were continuing to occur. I contacted the staff at the Mail Processing Center again, telling them that all they had to do was call my Rural Unit and someone would come there to pick up those pieces. We did not receive any calls, and the failures continued. My next step was to have my Rural Supervisor send someone down the hall to the Express Mail Unit to try to intercept the items on a subsequent day. The individual who went to that Unit was met with hostility. They did not have the time to be bothered by my employee. I then ratcheted things up to by boss, Dick. I sent him attachments of the Express Mail reports that showed the scan times that they arrived at the Mail Processing Center, and the scan times that they were received at my Post Office from the 12:30 p.m. truck. Dick assured me that he would follow up on this.

As expected, the staff at the Mail Processing Center took a very defensive posture. Dick called me back and told me that they said they had tried calling my Rural Route Unit a few times but didn't get any answer. I told him that the phone was always answered whenever I called there, so I doubted that had occurred. I reminded him that I had sent an employee to the Express Unit and the workers there wouldn't talk to my employee. It always amazed me that there was such a contentious relationship between many Mail Processing Center employees and employees who worked at a Post Office. We all worked for the same company, and we needed to work together to solve problems and make our company succeed. Dick assured me that they would be calling when the Express Mail arrived from that point forward.

The Supervisor who I had assigned to my Rural Route Unit was given the responsibility of calling me daily on my cell phone when the Express Mail arrived at her location. The drive from her location at the Mail Processing Center to my Post Office took from 10 – 20 minutes, depending on traffic. On many days there were less than ten Express Mail pieces, but on some days, there could be as many as twenty items or more with a guaranteed noon delivery. I needed those items as quickly as I could get them from the Express Mail Unit each day, and my staff at my Post Office needed to determine who they had available to attempt delivery of those items. If the Mail Processing Center staff at the Express Mail Unit delayed calling my Supervisor, the chances for getting those items delivered before noon deteriorated with each minute that passed.

It is important to note that this was not just a matter of revenue protection from the perspective of payouts that had to be made due to the failure of items being delivered by their guaranteed time. Those items were being sent to residential customers, and a large percentage of them were being sent to business customers. The items were presumably being sent through the much higher rate Express Mail class because those customers needed to assure that they were delivered in a timely manner. If the Postal Service failed to give them what they paid for, they did have alternatives. Our competitors would be happy to pick up that business. The rates that our competitors charged for individual items tended to be more expensive than the Postal Service rates, and we did have that bonus of Saturday delivery at no extra charge. However, unlike the Postal Service, our competitors had a greater ability to give discounted prices to businesses or individuals based on volume. We needed to retain that business.

Unfortunately, there was a period of growing pains in the process that was set up that we had to go through. I had to push back when I would see 10:30 a.m. arrival times scanned at the Express Mail Unit and my Rural Route Supervisor did not receive a call from them until after 11:00 a.m. There were a few occasions when the system broke down and we received no call. I would have to attach the reports for each Express Mail item that arrived on the 12:30 p.m. truck from the Mail Processing Center, dead on arrival, and send them to Dick for his follow up. Things did eventually settle down, with everyone working together to get the job done.

There were a variety of services that could be used by Postal customers to send their products through the mail at that time. These included Priority Mail Express, Priority Mail, First Class Mail, Standard Mail and the most inexpensive of all – Media Mail. According to Postal Service regulations, Media Mail with its low rates is supposed to be for the shipment of books, tapes, CDs, DVDs or other educational material. A package sent through Media Mail is limited to just those items, and subject to inspection to assure that such packages contain no other items. For example, if a personal note or letter is found included in a Media Mail package, the sender is notified, and they are required to pay extra because it no longer classifies as Media Mail. Through my experience in different offices, I directed employees to check out Media Mail packages occasionally. If they found something that did not belong in the Media Mail package, they contacted the sender to come in and bring payment for a service other than Media Mail.

While I was serving as Postmaster in my level 22 Post Office, Media Mail checks became an issue. Lauren was my Supervisor at that Post Office, and her responsibility was primarily overseeing our retail operations. She saw that a customer was coming in regularly with Media Mail packages. She decided that it would be a good idea to make sure that the packages being mailed out of our office conformed to the Media Mail specifications. Lauren was a rather timid, conservative middle-aged woman. I was concerned when she approached me one day with flushed cheeks and asked me if we could go to my office to talk. When we got to my office, I asked her what was wrong. She hesitantly told me that she had opened one of the customer's Media Mail packages and found that he was sending out sex toys through Media Mail. While I inwardly chuckled at her embarrassment, I managed to maintain an appropriate business decorum as I told her to do what she needed to do. The customer came in and paid for the appropriate postage but was found to be doing the same thing again a week later. We contacted the Postal Inspection Service to handle the matter, informing that customer that we were doing so, and had no problem after that.

There were a few specific areas that were focused on by our Marketing Department to increase revenue. Setting up events for eBay customers was one of those targeted areas. I took the initiative to host a few of those events, pushing the envelope of what was typical Postmaster activity in the process. I did the necessary research to find the most inexpensive locations to hold those events, realizing that I did not have the space to handle them at my Post Office locations. Being a government entity, I was able to receive discounted pricing for renting rooms at my local library. I would set up the dates and send a mailing out to all my customers. If a recipient of my letter was not an eBay seller, perhaps they would tell someone they knew who was an eBay seller. I was always hopeful for that domino effect.

I would place advertisements in my local newspaper for events that were coming up. I had to receive advance approval to pay for those ads, and I'm sure that I made Dick uncomfortable with my outside-the-box activities that he had to approve or disapprove. I would choose a conservative sized ad to keep the pricing down. He reluctantly approved them, contingent on a review by the District Marketing Department prior to placing them. I also put notices up on the Chamber of Commerce website. The staff at the Marketing and Sales Departments were always happy when I would hold events. Their pay increases were contingent on increases in revenue, and I'm certain that I was the Postmaster who was doing the most to achieve mutually beneficial end results, even though I did not personally receive any increases in pay as a result of increases in revenue.

Marketing and Sales staff members would often come to events that I hosted, to provide whatever assistance they could. They would occasionally come to Business Expo events where I would have a table set up, and Chamber of Commerce meetings and events that I attended. During the eBay events that I hosted, the agenda that was outlined would typically allow at least one of them an opportunity to speak to the audience. They would also bring along a lot of different handouts for the attendees. The focus of those events was on showing how easy it was to order supplies online and use the Postal Service for their shipping. I would collect the names and contact information from all of those in attendance and, of course, they would get entered into my Business Connect account.

I knew that with the big ship that was my Post Office heading in the wrong direction for a prolonged period, it was going to take time to change the direction. I focused my staff on the areas that needed the most improvement, working our way down the list as things were improved. We were finally getting ready to close out a fiscal year being one of the best Post Offices in our District in several key, measurable areas. Along with large improvements in work hours being used in all our operations, I was responsible for increasing new revenue coming into our District from my Post Office for a few years running. With only a few weeks remaining in the fiscal year, my office was responsible for approximately 50% of the new revenue coming into the District.

I called Dick to talk to him about the possibility of getting cash awards for some of my staff members. The Postal Service had not yet frozen the awards programs that were in place, but since I would need Dick's approval for any awards, I wanted to find out in advance how he felt about it. I was happy to find that he was very receptive to the idea. I assured him that the awards would only be going to the staff members that deserved them, and they would be based on measurable improvements in their operations. The awards would be submitted electronically through the Spot Award program by me to Dick for his approval and it would be done. I asked for some direction on monetary amount I should award, starting with the Manager who reported to me. He said I should give him the maximum amount. I had to look it up to see that it was set at $3,000. I gave lesser amounts to 3 other members of my staff based on their performance, providing elaborate narratives to support their accomplishments, and all were approved by Dick.

The awards arrived at my office within a few weeks, and I brought each of those staff member recipients into my office separately to give them the checks and the congratulatory folders that accompanied them. I advised them to keep this private, since not all the staff would be receiving awards. Despite my advice to keep the awards private, I knew that the news of them would inevitably leak out to the rest of my staff. I hoped that it would leak out. Hopefully that would achieve my desired result of getting the non-achievers motivated enough to produce better results, to enable them to receive an award in the future.

I assumed that since Dick had recommended giving my Manager the maximum award, that he would be doing his part in recognizing his Postmaster (me) in a likewise manner. After a few months passed and I hadn't heard anything from Dick about this, I was called to come to his office to discuss a few different operational issues that were coming up. Before leaving his office, I felt compelled to talk about the situation. I directly asked him if he was going to be putting me in for an award, since my office had done exceptionally well, and he had recommended and approved the award for my Manager. He gave me a deer in the headlights look that I had seen many times before, and he assured me that I would be receiving the same monetary award that he had recommended and approved for my Manager.

Another few months went by and I was still waiting. I received a call from my MPOOs secretary to come to his office, without being given a reason for the visit. He was involved with Postmaster training that was going on at the time in the basement of the building. When I arrived, his secretary directed me to go there with my peers who were being trained. I sat with the Postmasters waiting for him. He returned and called me up to the head of the room to read an official letter of praise that he had for me from the District Manager in an official folder that typically contains an award check. The District Manager's letter highlighted how he was thankful for the achievement I had accomplished in capturing over 3 million dollars in new revenue for my office and the District.

The District Manager referenced a letter of acknowledgement and gratitude that he had received from Headquarters. I took my folder and letter back to my seat. The Postmaster sitting next to me leaned over and asked how much I had received. I told him it was just the letter, that there was no check enclosed. That Postmaster had a look of shock on his face, but I told him that money was not given out for sales that were achieved. I had never received a cash award for sales in the past, and I did not expect to receive a cash award simply for increasing sales. I did finally get my cash award for my Post Office's performance a few months later.

A little bit about Dick... He was promoted to his position as my Manager after I had been in my position for about 3 years. He was a good Manager over his Post Offices within his responsibility, and he achieved results. He was always meticulously dressed in smart, fashionable, expensive business attire and he drove a new Mercedes Benz sedan. The rumor was that his income was secondary to what his wife earned at her job. He always received his paychecks by paper, versus direct deposit, and his checks were processed through my Post Office, since his office was located within one of my branch offices. He had a problem on two different occasions while I was Postmaster receiving his paycheck. We checked through all our mail for his office, and in both instances, there were no checks to be found. We would constantly encourage our employees to use direct deposit. It was the most dependable way to get paid. I bit my tongue when he had these two problems, but I could not understand why he didn't use direct deposit. It may have had something to do with his wife being the primary bread winner.

Dick knew that I had problems with the District Manager in the past, specifically while my office was going through its growing period of getting on the right track. I would joke with Dick whenever my office achieved an accomplishment and ask him if he mentioned it to his boss. He would tell me that his boss had no comment, or that his boss would bring up a list that my office was negative on. It was probably because of this past that I had with his Manager that Dick was reluctant to submit my name for his boss' approval of the bonus I ultimately did receive. By the time I received my award, we were 6 months into a new fiscal year, and I was already starting to think about awards I would be giving to members of my staff for the accomplishments that were continuing to add up. Unfortunately, I did not have to think about that for too long. The Postal Service announced that all awards were being suspended due to the financial condition of the organization.

Every Door Direct Mail (EDDM) was another program that was put into place within the Postal Service. EDDM was a program that allowed customers to bring in a full coverage mailing that was going to pinpointed locations in a Post Office delivery area. One of the benefits of this was that rates comparable to Bulk Mail were charged, without the hassle of needing to have a Bulk Mail permit, mailing list or other complicated paperwork and forms. The customers using EDDM could go online to identify specific areas where they wanted their items to be delivered, defining those delivery areas down to the streets within carrier routes. The simple paperwork could then be brought to their local Post Office and dropped at a retail window.

The Marketing Department at Headquarters was hot and heavy to make this new program a success, and the pressure to do so rolled out to all the Districts. The Postal Service wanted Postmasters and Managers aggressively going after new business and sales through EDDM. Tracking was put into place to put out reports about activity and successes achieved through EDDM at Post Offices. As usual, I was determined to be dominant on those lists. I recognized the potential that was available for customers and the Postal Service and jumped right on the bandwagon.

I started the campaign for EDDM business in my customary way. I used existing Marketing advertising flyers and developed my own for placement in each of my lobby locations. I sent out letters targeting the businesses in my city, making them aware of this new program and inviting them to call me for additional information. I gave tutorials to customers in my conference room, showing them how user-friendly the website was for EDDM. The only real hurdle for EDDM users was that their single piece mailing had to conform to specific dimensions that the Postal Service gave on the website. Another drawback was that a customer could only bring in a limited number of pieces daily. Mass mailings had to be made through the Bulk Mail Unit, with all the necessary paperwork filled out for approval.

There was great potential for restaurants, doctors and dentists, hair salons, etc. to target specific addresses close to their businesses for their EDDM mailings. If the conformance to Postal Service sizing standards wasn't so restrictive, many of them could have used menu printouts or other handouts they already had printed for use. The Postal Service recommended that Postmasters and Managers work with printers in their areas to accommodate the businesses that wanted to use EDDM. To that end, I contacted several printers in my city to solicit their involvement in this new venture. I told them that I would be able to include them on a list of providers to my customers, and of course they were interested.

One of the print shops that I contacted just happened to also be in a prime location where I wanted to establish a Contract Postal Unit (CPU). I went to that location and spoke to the owner. He was also very active in the Chamber of Commerce, so we had a good conversation about EDDM. He did express an interest when I brought up the topic of his business becoming a CPU. His print shop was in a corner of my city where there were a lot of businesses, but none of my Post Office's Retail Units were in proximity. It was very close to the boundary between my Post Office and a smaller, neighboring city that had a lot of businesses in that area. If I could get that CPU open, I would target a mailing to those businesses in my neighboring city as well. I would potentially be taking the revenue from my neighboring Post Office, but if it was convenient to the customers, oh well.

My Post Office's ranking on the EDDM list was at the top, but the real big break came from an unexpected source. The Postal Service had started a process of selling real estate property that it deemed non-essential. That property typically included original Post Office locations in cities and towns that had been outgrown, and the business had been moved to new locations. The Postal Service has a Real Estate Department in place to handle the transactions involving property. I was contacted by that department, letting me know that one of my Stations was going to be put up for sale.

The Station that was identified to be sold was the original Post Office location, in the very busy downtown area of my city. It had long ago been outgrown, and over the years the carrier routes and operations had been moved to a few different short-term rental locations, prior to a new Post Office being built. There was a Retail Unit at that location and a Post Office Box section. I had concerns about how the Post Office Box

125

customers would react to the closing of those boxes.

Those boxes had been held by families and businesses there literally for generations. I had a large section of Post Office Boxes at my Main Post Office that were vacant, so I knew that I could move all the Post Office Box addresses to that section to accommodate those customers. But they would have to make that long two-mile drive, instead of being able to stop at the Starbucks along the walk to my Downtown Station. Such an inconvenience was not going to go over well.

I also had the concern of not having a Retail Unit in the downtown business district. I started the efforts of trying to pursue a CPU opportunity in that area, hoping to have one up and running before my station was sold. I visited several businesses in that area of the city, getting some interest, but not enough interest to seriously move forward. The District Marketing Department was also considering renting office space to set up a Retail Unit in. I knew that the real estate in that area was prime, and I would be incurring the cost of rental if that occurred. That prompted me even more to step up my search for a CPU location.

There was a lot across the street from my Downtown Station that was used for parking for the customers that would come into that branch. There was also a large collection box that customers could drive up to drop their mail without having to leave their vehicles. I received a call advising me that the parking lot property had a buyer, and I knew I would have to make changes to accommodate my customers while the station itself remained open awaiting a buyer. I was given a date to have the parking lot property vacated and the driveways to it blocked to keep customers from entering and parking there. I had signs made and put up, notifying my customers of when the lot would be closed.

There were a very few numbers of parking spots on the

Downtown Station property. The employees who worked there parked there, and so did my boss, Dick. Dick had his office located in my Downtown Station, along with another MPOO who managed a group of smaller Post Offices in the area. Because of that, I rarely visited that location of mine, unless summoned to go there. Since the building and property were listed to be sold, Dick and his MPOO associate were going to have to find office space elsewhere. Break my heart. I didn't really care where he moved his office to, as long as it was out of my city. I was hopeful that he wouldn't have the bright idea to move into my Post Office, perhaps into my Postmaster office.

There was a city parking garage located directly next to my Downtown Station. I instructed the employees who worked at that location that they were to start parking in the city garage next door, effective the date of the sale of the parking lot property. I needed parking for the Retail Unit customers, but I did not insist that Dick park his Mercedes Benz in the city parking garage. That would probably not have been a warmly received idea. I did go to meet with the City Manager about my parking situation. I was able to get him to put signs up in several spots closest to my Downtown Station, saying that they were reserved for Post Office customers. I told my employees that those spots were not for them. When the parking lot did shut down, I heard the complaints from my customers. Some even tried to drive around the barricades that were put up to prevent their entrance. Things did eventually calm down, and I found a solution to the collection box placement that is covered in the OPERATIONS and AUTOMATION chapter.

After a short period of time, I was contacted by the Real Estate Department and told that there was a contract pending for the Downtown Station and its property. It was being purchased by a bank in the area. I scheduled a meeting with the owner of the bank, Harold, at his office. He was a very friendly person, and we made a good connection throughout several meetings we had at my office and his. I was pleasantly surprised to find out that Harold wanted to open a branch there, but he wanted to maintain an old Post Office motif. To that end, he requested that I allow him to use some old artifacts that were stored in the building. I received permission to take Harold on a tour of the facility he was purchasing, and he was going to be allowed to sign for some of the artifacts he would be using in his new branch.

The basement of my Downtown Station was filled with many old Postal items in isolated rooms. Harold was interested in a few antiquated scales that I had, old photos, original Post Office Boxes that had long ago been updated and many other items. He showed me the plans that were being drawn up for the renovation, and I was most thrilled to see that he wanted to include constructing a secure separation between his branch and my Retail Unit and Post Office Box section that he was going to lease back to us at a very fair rate.

Of course, during our conversations I brought up my own business matters. I told Harold about EDDM, and he loved the idea. I helped one of his staff set up an account for EDDM, and within a few days the bank brought their first mailing into my Main Post Office's Retail Unit. Because of the limit on the number of pieces that could be mailed daily through EDDM, it took more than a month for the bank to send out their mailing to my entire delivery area. Those mailings were brought in daily, without fail, until the whole city had been covered. My standing on the EDDM list was securely on top with all the other businesses I attracted to use that process.

I asked Harold to partner with me in holding an event in his bank that would allow me to present EDDM and other services that the Postal Service had to offer to interested customers of his. He thought that it was a good idea, and we set things into motion to do so. Harold attended some of the meetings that were scheduled over several months, and he had one of his staff sit in when he was unable to attend. I attended a few events that he held for his customers, and to attract new customers to his bank. I didn't miss many opportunities to press the flesh and hand out one of my business cards.

As the date came near for the sale to take place, I was going to have to temporarily shift the Downtown Station's Post Office Box delivery to my Main Post Office. To accomplish this, I sent out letters to all the existing box holders, advising them of the start and anticipated end dates for this change. They were advised that they would have to come to my Main Post Office prior to the temporary change, to sign for the keys they would be using and identify where their temporary Post Office Box was in my lobby. The grief that I was catching from customers over this made me very glad that this was not a permanent change. I would have had to have made counseling available to some of those customers.

Dick and his MPOO partner ended up moving their offices over to the Mail Processing Center. Even though he was now located in the same large building as my Rural Route Unit, it was a few miles away and outside of my city, so I breathed a sigh of relief. I had to fight with him and my District over wanting some of the furniture that was in the Downtown Station for use at my Main Post Office. I was told that most of the furniture in my building was not mine. It belonged to the District. I had Supervisor's desks and other furniture at my Main Post Office that were falling apart and receiving approval to purchase new furniture was not an option. I was able to receive approval for a small number of items, though not enough to quell the chagrin of my staff and employees who had aged and damaged items.

I had to use my employees to move out all the furniture, equipment, files and supplies out of the Downtown Station. Since this was mostly "District" property, I was able to get Dick to authorize the transfer of the hours that were used by my employees who were doing the moving over to the District. Many of the items went into Dick's new office or into storage at the Mail Processing Center. Other items had to be moved to the District offices, located about 30 miles away. Most of the items moved to the District went into storage as well. It amazed me that so many items could be placed into storage, but I could not have them to put them to actual use. Finally, after several weeks of moving things, the building was emptied out for the bank to take possession.

Harold decided to hold an event at his new building after the sale was completed. Invitations were sent out all over the city, and the local cable channel was going to have a film crew there to record it for viewing on their station. When I arrived there on the day of the event, the place was packed. It was strange for me to walk through the building that was once full of Postal items. Conference room walls and other office partitions were gone. Everything was now opened, and there was a stage set up for the festivities. Coffee, juice, bagels and donuts were provided for the attendees, and Harold asked me to meet with him and a few other people to go over the program that was going to take place. The flamboyant Mayor of our city was there, and I was told that he was going to be speaking first. I would be following him on the stage, and that was the first I was hearing of this. Fortunately for me, I had long ago lost my fear of public speaking, and I at least had a few minutes to think about what I was going to say.

Each of the speakers took their turn with the camera rolling. The mayor of the city was always able to get a crowd going. He looked like he was in his late sixties, perhaps his early seventies. He was retired from the Police Department of that city, and he had been the mayor there when I was a Supervisor at that office almost 20 years earlier. Quite a long run of reelections. He was about five feet tall and a bit round with his tummy, a rather comical looking figure. He was always well dressed in a suit, looking sharp, and we were friends. The first time I went to his office to discuss Postal-related business, I was surprised to find that he was not the decision maker. He took me to the City

Manager's office, and he obviously deferred to him during our discussions. He was more of a figurehead in a PR position. He stood in front of the crowd and assumed his typical position, slightly bent over with outstretched arms and a big smile on his face. "Heyyyyyyyyyy everybody!" he would shout out, and the audience erupted in smiles and laughter as he spoke. He was a tough act to follow.

I filled my allotted five minutes, largely expounding on my appreciation of Harold and our city's Historical Society, working together to preserve the memory of the original Post Office. When all the individuals with speaking parts finished their turns, Harold introduced the architect who was handling the renovation. The architect had his computer on, with screens and projectors in place to give his presentation. His presentation showed a 3-D rendition of the work that was scheduled to take place, with realistic looking drawings of the finished product. It was a very impressive show. When that presentation ended, I went into hobnobbing mode with the crowd that was in attendance. I did get nervous when I was speaking with a lady who I had not previously met. She told me that she was going to go up to see what the catwalk was like.

As I know I mention at other points in this book, the Postal Service Inspectors had an elevated catwalk that been in place within my Downtown Station since it was built. Those walkways were in place in most Postal facilities. The Inspectors would use them to covertly view what employees were up to, to assure that everyone was being honest and that the security of the mail was not compromised. Postal Inspectors would typically utilize those catwalks to make observations when there was suspicious activity reported to them, whether it was from an employee or from customers who had experienced problems. You never knew when the eye in the sky was watching.

While everything else had been removed from the facility, the catwalk was still in place. Harry's team were allowing people to go up there to walk through it. You had to climb up a ladder to get to the enclosed catwalk, and I thought it was a bit immodest for the lady I was speaking with to be climbing up the ladder. She was wearing a rather short skirt, as were many of the ladies and daughters of attendees who were there. I did not go up the ladder to the catwalk. I had been in catwalks before at other facilities, so it was nothing new to me. I also had a concern about the stress from the weight of all the people that were climbing up to walk through it. They would climb up and walk around the perimeter of the workroom floor, peaking out the same windows that Postal Inspectors had used for their viewing. I hoped that the structure would be able to handle all that traffic, as I am certain it was not built for that much traffic. The catwalk held up, the event was a big success for the bank, and the construction project soon began.

When I had initially arrived at my level 24 Post Office as Postmaster, the memories of being a Supervisor at that office came back to me as I spent time in the mornings on my workroom floor. There were close to 200 carriers working on routes there in the morning, along with many clerks, mail handlers and custodians. The Supervisors on duty had a lot of work to do, monitoring what all those employees were doing, with all the phones for our different Zip Code zones ringing incessantly. There were four delivery zones in that city, and each had its own published phone number for customers to call in on. There were two other lines that were available for calls from internal Postal Service sources. Supervisors were constantly being pulled from their monitoring of employees to answer the phones, and it had been that way since way before I was a Supervisor there.

I was aware that many Post Offices throughout the country had their local phone calls go to an 800 number that was in place to handle incoming calls. I contacted Gary, the MPOO who had promoted me to that job, to talk to him about getting my delivery zone phones channeled to the 800 number. Without hesitation, he said no. My Post Office was his largest one, with very affluent, "needy" customers, and his office was located right in the downtown retail area of the city, at one of my branches. He wanted the phones to be answered by real people, not an automated system. And that was that, for the time being.

Gary moved on to a different position in our District after a few years, and he was replaced by Dick. After Dick had taken over the office that Gary had occupied in my Downtown Station, I felt a lot less pressure on my job. Dick was more laid back in his management style than Gary had been, and my Post Office's numbers were moving in the right direction. As my attention turned more towards sales and increasing revenue, I decided to investigate making changes with my Main Post Office's incoming calls. I was not going to pursue the 800-number idea with Dick, but I could find ways to ease the impact of calls on my staff.

I had a clerk in an office who was accessible through my Retail Lobby. That job had been vacated during my tenure as Postmaster at that Post Office, when the individual who held that job retired. It was a day job, and most of the clerk jobs in my office were scheduled at night, sorting mail for the carriers. The job was posted for all the clerks to bid on, and it would be filled by the clerk with the highest seniority. I was fortunate that the successful bidder was perfect for the high demands of that job. She would answer the phone calls that came in on our general phone line, the number that received the most calls at my office. While doing this, she would also process Passports for customers who came in through the Retail Unit. There were many other duties that she handled, and her ability to multitask made her the perfect fit for that job.

I tasked her to start a daily process of tracking the types of phone calls that she was receiving. My intent was to find out how to put a phone system in place that would best serve my customer's needs. I contacted the company that handled our phone system and scheduled someone to come to my office for a meeting. There were nine different phone numbers at my Main Post Office. Based on the tracking of calls that had been finished, I would have preferred to have added a few more phone numbers to achieve optimum results. I was told that I had the maximum number that I could have on my system. I would need to upgrade to a new system to get additional phone lines, and that would not come cheap.

I did not want to draw any outside attention to what I was doing with my phones. I knew that if I had to request funding for my phone system, that could put a stop to the whole project. There was always some meddlesome higher up who knew better than I did. I would have to settle for the nine lines that I had. The telephone system representative walked me through what would need to be done to get an answering system into place. The telephone line in my office was the only one that would not be affected by the changes that were going to be made. I wrote out appropriate scripts for the messages that would play when anyone called each of the different phones in my office.

The changes that I was about to make were going to provide much needed relief to my Delivery Supervisors. I had a meeting with my titled Delivery Supervisors, the 204Bs who most often filled in for them as needed and my Customer Service Manager. The meeting was to inform them of the changes that were going to be made. I told them that each of their Delivery Unit phones were going to be set to record messages from incoming calls during their busy morning hours. The message would ask the customers to leave their name, contact info and the purpose of their call. The message on each of the phone numbers assured the customer that they would be called back before the end of the day, depending on when their call came in.

I firmly made the point that they each needed to be checking the messages that were coming in on their lines daily. They could do this after their carriers were out of the office delivering mail each day. I also firmly made the point that I expected to see further improvements in the productivity of their carrier groups. Since they would not be getting pulled away to deal with phone calls, they would be able to focus much more on the carrier activities in their units. I expected that there would be an increase in the amount of discipline they were issuing, as they would be able to more easily identify potential time-wasting practices of their carriers.

I took a phone line that was being used by one of my departments to use for my sales pursuits. Once the changes were made, when customers would call my general number, the call would go to menu choices for them to make. They would push the appropriate number to take them to the department they wanted to reach. If it happened to be a Delivery Unit they were trying to reach, and it was in the early morning hours, they would get that unit's recording and leave a message.

The different departments included Business Mail Entry (Bulk Mail), Retail Operations and the Delivery Units. Customers were invited on the menu choices to leave a message on my Business Line I had freed up. I checked that line daily, to follow up with customers who had questions about opening Click-N-Ship and EDDM accounts or were generally interested in finding out ways to cut their shipping costs and improve their service.

On the plus side, my clerk was freed up to handle Passport processing and additional duties I assigned to her. I did begin to see improvements in my carrier productivity in most of my Delivery Units. My Manager had to work with a slacker Supervisor or two to get them motivated to properly use the free time they now had. Discipline was being issued to the most flagrant time wasters. And I was increasing my sales contacts and getting new revenue through the line that I had set up for that purpose.

On the negative side, I called a few of the Delivery Unit phone numbers to see how they were being monitored. A few of them were not being checked consistently enough to give the customers the responses they were expecting. I found that one of them had a full inbox, with messages that had not been checked for about a week. Discipline was issued to the offending Supervisor, and I ended up moving that Supervisor to my Retail Unit due to problems she was causing in my Delivery Unit. The Supervisor was vocal enough in her outrage over receiving discipline that the other Supervisors were much more diligent about checking their message boxes and getting back to their customers. Greater detail about that disciplined Supervisor and others will be covered in an upcoming chapter.

I had read some internal information about Post Offices in another part of the country where Passport Fairs had been held. I had held a few at my level 22 Post Office prior to leaving there, and I knew that my new Post Office would be a ripe location to hold Passport Fairs. Both locations were populated largely by upper middle-class residents, but my new location had about four times the number of customers. And people who do have money like to travel. The Postal Service earned revenue for processing the Passports and for any photos taken. At my level 22 office we had sent a postcard mailing out to our residents, advertising the Passport Fairs that took place on occasional Saturdays. I had to schedule some clerk overtime in anticipation of good turnouts, and we made about $6,000 for the first one and another $5,000 for the second one. I also learned that backup cameras and loads of film were necessary to have on hand.

We had 4 cameras ready to go for the first Passport Fair at my level 24 office. There were tables set up in my Post Office Box lobby hallway and 6 clerks were ready to process. We had a station set up for picture taking and one for application reviews. I did not anticipate the large numbers of families and individuals who would come in, waiting in line for an hour or longer for processing. We took in close to $20,000 of revenue on that day. That caught a lot of attention at the District and Area offices, and they started to message other offices encouraging them to hold Passport Fairs. Paul was the new District Manager that was assigned to my District soon before I held that first Passport Fair at my level 24 Post Office. He was replacing the retiring District Manager, a much less intense man who had occupied that position when I was promoted to my new job.

I had taken pictures of the long, winding line of customers waiting for my first Passport Fair to open. I stood a few steps up on a ladder to get a good view of the line, chatting it up with the customers and getting them to smile for the pictures. I sent the best picture to a Postal Service news email address, along with information about the revenue that was made on that day and the number of Passports that were processed. The news group put out a daily newsletter that was sent out to all internal Postal Service email addresses. I was very happy when I opened one of the daily newsletters and saw the picture and the story I had sent in had been published.

I received an email from my new District Manager Paul, the first contact I had with him. He attached a printout of the newsletter and wrote "Nice job. Good results." on it. I was pleased to have made a good first impression on my boss' new boss. I knew very little about Paul at that point in time. I knew that he was an executive who had been working at our Area office, located about 15 miles away. Paul had the reputation of being a tough, no nonsense man. My future interactions with him, covered elsewhere in this book, would not be so pleasant.

I scheduled another Passport Fair 3 months later, and that one took in about $18,000 of revenue. I did not expect to see the number of customers and the revenue results come in so high again. It appeared that there was going to be a lot more revenue to be made. I used my discretionary spending to order a standing popcorn machine. I kept it below my $2000 limit that would have required approval from my boss. I would have my custodians set up the popcorn maker, a large coffee maker and condiments prior to the opening of the Passport Fairs. I would also schedule an occasional Popcorn Day for my employees on the workroom floor. I continued to schedule additional Passport Fairs every Quarter, until the revenue finally dropped down below $10,000.

I always went in to work on the Saturdays when we had our Passport Fairs. I made sure that lunch orders were taken for the clerks and others who were working the fairs, and I mingled with those who were waiting in line. I remember being approached by a woman who was there with her family. They had just come into the building and the line was long. She asked me if they could get Passports any other time. I told her that we processed Passports every Monday through Friday from 8:00 a.m. till 5:00 p.m. and every Saturday from 8:00 a.m. till noon. She looked at me quizzically and asked, "Then why are all of these people waiting here today?" I smiled at her and said, "Because this is a Passport Fair." She said they would come back another day and left with her family.

On the downside of holding the Passport Fairs, once I had cycled out of holding them, my retail revenue took a downturn compared to Same Period Last Year (SPLY) numbers on my Post Office's financial reports. I had to explain this to Dick when he called me expressing concern about those numbers. Even without the Passport Fairs, my Post Office made a lot of money processing Passports. Because her desk was located close to my office, I could hear the conversations that would take place between my clerk and Passport customers. It would amaze me when customers would show up, telling my clerk that they had their trip planned and paid for, and it was only a few weeks away. They obviously had no idea how long it took for the Department of State to get them their finished Passports after the Postal Service had sent everything in for them to process. The associated fees close to doubled when an expedited

Passport was needed.

At one point, I needed to get a new copy machine for my Main Post Office. The copy machine that we had was the same one that was there when I had been a Supervisor at that office years earlier. We had been putting band aids on it since I had gotten to the office, but it was not going to work any longer. The purchase of a new copy machine was going to require the approval of my boss, Dick. I was annoyed when Dick told me that I was going to have to provide justification, data that would show the return on investment. I was the Postmaster of his largest office, the greatest revenue earner in the District, and I had to go through this crap to get a new copy machine.

It was necessary for Post Offices to make copies of paperwork that was sent out to the State Department when Passports were being processed. I printed out reports that showed how much revenue my Post Office had taken in processing Passports, something he was already aware of. The revenue my office had brought in from Passports was enough to buy about 20 of the copy machines I needed. While our copy machine was out of service, we were having to use our office printers to make copies as needed. Dick approved the purchase within a few days of receiving my justification, and we were able to get back to business as usual.

Another area that I aggressively went after was postage avoidance. Carriers would go out on their routes, placing mail into mail receptacles, sometimes having to deal with flyers or other items attached to the mailbox. Items would be rubber banded onto the boxes or stuck between the flags used to indicate there was outgoing mail in the box, getting in the way of the carrier's access. Items would be placed within the mail receptacles without postage on them. As I investigated our manuals, I found that items could not be placed into mailboxes without postage, of course. But the policy went on to state that items could not be attached to mailboxes in any way.

I instructed my carriers to bring back just one item when this occurred on their routes, and to leave the rest of the items in place. I also wanted an estimate of how many items were out there on or in the receptacles on their routes. I would get the contact information off the item I received, calculate the postage that should have been paid for the estimated number of items, cite the Domestic Mail Manual violation and send the violators a bill. Payment would come in from them, adding more revenue for my Post Office. On a few occasions, I was aggravated when the carrier took the time to bring every piece back in to my office. I had to explain to them that I could not charge the perp for the postage if we didn't leave the items out there.

Priority Mail Delivery Confirmation was something that received a lot of attention from Headquarters on down to the individual Post Office zones. Every week the numbers were internally published showing the percentages of Delivery Confirmation pieces that had been delivered on time. The attention would roll downhill from Headquarters, to the Area offices, to the District offices and finally to the Post Offices and Mail Processing Centers that had the lowest scores. I understood the importance of the attention, and it meant a lot to me personally in my job. The leads that were being turned in from our carriers and other employees were usually geared towards customers who were using one of our competitors. We were trying to steal that business from our competitors, and we needed to be handling our Priority Mail correctly and efficiently if we were going to not just gain that business but retain it as well.

Priority Mail was a rapidly growing product during my latter years as a Postmaster and Manager with the Postal Service. Customers were doing a lot more online purchasing, eBay businesses were growing and expanding and there was competition to get that business between the Postal Service and other companies. Unlike Express Mail, there was no built-in refundable guarantee to the customers who used Priority Mail. The Postal Service gave expectations that delivery would occur within 2 – 3 days. The 3-day standard was only expected if there were unusual distances between the sender and the recipient. I considered Priority Mail and Delivery Confirmation to be very important elements to the success of the Postal Service, giving them the attention that I felt was appropriate. Further elaboration of nuts and bolts of those services will be covered in the TRAINING chapter.

Postmasters had the ability to pull a variety of reports from the system where our scanners were downloaded daily. I tasked one of my Supervisors to pull up the results from each previous day for all the scans that had been made. There were hundreds of scans downloaded daily, and I had to develop an Excel spreadsheet to hone down to the Delivery Confirmation results. Items that came in prior to the carriers departing on their routes received an Arrival at Unit (AAU) scan by the clerks who sorted the mail. Those scans would show which route the item was sorted to. The expected scan that followed on each item would be a Delivered scan. A Notice Left scan was made if the customer was unavailable to receive the item because it was too large to fit in their receptacle, or to be left securely at their address. The items that did not have any other scans following the AAU scan were the ones that needed attention.

Supervisors were required to daily check all the carrier cases for anomalies. One of the items that they looked for was undelivered packages. If a Delivery Confirmation item was found that had not been scanned by the carrier, it needed to be initialed and dated by the carrier on that route, indicating that such items may have been for a business that was closed. If there were no indications as to why the item was there, discipline would be pursued. Items that had notices left for the customers to pick up were sorted in a large row of shelves located near my Retail Unit. Those shelves were reviewed daily by one of my Supervisors. The Delivery Confirmation items were checked to see if an item was there that had not been scanned further following the AAU scan. Carriers would occasionally leave notices but forget to scan that a delivery attempt had been made. That would mean poor scoring for my office.

Unscanned items that were awaiting pickup had to be left on the shelf, in case the customer came in to pick up the item. The name, address and Delivery Confirmation number would have to be written down by the Supervisor for follow up with the offending carrier. If that carrier happened to be on a day off, we would hold on to that information until they returned to work. I was patient. If it was found that the carrier was at fault, their failure to stop the clock on those items with an appropriate scan would result in discipline.

Saturdays offered additional challenges on business routes. There would be stacks of packages at the carrier cases for business routes. Most of the carriers who were regulars on my business routes were very good at their jobs. Nevertheless, being an equal opportunity employer, those checks were conducted on all Delivery Confirmation items. Problems typically occurred on business routes when the regular carrier was not scheduled to work. PTFs or the Carrier Technicians that handled the business routes on the regular carrier's days off were often not as experienced, or perhaps just not as conscientious as the regular carrier. Either way, discipline was the corrective action that would hopefully get their attention and prevent further failures from occurring.

As I shared earlier, I was responsible for approximately 50% of the new sales within my District, as measured through the Business Connect system. As I prepared to leave that Post Office for my new Manager position, I was hopeful that my replacement at my Post Office would continue to focus some attention on sales. I had left him the tools he needed to succeed, but I was not optimistic. I had been in Postmaster positions long enough, having attended many meetings with and talking to my fellow Postmasters, to recognize that my focus on sales was very uncustomary. Postmasters were focused on operations, driving performance numbers and cutting costs. Any pressure that came from above concerning sales and business connections did not receive a lot of attention from my peers. That was obvious to me as I looked at reports that showed how many business connections were made throughout my District. I was always on the top of the list, and many of my peers had zero connections listed.

There were not metrics in place to reward Postmasters and Managers for any sales that were achieved. There were clearly defined goals given to Postmasters for a variety of topics, and potential pay raises would be given in correlation to those goals. Since there were no goals for sales for Postmasters, I had to conclude that the Postal Service decision makers did not have high expectations for sales from Postmasters. I knew that the organization needed to be focused on hours and productivity, since employee pay and benefits were the single largest expenditure that the Postal Service had. I did not dramatically shift my attention to sales until I did have hours and productivity at acceptable levels, and I did not have expectations of receiving any additional compensation for sales achievements. I did it because I knew it was the right thing to do. I could not help but think, however, that there was something askew with the goals that were being driven by the company.

When I did finally move on to my final position with the company as a REC Manager, my passion for sales did not end. I did my customary digging into my new job, focusing on things that affected productivity and hours. I knew that I would have to eventually put some focus on sales. I'm sure that a lot of Managers within the Postal Service would think that putting any attention on sales with REC employees was a goofy idea. I considered that to be outside-the-box thinking, and I did not ever like being inside that box.

There were approximately 3,000 employees working at my REC. Many of them had come to work at that REC from different parts of the country, where their REC had shut down and they had relocated. RECs did not physically handle any mail, incoming or outgoing, other than our own business mail at our facility. RECs did not have contact with any customers, so what was the point of pursuing leads through the employees? I followed my basic sales philosophy, down the rabbit trail of everyone knows someone. Perhaps some of my employees were running an eBay or other business out of their home. Perhaps they had a neighbor, friend or family member who had that type of business in progress, or they were considering it. Any of those contacts might have been local, in the city where our REC was located. Perhaps they lived in some other state. That didn't matter to me. A lead was a lead. The Postal Service was a nationwide organization with Sales Specialists domiciled in every District.

I devoted one of the marathon meeting days that I held each Quarter at my REC to sales. I had my laptop and a projector set up in our large conference room. I showed each of the groups that came in, throughout the day and into the night, how to access the Postal Service online services. I did my best to fire each group up about our company. I passionately shared with them how we each had an obligation to do whatever we could, beyond doing our own jobs, to make our company succeed by growing our revenue.

There were internal forms available online for sales leads to be submitted, but I wanted to make things as easy as possible for my employees. I also wanted to make sure that my REC and the employees responsible were recognized for any leads that were turned in, especially if they resulted in sales. I created my own lead submission forms and had a stack of them available for my employees on the marathon talk day. I also called the Sales

Department of the District where my REC was located, making a contact within that group. I told the surprised Sales Specialist that I would be sending her leads that were turned in by my employees. She assured me that any of the customers outside of her area would be funneled to the appropriate District for follow up.

Lead forms for my REC employees were readily available at the front desk, close to where the employees clocked in, along with a variety of other forms that they needed for their jobs. We had a Master Form folder, containing the forms that were available at that desk. Copies were to be made by the Supervisors, to replenish any of the forms that were running low or were used up. I would check that desk occasionally, reviewing the items that were available there. I was most annoyed when I found at one point that the lead submission forms were gone, and they had not been replenished. Following my stern interaction with my three Operations Managers, that did not happen again.

I made an appointment to visit the Postmaster of the city where my REC was located early on during my tenure there. We met at her office, where I advised her of the leads that were being submitted by my employees. I wanted her to be aware of the potential increase in business for her Post Office, as leads turned into sales. We developed a good working relationship, and I met with her several times during my time at the REC. I also attended a few meetings that were held by the District Sales Department in that District. As my time wound down at the REC, I had to become more focused on the operations, staff and local union issues. My SALES days were over.

CHAPTER THREE: THROUGH THE SNOW, RAIN, HEAT, AND CRITTERS...

There is no actual official creed claimed by the Postal Service, but this is as close as it gets:

"Neither snow, nor rain, nor heat, nor gloom of night, stays these couriers from the swift completion of their appointed rounds." - Herodotus, 503 B.C. (Inscribed on the General Post Office facility on 33rd Street and 8th Avenue in New York City.) And then there were also a variety of mostly furry creatures that would have to be dealt with daily...

The first memory I can recall of delivering mail was during a snowstorm in the winter, a few weeks prior to Christmas. I was working out of a Postal Service car and there were a lot of packages in the trunk of that car. Back in those days, the Postal Service had official small jeeps and larger vehicles that were used for the delivery and collection of mail. Those vehicles had the colors and wording that clearly identified them as Postal Service vehicles. There weren't enough of those vehicles to go around, especially as routes grew in different areas across the country. Cars would be purchased or leased and used wherever possible to make up for the lack of official vehicles.

I was freezing and it was dark outside. I would walk up to each house and stand under their lights on their porches to read the addresses, trying to get the correct mail delivered at each stop. As it got later, colder and the snow continued to fall, I finally gave up on delivering the packages I had. I was hoping that someone would be sent out to help the newbie (me), but I was the help. I don't remember what time I made it back to the office, but I wasn't the last carrier to return that day. That was my true initiation into life as a carrier, and I wasn't too certain that this was the right work life for me at that point. Things did get easier, though, with the passage of time.

Over those early years I tried a variety of things to help combat the weather. I was a City Carrier and we received a uniform allowance annually. New carriers were not able to purchase all the clothing that they needed for the different seasons for a few years. The uniform allowance received would only go so far. Postal Service management understood that, and partial uniforms were not a problem during the first few years of employment. I tried battery heated socks, with wires running up my legs to a battery pack on my hip. I had to either buy gloves that had the fingertips exposed or cut the tips off the fingers of the gloves. That was just my thing. I had to feel the mail as I flipped through letters walking between the houses on my route. I wore a safari helmet in the rain to keep my eyes clear. Each carrier finds the uniform items that works best for them, through whatever seasonal changes that may occur where they are located.

Early on in my carrier career, I was filling in delivering mail on a carrier's route while he was on vacation. It was hot and sunny out and I took my shirt off while I delivered the mail. I was young and vain, and I wanted to work on my tan. As I approached one of the customer's doors, a woman asked me if I was thirsty. I told her that I was, and she invited me into her house. She poured me a glass of ice water and we chatted in her kitchen for a few minutes until I finished my drink. I left her house, finished the route, put my shirt back on and returned to the Post Office. When I got back into the office, my Supervisor, Jim told me that he wanted to talk to me. He took me into an office and asked me if I was delivering the mail without a shirt on. I sheepishly told him that I was, and it wouldn't happen again. He told me that it had better not happen again, or he would have to issue discipline to me. I asked him a few questions and found out that it was the woman who had invited me in for the ice water who had called in to complain.

As a PTF carrier, I would be assigned to fill in for regular carriers on their routes when they would take scheduled vacation time off. Jim was planning on scheduling me to fill in for an older carrier who had vacation time coming up soon. The delivery pattern on the route was complicated, so Jim had me accompany the carrier on his route for a day to learn it. He delivered to a lot of mini mansions in a very affluent part of town. The customers on his route received a large volume of mail and packages, and there was no rhyme or reason to the delivery points. Some of the customers had large mailboxes, and I mean LARGE, at the end of their driveways, at the curb. Some of those mailboxes were able to hold large packages, which was convenient to the carriers delivering their mail. The inconvenient part was that this route had a regular car with left-hand drive assigned to it, unlike the right-hand drive Postal delivery vehicles. The carrier couldn't just reach out his window to put the mail in those mailboxes. He had to get out of his vehicle to get to them.

As I rode along with him, he spent a lot of time moving his car around and driving up to several of the houses to deliver their mail. I was a little nervous when he parked the car and a few dogs started running towards us. He told me not to worry. He reached in his mail bag and took out a few dog biscuits. He tossed them to the dogs, and they followed us around while he delivered the mail. He told me that he would leave the dog biscuits in the glove compartment of the car assigned to his route for me. I was glad that he did. During the weeks that I filled in for him I don't know what the dogs might have done if I didn't have those biscuits. Years later, as a Postmaster in different Post Offices, I directed the carriers not to give treats or biscuits to the dogs on their routes. It was too risky for the fill in carriers who did not have those treats, and I did not want to risk the health and welfare of the fill-in carriers when the dogs did not get what they were expecting.

Carriers were given spray cans of Halt to take on their routes each day. Halt was an orange colored pepper spray that hooked on to the side of our mail satchels. It was to be used as necessary if a dog was attacking. We were taught the technique of pulling the mail satchel off our shoulder, to position it between ourselves and an attacking dog. We would then have access to the spray can as well. I paid attention to that training, and I made sure I always had my can of Halt attached to my satchel when delivering mail. I was delivering mail in an area of town that was new to me one day, when I had the opportunity to test the effectiveness of this technique out. It was a very windy day out, and I had to climb about 15 concrete steps to get to the mailbox that was next to the door on one of the houses.

As I was putting the mail in the box, I saw a very angry looking dog running up the stairs towards me. It was a large, mixed breed dog, baring its teeth as it growled and barked at me. I dropped my satchel and the dog bit at it, trying to get a piece of me. I grabbed my can and started spraying, but the wind had the spray flying everywhere, including back at me. I was backed into a corner on the small porch and there was no way of getting past the dog to the stairs. After a few long minutes of this standoff, a woman came out of the house. She called to her dog, who was still trying to bite me, and she began to yell at me for spraying at her dog. I told her what she could obviously see for herself, that her dog was trying to bite me. She put her dog in the house, continuing to yell at me as she did. I kept my mouth shut and walked away. If I had a nickel for every time someone said "Don't worry. My dog doesn't bite", I'd have a hell of a lot of nickels.

Sometimes those dogs were just too fast, and it was difficult to be on guard all the time. I was delivering mail on a route that I was somewhat familiar with, filling in for a carrier on vacation. I was driving up a long driveway to a customer's house to deliver their mail. I knew that they had a small poodle. I had seen it in their house when I delivered their mail. I could see through a window next to the door. The poodle would run towards the door barking and growling. It would jump up and grab at the mail as I pushed it through the slot in the door. What I didn't count on was stepping out of my vehicle and the dog running at

150

me outside of the house. The poodle came up behind me, not barking to give me warning, and bit me in the ankle. Then the barking started. Fortunately, no blood was drawn. I didn't want any medical attention and I didn't want an accident on my record, so I kept it to myself and nothing ever came of it. Failure to report an accident, which is what I was guilty of in that instance, is an issue in and of itself. More will be covered on that in the DISCIPLINE chapter.

Letter carriers on walking routes were always instructed to walk across the lawns from house to house, to expedite the delivery of the mail on their routes. Rarely a customer on a route would insist on the carriers using the sidewalk rather than walking across their lawn or cutting through the bushes or landscaping at the edge of their property that separated their house from their neighbor's. One of the houses on a route that I serviced had 3 very large dogs. The owner of that house was always careful to have the dogs inside the house at the approximate time that their mail was delivered each day. That was a good thing, but it did not alleviate the problem that I faced with the major poop field that their front yard had become. The grass was all but gone, killed off by the poop piles that covered it. Even the sidewalk leading up to their house was covered with dog feces. Tiptoeing through those tulips was a necessary daily event to avoid getting my shoes coated in feces. It did make me wonder what the inside of the house looked like.

Filling in on routes when the regular carriers were on vacation, or otherwise absent from work, was often the most challenging part of being a PTF carrier. The first day of delivering on a route would often be difficult. I would have to learn about any peculiarities on each route, things like best places to park, where to take breaks and lunch, where to cut across lawns and where all the animals resided.

One Saturday when I was called in for overtime, I was given pieces of routes to carry to assist the regular carriers on their routes. One of the pieces I was given was delivering the mail to my dad's house. I was living there with him at the time, and I had a big, floppy eared German Shepherd. I walked around a building that was next to my house. My dog was chained out front. When she saw me coming up the walkway in my uniform, looking down at the mail in my hand, she started barking and running at me. She looked fierce and I thought she was going to bite me. I yelled out to her "Hey dummy! It's me!" Fortunately, she recognized me and backed off. Her tail went between her legs and I breathed a sigh of relief. I sat on the porch of that house when I wasn't working on another day, watching as a carrier rounded that same corner to approach my dad's house. The carrier was wearing a headset and didn't hear my dog as she ran towards him. When my dog was almost on him, the carrier went into panic mode when he finally noticed her. I called my dog before she reached the carrier and she immediately came back to me.

I would remember that and other incidents years later when I became a Postmaster, ever mindful of the dangers that letter carriers face daily in the performance of their duties. I made certain that warning cards were used by the carriers on their routes. There were different colored cards that were used to alert PTFs, or any carrier other than the regular who was not familiar with the route, to potential problems that might occur. The cards were typically sorted to an address prior to the affected address. If there happened to be a dangerous dog at an address on a route, the replacement carrier would see the orange warning card while sorting through the mail a few houses before they arrived at that house. If a customer happened to be on vacation, or a house was vacant, the warning cards would alert the replacement carrier to avoid mail being left at those addresses.

As a carrier, I had the misfortune of walking along, delivering the mail on a route that I was unfamiliar with, unaware that a customer was on vacation. I moved along the houses on the street, depositing the mail into the door slot of the house where the residents were on vacation. I noticed when I reached the next house that the mail addresses were off, then realized what I had done. I could not retrieve the mail that I had deposited incorrectly into the previous house's door slot, so I had to advise my Supervisor of what had occurred when I returned to the Post Office. The warning card system would have prevented that error, and the neighbor of the vacationers wouldn't have had to wait until their return to get their mail from them.

After a few years in my new carrier job, I reached the point where I had my own route. I had many customers on my route who were appreciative of the service I provided, bringing them their mail every day through the gamut of weather conditions. My route began with houses that had some of the wealthiest residents in town and ended literally across the tracks with the absolute poorest residents in that town. It didn't matter which side of the tracks they were on. Certain customers showed their appreciation by offering me hot or cold drinks, depending on the weather. Some of my customers would have cookies and other food they would occasionally offer me as I worked my way through my route of about 350 customers. One of my customers gave me a pink blanket with postage stamp designs on it when she learned that I had a new daughter. That was my daughter's "blankie." She had it for years when she went to bed and may still have it. I'll have to ask.

Working as a letter carrier is certainly a rewarding experience. A carrier can make a great number of friends on their route. They can also unwittingly make enemies. Some of those enemies are often of the four-legged variety. I had been delivering mail on my regular route for a few years, so I got to know quite a few people on the route. Most of my customers were very friendly. While the people on the route that a carrier delivers get to know him or her and develop friendships, their pets can be an entirely different story.

There was a young married couple that lived on my route, and they were always friendly to me whenever I saw them as I delivered their mail. The husband was a doctor and the wife worked part time out of the home. They had no children when they moved into the house, but after several months of living there, they had a baby on the way. They also had a large dog that looked like it was part wolf, and he let me know on a regular basis just how much he would like to make me a part of his lunch. If he happened to be out, in their fenced back yard, I often wondered whether he would jump over the chain link fence as he rushed it when he saw me approaching. He would snap, snarl and salivate as he rushed towards the fence, banging his paws against the top of the fence as he barked at me. If he happened to be in the house, I would deposit their mail into their front door's mail slot as quickly as I could and back away. I could hear him barking and banging against the door as I walked away.

As I mentioned earlier, those front door mail slots can be one of the many sources of nightmares for a letter carrier. Even without animal involvement, if a carrier sticks his fingers too far into the mail slot while depositing mail, he or she will lose skin off their fingers while retracting them. This situation becomes much more serious when there is an animal involved on the other side of that slot. If the deposit is not made quickly enough, the carrier's fingers can be a nice little "finger food" for a hungry hound. I knew of some carriers that would intentionally take their time making the deposit, all the while carefully protecting their fingers, so that the animal would have time to get sufficiently excited to grab and chew the mail apart with its teeth.

But back to my expectant customer mom. Eventually, the blessed day finally arrived, and the new mom and baby were soon home. As I made my daily rounds delivering their mail one day, mom came to the door and asked me if I wanted to see her baby. Of course, I said yes, and she went to bring her baby to the door. As she opened the door to give me a view, her dog ran past her, came out the door, ran behind me and bit me on the back of my thigh. Of course, she was very apologetic, as she somehow managed to get her dog back into the house. I think her dog was just satisfied that he had finally gotten a piece of me. I called the Post Office and went to the local emergency room as advised. The thing that frustrated me the most was not the dog bite. I didn't need stitches. I waited a long time, got bandaged up and left the emergency room. What frustrated me was when I received my paycheck and saw that I was not paid for the time spent in the waiting room. I was there for about 2 hours past my 8 hours, and I expected to get paid overtime for those hours. I talked to my Supervisor about it and I was told that once the accident occurred, the clock stopped.

I returned to my route the next day, a bit anxious as I approached and delivered mail to the customer's house where I had been bitten. My apprehension continued for some time. When I finally got more relaxed the delivery to that customer became routine again. Several weeks later, I was delivering mail to that block on a Saturday. As usual, I tensed up a bit as I approached the house with the wolf dog. I didn't see any sign of the dog as I approached the house. I didn't hear any growling or barking as I put their mail through the door slot. I did breathe my usual sigh of relief as I continued down that side of the street delivering mail. I reached the last house at the end of the block, crossed the street, and began delivering the mail in a loop down the other side of the street.

As I was fingering through the mail to have it ready to place in the mailbox of the house across the street from the wolf dog's house, my eyes were focused downward, looking at the letters in my hand. I suddenly heard a ching, ching, ching sound coming my way and getting louder. I looked up and saw the wolf dog running right at me. He wasn't barking, just running full throttle, focused on getting another bite at me. I instinctively dropped my bag to attempt to stop the bites that would be coming my way, grabbing my can of Halt and getting ready to spray. I saw his owner, the doctor come around the corner of their house. He yelled the dog's name once, and the dog turned around immediately and went back. The doctor apologized to me profusely, and I finished delivering mail to the houses looking over my shoulder.

I had a female Carrier Technician assigned to my route and four of my neighboring routes at that time. Carrier Technicians were assigned groups of five routes that they would cover on the regular carrier's rotating days off. They were paid at a higher level than the regular carriers because it was expected that they would be able to keep track of the customers who were having their mail forwarded, customers who had their mail on hold, vacancies and other pertinent data on all five of those routes they covered. My Carrier Technician was a mother of five young children, and she had a sixth on the way while she was covering my route. She was a very hard worker and rarely called in sick or missed work for any other reason. She worked all the way up until she delivered her baby, finally calling in when she went to the hospital to deliver. After four weeks, she was back on the job and functioning at her normal capacity. I recall her telling me that her baby's soft head had a dent in it from the bag full of mail she would carry each day. She said that the baby's head would not be permanently affected by that, but I did question the accuracy of what she was telling me.

As diligent and hard working as she was, she had a bit of an irrational fear of animals. I know that she was as cautious as I was when delivering mail to the area where I had been bitten by the part wolf dog. That was certainly understandable and rational. On another part of my route, one of my customers had a cat that was deaf. He was an older white cat, and my customer told me that he was deaf and liked to be outdoors a lot. The customer was making me aware because she did not want me to be alarmed when I was delivering her mail, letting me know that sometimes her cat liked to follow the mail carriers and jump up at their legs. My Carrier Technician was aware of the cat and was very fearful of that cat. She would typically come and talk to me at the beginning of the day after she had delivered my route. She would make me aware of any changes that had taken place on my day off. Occasionally, she would also inform me of any encounters she had with any of the pets on my route. Sometimes that would be about the deaf cat.

When I delivered the mail at the deaf cat house, I would often see the cat crouching down in the grass between his house and the neighbor's house, weather permitting. I would deliver the mail to his house, then cut across the lawn to get to the neighbor's. I would finger through the mail that I had, getting the neighbor's mail separated out for delivery to their mailbox. I would glance around while doing so, keeping an eye on the deaf cat to avoid being surprised at anything that might happen. As I walked past the crouching cat, he would often run over to me and jump up at the back of my pant legs. He had nails, of course, and he would scratch at my pants as he jumped up at me. He wouldn't hurt me, but an attack like that could be startling if you weren't prepared for it. My Carrier Technician wore a skirt when the weather was warm enough to do so. I presume that this had a large impact on her fear of the deaf cat jumping up at her. She would get her legs scratched at times, and she would show me the next day when it occurred.

On one morning, after she had delivered on my route, she did not do her usual coming to me to talk about the previous day's events. I remember thinking that this was unusual, so I approached her on the route where she was sorting mail. I asked her how things went the day before and she gave me a quick and unemotional "Fine. No problem." I went back to my own route and assumed that she just didn't feel like talking. When I left the Post Office to deliver the mail on my route, I discovered why my Carrier Technician was not talkative about the previous day's events. I delivered the mail to the deaf cat's house and started my walk across the lawn towards the neighbor's house. I could see the deaf cat crouched down in his usual position in the grass. He was not moving closer towards me like he usually did before he charged and pounced. He kept his distance, but I could see something that was amiss as I passed him. I could plainly see an orange tinge on the cat's white face.

Orange was the color of that Halt dog spray that every delivery carrier had to take with them on their route each day. I had used it a few times, so I was aware of the color and how it sprayed in a thin stream of about ten feet when used. I could only deduct that my Carrier Technician had given the poor deaf cat a face full of spray the previous day. That explained why she was not very talkative with me earlier in the day. I did confront her about it the next day when I saw her. She reluctantly admitted to me that she had sprayed the cat. The only comment I could think of was to advise her that it might be a good idea to wear pants on the days she did my route, rather than skirts. At least her legs wouldn't be exposed to getting scratched or bitten, and the cat wouldn't need to be getting unwanted orange makeup applied each week to its face.

As I have mentioned in other parts of this book, the route that I had at that time ranged from houses that were very expensive to houses that were very old and many of them were in disrepair. The owners of the houses correspondingly ranged from very wealthy to very poor. The older houses were literally on the other side of the tracks from the more affluent area, and the residents who lived in that area were exclusively African American. Since the Post Office where I worked did not have enough Postal vehicles assigned to cover all the routes, the Supervisors would solicit carriers on walking routes to use their own personal vehicles to deliver the mail. Carriers on walking routes did not need right hand drive vehicles since they had no curbside deliveries, so they were the only ones who could use their personal vehicles. We received a daily compensation for the use of our vehicles of $6. I used my own vehicle that had a hatchback and was very convenient for delivery use. It was an added benefit having air conditioning that I could turn on occasionally, unlike the Postal vehicles that did not have such luxuries.

My first parking point on the other side of the tracks was on a corner where two little girls lived. They would often be outside playing when I would park there to start walking and delivering mail. When they would see me getting out of my car, they would usually approach me from the parkway at their house and call to me in unison "Heyyyyy Mailbox." That was their name for me. I would chat with them a bit as I embarked on my journey down their street, delivering the mail to their house and to their neighbors.

One day as I was returning to my vehicle, I saw the two sisters with their faces pressed up against the back window of my car. As I approached my vehicle, they looked up at me and asked me who the dolly belonged to that was in the back seat. I told them that it belonged to my daughter, as I opened the door to look inside. My daughter must have left her doll in there the last time she was in the car. The sisters were obviously interested in that doll, and I would have liked to have given it to them, but it did belong to my daughter and I wasn't going to give away what belonged to her. I did purchase a few small toy items that I gave to them a few days after that occurrence.

As I would continue delivering mail on that section of my route, I looked forward to parking at one spot on particularly hot days. I would do my usual walking down one side of the street and return up the other side delivering the mail. An older African American man lived at the last stop of that loop, and he would often have a can of ice-cold soda waiting for me on his porch when I arrived there. Sometimes he would be outside and chat with me while I drank the soda. At other times, the soda would just be sitting there waiting for me, ice cold with the condensation dripping down the sides of the can. I remember the joy that I felt seeing that soda waiting there for me, and the gratitude I felt for my caring customer.

On one particularly hot day, I continued walking the next loop from that parking point. I was walking past a recreation center to get to the first house for delivery. There were several teenagers playing basketball on the court there. As I walked past them, I saw a tall, muscular young man walking towards me. He was wearing cut off shorts, tattered tennis shoes and no shirt. While I was walking towards him, I noticed that as I would move from one side of the sidewalk to the other, his movements were mirroring mine. He had an angry look on his face, staring at me as we got closer to each other. He continued to mirror my steps until he was standing right in front of me, blocking my passage. We were both at a standstill at that point. I tried to step to the side to pass him, and he again moved in front of me to block me. I am a shorter guy, and he was at least six inches taller than me. I looked up at him and said, "Excuse me". He looked down at me, eyes fixed on mine, and snarled "You suck." I did not respond to that. As I stood there for a very uncomfortable 10 or 15 seconds that felt like an hour, I pondered about what I should do. I remember thinking "I wonder if this orange spray I have clipped on my bag works on people". Fortunately, he finally did step aside and let me continue on my way.

Finally, I became a Supervisor at the level 24 Post Office. There was sometimes a lot of turnover with Supervisor positions, especially at the larger Post Offices. We had been short 4 Supervisors for several months, filling in with 204Bs, when finally, my Postmaster was given the authorization to fill the vacant positions. Before long, we had 4 brand new Supervisors in our office. There was always a learning curve when starting out as a Supervisor. Some newbies had a harder time than others. On one very snowy afternoon we still had about 4 hours of mail that needed to be delivered sitting on our workroom floor. The Postmaster was leaving for the day. Before he left, he told me that all the remaining mail had better be delivered. Whatever it took to accomplish that, he didn't care. One of the last things that any Postmaster wanted to do was to report to their MPOO that mail had not been delivered. Information like that had to be reported all the way up the food chain to Headquarters. And it rolled back down to that office a lot harder than it went up the chain.

The carriers were returning from the street and it was dark outside. I talked to the other 3 Supervisors who were still there with me. Liz was one of the new Supervisors who was still trying to get acclimated to her new job. I told Liz and the other two Supervisors to wait by the doors coming into the building. There were many carriers still out and we needed to catch them as they were coming back in. I didn't care what kind of Overtime List they were on, if any. They were to be instructed to take mail that was still inside the building out for delivery. If they refused, they were to be told that they were being given a direct order and that if they didn't do as instructed, they would be disciplined. More than a few of the returning carriers refused to go back out, even under the threat of discipline. We did end up finding enough carriers to go back out and get the mail delivered. What amazed me was that in the middle of this hectic event, trying to get all the mail out with carriers refusing to go back out, Liz was frustrated to the point where she was standing in the middle of the workroom floor crying. The carriers would joyfully remember that for a long time to come.

During each of my managerial positions with the Postal Service, I have always taken the safety of my employees very seriously. I made certain that safety talks were given to the employees on a regular basis. It was important to me that they received constant reminders of potential dangers that could face them, whether in the office lifting heavy objects or out on their routes delivering mail. I had only been in my first Supervisor position for a few weeks, working the late afternoon shift at a large Post Office. I received a call at the Post Office from someone advising me that one of my carriers had been involved in a serious accident. The carrier was driving along a route picking up mail out of collection boxes. It was dark outside and snowing at the time. I went out to the location and found that the carrier was injured, and someone had already called for an ambulance. Outgoing mail was spread around all over the interior of the vehicle. I called back to the office and had another carrier meet me at the accident location. We transferred all the mail from the truck that was totaled into another Postal vehicle, to assure that the mail was kept moving through the system to the Mail Processing Center and getting to the proper destinations.

I kept in close touch with the hospital and was advised that the carrier had broken a few ribs and was being kept overnight for observations. I visited her in the hospital the next day before going to work. I was concerned about her health and safety, but my Delivery Manager also tasked me with carrying out the unpleasant task of getting information from her to follow up on issuing discipline to her. As you may have deduced by now, I normally did not get squeamish when it came to issuing discipline. In this situation though, I did feel bad about questioning her while she laid in a hospital bed about the circumstances leading up to the accident. About a week later, after she had recovered sufficiently and returned to work, I did my job and issued her a suspension for Failure to Work in a Safe Manner. I did understand the necessity of this course of action. Her accident had not only caused her personal injury. It cost the Postal Service a vehicle, the expenses of her ambulance and hospital stay, paying her during her recovery time and the overtime to handle the mail she had been collecting at the time of the accident. Hopefully she would bear this in mind as she continued to perform her job, heightening her awareness of her surroundings and the need to be safe.

The location where I served in my last Postmaster position was largely inhabited by people ranging from upper middle class to outright rich. There was a small percentage of people who were at the lower end of the financial spectrum, but they were few and far between. I accidentally became aware of one such individual one day when I was inquiring about one of my carriers who delivered mail in the business district of the city.

One of the many reports that I viewed daily was a Managed Service Point (MSP) report. Barcodes were placed at various delivery points along each carrier's route for them to scan as they progressed along their route each day. The Variance Report would show abnormal differences in previous day activities. Those differences included the actual time that a carrier scanned barcodes at each point versus the "normal" time that mail would be delivered. Scheduled lunch and break points were included in the MSPs on each route, enabling management to view whether the allotted times for lunches and breaks were being followed. The report would also show if scans were made out of sequence or if there was a larger than normal span of time between two of the MSP barcodes. On the day in question for this carrier who delivered in the business district, I had the carrier's Supervisor inquire as to why there was a longer than acceptable variance between two MSP scans on his route.

The matter of fact response that I received from my Supervisor about his carrier's variance surprised me. I was told that the carrier had a Priority Mail envelope that was addressed to a homeless man on his route. Apparently, this was a situation that occurred occasionally with the homeless individual. Items were addressed to the homeless individual by name, and the address was that of a parking garage on the carrier's route. The carrier knew that this homeless individual often slept in the parking garage. When he would receive an item for the homeless individual, he would drive around the multi-level garage attempting to find the man. I had the Supervisor bring this carrier to my office to find out more about this situation. As I asked questions, I found out that sometimes the carrier would drive around for 10, 15 minutes or longer looking for the homeless man. If he was unable to find the man on a given day, he would bring the item out the next day to search for him again. I told the carrier that he was to cease and desist from trying to locate this man. If there was no valid delivery address, the items needed to be returned to sender marked as such. I also included this topic in a service talk to all the carriers, letting them know that we only delivered mail to valid, verified delivery addresses on routes with authorized mail receptacles. I needed to make certain that there weren't similar situations going on elsewhere in my delivery jurisdiction area.

It would be unfair of me to attempt to explain the rationale of why that individual chose to remain homeless, especially since I had no personal conversation with him about that specific topic. I was told that he had been a successful businessman in the community and that he stopped paying taxes at his home, in protest of where his tax dollars were being spent. He eventually lost his home and his job. I do not know if he had any family involved, but he had been alone for several years. He often slept in the covered, multi-level garage where my carrier would find him, particularly when the weather was inclement. At other times, he would sleep out in the open, in parks and other public locations. He had a bicycle that he drove around, with all sorts of items attached to it. The local police were aware of him and his situation, and they never bothered him. I only had one conversation with him over the telephone after I instructed the letter carrier who had been delivering mail to him to stop delivering mail to him.

I received a call at my office from this homeless individual. He was outraged that I had instructed my carrier to no longer deliver mail to him. He went on a rampage about how he was entitled to have his very important mail delivered to him, and that this had been going on for years. I explained to the man that specific rules were in place regarding the delivery of mail. I read the regulations from a manual to him, sharing in part that

"The Postal Service may withdraw service to a delivery point if a customer does not provide a suitable mail receptacle in the postal-approved location for the delivery of mail after being so notified by local officials..." I told him that he did not have a mail receptacle for the carrier to deposit mail into and he did not even have a specific address for delivery. I told him that Post Office boxes were not very expensive and offered that as a solution to this problem. He told me that he would not pay for a Post Office Box, even if he did have the money to pay for it. He remained outraged and cursed at me, telling me that he was going to report me and that I would lose my job for denying him delivery service. I told him that there was nothing further I could do for him, ended the conversation and never heard from him or anyone else about the matter again. He may have solicited a business or private individual in the area to receive mail at their address on his behalf, but I do not know for certain.

Time changes were always a thorn in my side, particularly in the fall. When the clocks were turned back, that meant it would get darker earlier each day. Carriers were always still out delivering mail in the dark. On really rough days, with a lot of sick calls or late processing of mail, it was all the worse. As a Postmaster, I vividly recalled my experiences when I was a carrier delivering mail in the dark. It was bad enough that the carriers didn't have enough light to see the mail they were handling, especially on walking routes, but they also had their vision restricted from seeing pets or obstructions in their paths while they delivered the mail. And that meant the potential for injuries.

One of my local carrier union representatives informed me of a business that sold official Postal Service hats with headlights on them. I didn't hesitate to purchase dozens of them for my carriers. A button could be pushed in the brim to turn the headlights on, and the batteries could be replaced when needed. I made certain that these hats were distributed to carriers on walking routes and to each of my PTF carriers, since they would likely be out later helping on or assigned to walking routes. I didn't have data compiled to support my premise, but I suspect that equipping the carriers with those hats helped prevent any number of accidents that may have occurred.

Inclement weather is always a concern for employees who work outdoors. As I shared earlier, it took a year or two before carriers were able to amass the official Postal Service uniform items that they needed to get them through the season. Staying warm and dry wasn't the only concern that my carriers had in bad weather. While I was serving in my last Postmaster position, one of my carriers was struck by lightning while out delivering mail. Fortunately, she was not severely injured from what could have been a life-threatening occurrence. I was surprised to learn, however, that this wasn't the first time this had happened with this same carrier. Years earlier, while I was working elsewhere, I was told that she had been struck by lightning while out delivering mail. It is a disproved myth that lightning never strikes the same place twice. Obviously, there is no old adage or other protection that applies to individuals as well. Fortunately for her, prior to my leaving that Post Office, I assisted that lightning rod carrier in obtaining a promotion to an indoor office position in the Postal Service. Hopefully she has not had any other electrifying encounters. We all know what happens when you get three strikes.

The first regular assignment that I had as a City Carrier was on a Collection Route. My hours were 12:00 p.m. to 6:00 p.m. daily, with Saturdays and Sundays off. I signed the overtime desired list, so I would often be called or scheduled to come in and work on Saturdays for time and a half. Sometimes I would be called to come in a few hours before 12:00 to carry mail for overtime. I drove an old, presumably long ago retired half-ton Postal vehicle. My route had me going out for about an hour, then returning to drop off the mail that I had collected after each hour. The Post Office where I worked had very large and busy business areas, with more than a few corporations that had their national headquarters located there.

One of my collection spots was at the headquarters of a fast food restaurant chain that had locations worldwide. I tried to get them to call ahead when they were going to have a shipment going out to their locations all over the world. Unfortunately, they didn't always comply with that request. I can recall several times showing up there for my first pickup of the day to find stacks and stacks of boxes that needed to be picked up. Depending on the size of the boxes, which typically contained promotional material going out to all their locations, I would have to make several trips to pick up all the items they had going out. I did love seeing all those meter strips with all that money coming into the Postal Service, but it was a pain getting behind on my collection route because of having to make several trips to that one stop.

Postal Zones were implemented for large cities in the United States in 1943. Zip Codes were introduced to the public for use in the early 1960's. For those who may not be familiar with the early beginnings of Zip Codes, Zip is yet another Postal acronym for Zone Improvement Plan. Mr. ZIP, sometimes referred to as Zippy, was the cartoon character that the Postal Service used to help enlighten business and residential customers about using the ZIP Code. During my first carrier job, in the mid to late 1970's, there was no automation of mail in progress. When I returned to a carrier job, after a several year absence, automation was just starting to impact the carrier's job.

In the early 1980's, the ZIP plus 4 Code was instituted. The 4-digit add-on number identified a geographic segment within each 5-digit delivery area, such as a city block, office building, individual high-volume receiver of mail, or any other distinct mail unit. The automated letter mail that carriers started to receive, in the mid 1980's, was not yet in delivery point sequence (DPS). The letter mail was grouped together by the 4-digit add-on numbers. We would receive trays of letter mail that were basically grouped into blocks. Sorting that mail was a lot faster when a carrier didn't have to twist and turn, putting the letters in random locations on a 6-shelf sorting case. Of course, the expectation was that the routes would not take as long to sort in the office. This was the advent of what would increasingly change the processing and delivery of mail for years to come.

In 1990, the Postal Service awarded two contracts to private firms to independently measure First-Class Mail service and customer satisfaction, providing benchmarks for evaluating service improvements. In 1993, the Postal Service awarded an additional contract to measure the satisfaction levels of business mailers. First-Class Mail service performance is independently measured under the External First-Class (EXFC) Measurement System. By 2000, EXFC scores for on-time delivery reached a record high of 94 percent for the first time. In 2006, the Postal Service reported a national 95 percent success rate in on-time overnight delivery, with several service areas achieving 97 percent on-time delivery.

The independent companies that the Postal Service contracted to perform the tests that produce the EXFC results have a process that they use for their testing. They would pick collection boxes throughout the country to deposit bundles of mail. They then tracked how long it takes each of the pieces within that bundle to reach its destination. If 95% of the items reached their destination on time, that was the score given to that group of items. The Postal Service was, and presumably still is very serious about those scores, and there are a variety of processes that must be followed throughout the organization to assure that failures do not occur.

In each of the offices where I served as a Postmaster or OIC, in 3 separate Districts, the same rules were followed to assure compliance. Barcodes were placed in each of the collection boxes. The carriers who collected from those boxes needed to scan the barcode when they were picking up the mail. Their scanners were downloaded when they returned to the Post Office, and the Supervisor in charge had to print out reports for however many collection runs were in place. The Supervisor was responsible for validating that all the collection boxes were scanned, and that the scans were completed no earlier than the pickup time posted on the collection box. If a scan showed that a box was hit early, or that a box was missed, the Supervisor had to send someone out to collect the mail and scan that box. If there weren't any carriers left in the building, the Supervisor had to go out and take care of the collecting and scanning.

The District Offices and the Area Offices would occasionally send "support" staff out to validate that these reports were being filed correctly and that they were validated daily by the Supervisor in charge. It was necessary to keep these reports on file if there were EXFC failures that occurred and had originated from a specific office. The reports were the proof that everything was done correctly, sparing that office's staff from the stern retribution they would receive if those reports weren't in place to verify that correct practices were followed and in place.

The worst possible thing that could happen to an office, where the most unpleasant attention and possibly even career altering results would roll swiftly down from on high, was a Zero Bundle Failure. The mere mention of that term stopped managers in their tracks, thinking "Please not me. Please not me." A Zero Bundle Failure occurred when every piece in a test bundle dropped into a collection box failed to arrive at its destination on time. Receiving a notice of this having occurred set a tumult of activity into motion, with a team of District and/or Area staff descending on the responsible office.

It is important to note that EXFC scores were always one of the numerous items that were used to factor into whatever performance pay programs happened to be in place. There have been numerous different programs in place over the years, and of course the executives in District and Area offices received the greater share of rewards, based on their higher salaries. They have a vested interest in the offices beneath them achieving the highest possible scores. Having a higher EXFC score than an executive peer is also a matter of pride among the executives. Nobody wants to be among the bottom performers.

The Managers, Post Office Operations (MPOOs) have groups of Post Offices under their responsibility within each District. They would be notified each night of the status of the collections throughout their offices. If they received notification that a box was scanned early, a box was missed, or an entire collection run was missed, they would be on the phone with that Postmaster. If mail was collected late enough to have missed the regular transportation that took outgoing mail to the designated Mail Processing Center, the Supervisor or the Postmaster was responsible to drive the late collected mail to the Mail Processing Center. That was necessary to assure that it was processed that same day and moved along towards its ultimate destination.

As I have shared elsewhere, while serving in my first official Postmaster job, the MPOO I was assigned to had an office in the same building where my Post Office was located. He would occasionally ask me to fill in for him. Even though he did have higher ranking Postmasters working in his group, it was convenient to just have me go up the stairs to his office and take over. During one of the occasions when I was assuming responsibility over the group of Post Offices, I received a pager notification at my home at about 7:30 p.m. The notification told me that one of the collection boxes at an office in the group had not been collected. I referred to the list that I had of telephone numbers for all the Postmasters in the group and called the Postmaster of the offending office at his home.

I knew the Postmaster, and we got along well and were friendly to each other when we would attend meetings together. He was a higher level than me, but I was his Acting Manager at that point in time. I told him what happened, and he attempted to joke with me about it, chuckling as he told me there was nobody left in the office to deal with it. I told him that he was going to have to go to his office and take care of what needed to be done if he couldn't get someone else to do it. I knew that his residence was about 20 miles from his office, and he was not happy, but he did it. He didn't talk to me much at those meetings we attended together after that night.

While I was serving as Postmaster at my largest office, I received a call at my home one evening from my MPOO. He informed me that one of my collection boxes was showing up as not having been scanned. It was early enough that I knew I still had a Supervisor and employees at my facility. I called my Supervisor to tell him about my boss' call. He told me that he was already aware of the problem, but there was nothing he could do about it. I asked him to explain. He said that he talked to the carrier who was responsible for collecting the mail from the box in question, and that carrier had assured the Supervisor that he had collected everything that was in the box at the appropriate time. Unfortunately, his word didn't mean much without a verified scan of that box. The problem was that the collection box was located inside of a bank, and the bank was now locked up for the evening.

I called my MPOO and informed him of the situation. He was not happy. He told me to have someone there to collect the mail out of that box as soon as the doors opened the next morning. When I had a carrier sent out to collect from the box the next morning, he fortunately returned with only about 15 pieces of mail. I did as my MPOO instructed and looked through all the pieces that were retrieved, focusing on the destination points. There were several letters that were going to neighboring offices. I was told to make sure that each piece that was going to offices within my District arrived at those offices in time to be delivered that day. This salvage effort was not uncommon in situations like this, but it did require a lot of carrier time and effort to drive to the various locations before their carriers left their buildings. If any of these letters going to nearby offices were from a test bundle and were not delivered that day, they would have been counted as "failures", negatively impacting our score from the originating office. Whatever it took to avoid a Zero Bundle failure, it was done.

Accountability was in place at both the originating and the destinating Post Offices. If a failure to achieve the expected delivery date occurred, every point was looked at between the originating and destinating offices. That included the Mail Processing Centers and their transportation as well, particularly if several pieces were involved. Finger pointing between Post Offices and Plants when failures occurred was a common place occurrence. There were many redundant checks in place at Post Offices to assure that all mail was collected and dispatched to the Plants for processing daily. In addition to verifying that all collection boxes were picked up in a timely manner, Supervisors had to verify by signature that all mail was dispatched in a timely manner from their Post Office on each departing truck to the Plant that serviced their office. If mail failed to make it on to a departing truck by the end of the business day, the Supervisor was responsible for personally driving that mail to

172

the Plant for same day processing.

Trust, but verify. That was the creed followed by Postal Service upper management. A few times while serving in different Postmaster positions, I was tasked by my District and Area office to visit other offices to check on them. Different Managers and Postmasters would be sent out with a schedule to follow. Checklists would be marked off during visits to offices very early in the morning, and again at the end of day. I would check each of the carrier vehicles in the early morning hours at a location to make sure they were locked all the way around, with no windows left open at all. I would observe the processes in place following the carrier's arrival, validating that any missorted mail did not get left behind and undelivered. There were numerous things that would be checked off at different times of the day, and the Postmaster and staff at the facilities being checked were almost always a bit intimidated by the attention. I know that I was when my office received this same scrutiny. Whatever it took to avoid a Zero Bundle failure, it was done.

As most people know, some of the federal holidays are only observed by federal agencies. Included in those are Martin Luther King's Birthday, President's Day, Columbus Day and Veteran's Day. Many of us who worked for the Postal Service referred to those holidays as working holidays. At least they were for non-federal employees. The difficulties associated with those holidays made me often wish we did not have them at all. Collections were one of the most difficult issues to deal with after one of those holidays. While the rest of the working world was engaged in regular business, we were dormant. I would often need to send out collectors to pick up mail out of full collection boxes to start the days after those holidays. If I did not do so, those boxes would certainly be overflowing with business mail by the time the regular evening collections occurred. At times they were overflowing already. It was not uncommon to have calls come into my office alerting us to the fact that a box, or more than one, were filled to capacity.

173

One of the problems associated with those extra collection hours was that they were typically not factored into our operating budgets. That meant we would exceed our planned workhours when those extra collections were conducted. Still, they were a necessary thing for service considerations. The dates on all items mailed on one of those working holidays were also incorrect. External service testing of Postal Service products would typically not be affected. The entities that are contracted to facilitate the testing would only deposit test items on regular Postal workdays. Nevertheless, a negative impression would be given to both businesses and private parties when they would receive mail and take notice of the dates that their items were mailed and when they were received.

Mail Processing Centers faced challenges as well. They would receive what amounted to two days of mail in a single day following a working holiday. Elaborate plans would often be formulated to expedite mail from the Post Offices to the Plants. Service expectations and commitments depended on expediting mail to the Mail Processing Centers to push those envelopes and packages. Since my level 24 Post Office was located relatively close to the Mail Processing Center that served us, I had several of my Collection Routes terminate directly at the Mail Processing Center, rather than return to my Post Office to handle that mail. I looked at it as my office helping the Mail Processing Center out with their operations. The Collection Routes that terminated at their facility gave them the opportunity to get their hands on that mail an hour or two quicker than if it was brought back to my office, awaiting the arrival of a truck to transport that mail to the Processing Center. Unfortunately, there was finger pointing that had to be dealt with between my Post Office and the Mail Processing Center.

Mail that was sent out from Post Offices to their supporting Mail Processing Centers had to be culled and prepared prior to loading it onto a truck. Separations into containers included stamped mail, metered mail, flats and several separations for Priority Mail. Mailhandlers and clerks on my dock would handle those necessary separations, and when they weren't made correctly, I would hear about it from my MPOO. Because some of my Collection Routes were terminating at the Mail Processing Center, the mail within each of those vehicles was not able to be separated to the same depth of the mail that was brought back to my Post Office. Soon after the changes were made that resulted in my collection vehicles regularly going directly to the Mail Processing Center, I began to receive complaints from the management staff at that facility. They said that the mail they were receiving was causing them hardships because it was not separated properly. It took more than a few meetings to work things out with the Mail Processing Center management, gaining their acceptance of the fact that my carriers could only do so much within their vehicles. Getting that mail earlier was worth the sorting that they would have to do, and specific docks were identified for my carriers to unload at each day.

There were telephone conferences (telecons) daily that I called in on during my OIC detail prior to being selected for my first official Postmaster position. Each morning, the Postmasters of all the medium to large sized Post Offices were required to call in, as well as the Mail Processing Managers within the District. Each of the Managers would report on a laundry list of topics, answer questions and listen to concerns raised by the upper management. I learned from my listening to these that you did not want the embarrassment of any problems within your office brought up on these telecons. During one morning telecon, there was discussion about a few Express Mail pieces that were reported to have been found high in the branches of trees in a rural area. The trees were in a village not too far south of a major airport within the District. I heard someone on the call say "Oh no. Not this again." There was no further discussion about it during the telecon, but out of curiosity I had to call and ask my MPOO, George about it after the call ended. He told me that this had happened once before, Express Mail pieces being discovered high up in tree branches south of the airport. The best anyone could guess is that somehow these pieces dropped out of the jet that was carrying them to a sorting facility in Georgia. That is certainly not the kind of Air Mail service the company wanted to provide.

At my level 24 Post Office, I had a Retail Unit located at a far end of the city where the Post Office was located. The Retail Unit was located at the end of a strip mall. I visited that Unit often, as I did all the facilities under my responsibility. I observed that there was a lot of traffic coming into the Unit involving customers dropping off mail. I had a large collection box (jumbo box) with a snorkel for depositing mail located on each side of it, and I knew that this location would be a nice home for it. There was a lane that was used by traffic driving by the outside of my Retail Unit and placing the jumbo box there would enable individuals in their vehicles to deposit their mail coming from either direction. Anything to keep the lines down at my Retail Windows. I didn't want to simply drop that jumbo box without seeking approval from someone. It was not Postal Service property, so I felt the need to seek authorization from someone.

I started with the city officials. They advised me that I would need to contact the owner of the mall where my Retail Unit was located. It was not on public property. I had to do quite a bit of digging to find the contact information for the owner, but eventually I did. The owner did not have any problem with my placing the jumbo box there, so it was a done deal. I did end up back at the City Manager's office when it came time to move a jumbo box away from my downtown branch office.

As I've shared elsewhere in this book, my downtown branch office, where my MPOO was domiciled, was being sold. The parking lot across the street from that branch was the first piece of property to be sold. There was a jumbo box located within the parking lot, and I knew that my customers would not be happy about its removal. I needed to make sure that they would have a location close by where they could drive up and deposit their mail, without having to leave their vehicle. I drove and walked around the downtown area, searching high and low for an adequate place to put my jumbo box. I found that there was a one-way street that passed by the train station that was in our city. It was located about five blocks from the downtown station, so not too inconvenient for my customers. A one-way street enabled me to place the box where customers could simply reach out their driver window to deposit their mail, without having to worry about oncoming traffic. Problem solved.

I became aware of another problem involving my collection operations when I was reviewing the hours that were used after a particularly cold, icy evening. I was told that one of my collector's vehicles had been stuck at the bottom of a driveway leading to the delivery doors of a prominent building in our business district. It was bad enough that a separate vehicle had to be sent out for the carriers to have to walk the outgoing mail up the icy driveway, risking injury from falling on that slippery slope. They also had to get a tow truck to get that vehicle out of its stuck position at the end of the driveway.

I spoke to the manager of the building and advised him that things were going to need to change. The manager did not want my carriers using any other entrance than the one that they were currently using, at the bottom of the driveway in the back of the building. There were more than a few prominent businesses located within the building, and they did not want their customers having to see the carrier riff raff entering and exiting their building. I explained to the manager that this was a matter of safety for my carriers, and I was not going to risk that or the delaying of mail due to my vehicles getting stuck in their poorly designed building entrance. The manager still did not want to budge. He finally caved when I told him that I was going to move the collection point from its current spot inside the entrance at the bottom of the driveway to the outside corner of the street. I knew he would not want to inconvenience his tenants with such a drastic move. They would have to exit their vehicles at the corner to deposit their mail if I did that, an especially bad situation in bad weather. Instead, the manager agreed to let me move the collection boxes to the first floor of the building, where my carriers could drive up and collect the mail without encountering the slippery slope.

One of the busiest times of year at any Post Office is Tax Day. There is a large segment of our population who insist on waiting until the last possible minute to get their tax payments in the mail. I must admit that I was one of those last-minute mailers, only once. I had miscalculated what my taxes were going to be one year after a work relocation, and I did not want that payment to go in any earlier than that last possible minute. I could relate, somewhat at least, to the mindset of those individuals who did the last-minute shuffle to the Post Office. A lot of planning had to go into the operations that occurred on Tax Day, with meetings and discussions and the customary redundancies that were put into place to assure the best possible service.

As I've shared often, the city where my level 24 Post Office was located was very affluent. Tax Day was a big day in that city. I had to have employees scheduled to collect from the jumbo box outside of my Main Post Office until the last pickup at midnight. Those rich people did not want to part with their money until the last possible minute. We had to coordinate with our Mail Processing Center to make certain that all the mail collected and sent to them received the cancellation date of that Tax Day. I decided to go to my Main Office on only one of the Tax Days during my time as Postmaster there. What I witnessed lived up to what I had heard occurs on those days/nights.

During the hours leading up to midnight, traffic was backed up on the highway leading to my Main Office. Customers would drive up and hand their mail to the employee who was stationed by the mail receptacles at that time. That was quicker than having customers slow down and come to a complete stop to deposit their letter sized and larger envelopes. Traffic was able to move more quickly through the procession line and hampers full of tax mail were filled and taken to the dock for trucking to the Mail Processing Center.

There would inevitably be customers driving up as midnight came and passed, and they were most unhappy when they found that they had arrived too late. Their tax envelopes would not receive the correct cancellation date and they would potentially be owing additional money for late filing. I'm not sure how often people were caught by the IRS and charged for late filing, but it certainly generated some excitement for those customers beyond the midnight hour.

The events of 9/11/2001 brought about a new paradigm of thinking in every aspect of society. I would venture a guess that most individuals will forever remember where they were and what they were doing when the jets hit the twin towers in New York City. I happened to be on annual leave that day, working on a project in my basement. My wife called down to me when the first jet struck. I joined her upstairs and watched in horror as the second tower was hit. That is a memory that will never be forgotten.

The United States Postal Service was drastically affected after that dreadful day. Security became a matter of significant importance beyond what it ever had been previously. One of the greatest concerns was the possibility of an explosive device being placed in a package and sent through the mail stream. The Postal Service has always used commercial airlines flights to transport mail to different destinations. If a commercial flight were to come down due to an explosive device that was placed in a package, the Postal Service would no longer be able to use commercial flights to transport mail. If all mail and packages sent through the Postal Service had to utilize ground transportation as its most expeditious means, trucking mail in semis across the country, that would incapacitate the organization's ability to compete for business.

After the discovery that anthrax had been sent through the mail, just one week after the 9/11 terror attack, the handling of letter mail and packages was no longer a routine matter. Over a period of just a few months following 9/11, there were several confirmed instances of anthrax having been sent through the mail. There were several confirmed deaths as well from that anthrax exposure, including the deaths of Postal workers who had handled that mail. The availability and use of gloves by Postal employees who handled mail became a commonplace occurrence. Gloves were purchased by the Postal Service and almost every employee used them, changing them often as they would work throughout their day. Although the use of gloves by employees did decline with the passage of time, they were still being regularly used by several employees more than a decade later when I served in my final Postmaster position.

I recall being challenged by my MPOO, Dick at that Post Office about the expenditure my office was incurring for the purchase of those gloves. I asked him "Do you really want me to tell my employees that we are no longer going to provide them with gloves?" He briefly thought about the impact that would have on the morale of my employees, the bad press that such a decision would bring about and the grievances that would certainly be filed by all the unions representing the craft employees. He backed down on his position and told me to keep purchasing what was needed to make my employees feel safe.

The Aviation Mail Security and Hazardous Materials Group was formed within the Postal Service following 9/11. That group was responsible for developing, implementing, and maintaining policies and procedures for the acceptance and handling of hazardous materials throughout the Postal Service. Warning labels have been in place on all collection receptacles throughout the Postal Service network as a follow up security measure. Those labels serve as a warning to customers that if the identified procedures are not followed, their item may be identified within the Postal Service as "Target Mail" and returned to the sender. Target Mail included any larger items that had stamps affixed to them, with no way to positively identify the sender.

Clerks who are working at Postal Service Retail Units have been trained to follow specific guidelines, including asking specific Hazmat questions when a customer brings a package to their window for mailing. Validation that the procedures and training are being followed is measured primarily through a Mystery Shopper program that has been in place for years. Referred to as the Postal Service's Retail Customer Experience (RCE) program, Mystery shoppers are customers unknown to the retail staff who fill out evaluations on their shopping experience, which helps determine how well retail units are performing. 40% of the "score" received for a Mystery Shop was based on how long the shopper waited in line at a Post Office. If a wait time for a Mystery Shop was longer than five minutes, that shop's score can go down significantly. Other areas that are weighted within a Mystery Shop are the neatness and cleanliness of each Window Unit and the availability of specific forms, supplies and promotional materials. The attentiveness and attitude of the Postal Service employee being shopped is also weighted in the score. There are other questions that are asked of the Mystery Shopper, but asking that customer if their item being mailed contains any hazardous materials is the one most germane to security. The failure of a clerk to ask a customer about hazardous materials within their package allows the possibility of a disaster to occur if something within that package ignites or explodes. The Mystery Shop program is covered more in depth in the Discipline chapter.

United States Postal Service Inspectors would periodically target Post Offices to assure that official security measures were being followed. There was a concern that a Postal vehicle could be stolen and potentially used as a bomb or transport for other weaponry in the wrong hands. Since Postal vehicles could go virtually anywhere unrestricted, they would make an excellent choice for nefarious purposes. The Inspectors would check our Postal vehicles at our facilities when the carriers were not out delivering mail. This would occur at any time of day or night. They would check all the doors and windows on each vehicle to make sure they were completely closed and locked. They would also go out on the carrier routes and similarly check the vehicles while the carriers were away from them delivering mail. Any abnormalities were reported back to our District Offices and to the Postmasters for follow up. Follow up would typically mean some type of discipline to the offending party.

At each of the Post Offices where I served as Postmaster, I would task my staff with going out and checking on the Postal vehicles used by carriers during delivery as well. I would personally do the same. I regarded the importance of security very seriously, and I occasionally would check Postal vehicles outside of my own jurisdiction. Whether I was in a neighboring city or travelling in another state, I would occasionally park my car to check the doors on a parked Postal vehicle to see if they were all locked. If I found them unlocked, I would find the carrier and show them my business card, letting them know that I was calling their Postmaster. The Postmasters I would call in such circumstances were surprised about what I was doing. I'm sure that many of them were thinking as many of you may be, "Get a life!" I do not know how other Postmasters handled situations where their employees left their vehicles unlocked, but I would always insist that discipline was initiated for offending employees of mine.

Following 911, fear ran rampant throughout the Postal Service individuals who handled the mail. There were situations that occurred throughout the country where suspicious materials were found travelling through Postal facilities. Powder leaking from a package, or liquid that could not be readily identified resulted in more than a few facilities being vacated and shut down in that fearful environment. Experts would be brought in, wearing their moon suits, to collect and test suspicious materials found in those facilities. This had an obvious impact on the ability to continue to provide uninterrupted service to the customers.

Each Postal facility was required to have a Continuation of Operations (COOP) plan developed and ready to implement in the event of a disaster. I was the Postmaster of a level 21 Post Office at that point in time. I had to have duplicate labels printed out for all my clerk and carrier sorting cases, which I carried within my personal vehicle. That amounted to hundreds of strips of labels, ready to be inserted into remote clerk and carrier cases as needed. Our District office had semi-trailers loaded with clerk and carrier cases, ready to transport them to backup facilities in the event of an emergency. This also required me, and all my counterparts, to have an adequate location where all this equipment and our employees could be housed in case of an emergency.

I visited a few different locations that I thought might fill the bill for these requirements. It took many meetings and a lot of correspondence before I ultimately found a suitable location. It was also necessary for us to have contact information for each of our employees, preferably a phone number. Gathering this information was not an easy task. Many employees did not want to give me their personal contact info, and thanks to the blessings of their unions and our contracts, they were not required to do so. The best that could be done with those employees was to let them know where to report, our alternate facility, if they came to work and found the facility shut down. The fact that I was also responsible for a centralized forwarding facility (CFS) at my location added additional backup criteria to my venue.

As shared earlier, my CFS unit was one of many across the country that handled the forwarding of mail. As all such units did, my unit processed the forwarded mail for the first three Zip Code numbers shared within my area. The daily backup information from my own CFS unit was able to be saved to a disk drive. That information would only be able to be uploaded and functional at another CFS site. The two nearest CFS units were located over 50 miles away. I had to take the daily backup files with me each day. They could be used at one of the other locations for processing forwards if our facility was shut down. My trunk was full of labels and CFS data files. I wonder what would have happened if my vehicle was in a crash and burned amidst a shutdown at my facility? Probably should have had a backup for the backup.

The area surrounding the city where I was serving in Supervisor capacity had been farmland for years. Those cornfields were sprouting up houses and subdivisions in virtually every direction surrounding the city. The city and its Post Office next to my work location were the same size, but the name recognition and the real estate value of property was much lower. The Postal Service District Offices had maps that clearly defined the geographic territories that were served by each Post Office. This was necessary and important for defining which Post Office would be handling the delivery to a new area. It was even more important in our situation where the subdivisions were springing up.

I received a phone call from a customer one day. He wanted to know what his Zip Code was going to be for his new home he was buying. I was unfamiliar with the area that he described, so I took down his phone number and told him I would have to do some research and call him back. I checked with my District Address Management office and I was told that this house and

184

subdivision were not located in my Post Office's delivery area. They were within the neighboring Post Office's delivery area. I called the customer back and informed him that he would not have a Zip Code in my Post Office because his house was not in my delivery area. I gave him the phone number for the neighboring Post Office and told him he would have to call them to find out what his Zip Code would be.

He became very upset and told me that the builder had told him that he would have an address in my city. I told him that the builder was wrong, and that he should have checked with the Postal Service before giving out this information. His voice was shaky as he told me that his wife would divorce him if she found out that the house they had bought was not in my Post Office's city. I told him I was sorry, but that there nothing I could do about it. There was a lot of political pressure brought to bear over the territories defined in several of these areas where new homes were being built. I found out after I had moved out of the area to my next position that the territory lines were redefined. That subdivision and other areas that were previously defined as belonging to the neighboring office were changed to my old office. The property values of those homes were greatly increased as a result.

I spent 3 years working in that Supervisor job. I spent time supervising employees on Collection Routes, City Carrier Routes and Rural Routes. I gained experience adjusting routes in City Route zones and in Rural Route zones due to the amount of growth we were having in the number of new deliveries. During my time at that office, letter mail began to arrive in delivery point sequence (DPS). DPS letters were sorted by machines at the Mail Processing Plant and sent to our office in trays for the carriers to take out on their routes for delivery. Clerks did not have to sort that mail to the carrier's routes. Carriers did not have to sort that mail into their cases to get it into delivery order, then pull that mail back out to place in trays for delivery. The reduction in hours meant that the adjustment of routes had to be completed to capture the expected savings.

There were 55 Remote Encoding Centers (RECs) opening up across the country. I learned much more about automation when I was promoted to my REC Operations Manager position from my Post Office Supervisor position. Each REC would handle the processing of letter mail for a designated group of Mail Processing Centers. If the address on a letter could not be read at the Mail Processing Center, a picture was taken of that letter and that image would be sent to the supporting REC. RECs did not handle any physical mail, only the images that came over dedicated telephone lines to the DCOs (Data Conversion Operators). The DCOs had to be trained for how to correctly input their interpretation of what they were reading on each image into their keyboard. The "result" of their interpretation would then go back over the telephone line and be paired back up to the actual physical letter. A barcode would then be sprayed onto that letter, removing the need for sortation by clerks and carriers from that point on. These letters would arrive at Post Offices in trays, following the sequence of delivery addresses on each route.

Following my promotion to REC Operations Manager, there was a lot to do before the new REC would even open to start operations. A facility had been leased, but it needed to be restructured to accommodate all the equipment that would be needed to function. The facility had been vacant for years. There were eight Supervisors promoted by Ben to handle operations at the new REC. Max would have five Supervisors reporting to him, since Tour 3 operations were the heaviest processing times, and I had three Supervisors assigned to me. They were all local to that area, and Ben was the only one of us who knew anything about REC operations.

We travelled as a group to a few existing RECs, to give us newbies an opportunity to see how they functioned. We also went through the training process that our DCOs would be going through at our new REC. That was particularly challenging for me. The keyboard used by DCOs was very similar to a standard alpha numeric keyboard. There were some different, additional keys that were needed for processing mail. My typing style is hunting and pecking. I did take a typing class years ago, but I ended up reverting to my hunting and pecking because of my comfort and familiarity with that style. I have amazed onlookers with the speed at which my hunting and pecking fingers can move. As far as the training class went, I did not pass. Fortunately, my Operations Manager job was not contingent on my passing. That was not the work I was being promoted to do.

RECs worked closely with the Mail Processing Centers they supported. The only Postal Service background that I had was working in Delivery, with City and Rural Carriers. My studying of a foot-high stack of paper about RECs was as close as I ever came to Mail Processing. I enjoyed listening to Ben tell the story several times to other people. He would say how this guy (me) came into the interview with only a delivery background. His application was well written, so I figured I would give him a chance. I was so impressed by how much he must have studied to be able to talk the terminology like he did that I hired him.

We advertised that jobs were available and rented a large enough facility to interview hundreds of applicants. Personnel from the Human Resources department of our Area office were sent to our location, to assist us with the interviewing and hiring process. We hired several hundred people to work on shifts during the 20-hour operating window, 7 days a week. Their hiring was contingent on them passing the keyboard training for the job. Their training was scheduled to begin as soon as the building renovations had been completed and the equipment was installed at the facility.

I moved out of the hotel where I was staying and into a furnished two-bedroom apartment where my family could join me. It was summer and we had to sell our home back at the old location while we looked for a home at our new location. The cost of living was much lower than it was at my previous job location, so we were able to buy a very nice 4-bedroom house for half the price it would have cost for a similar house at our old location. A nice raise and a lower cost of living were certainly a nice package. Unfortunately, that would go away when I took my next position back at the same higher cost of living area.

Everyone in the remote encoding environment knew that the RECS were intended to be phased out over time due to technology improvements. The workload that we had at the REC where I served as Operations Manager fluctuated with the seasons. Christmas was always the heaviest processing time. So many Christmas cards were being mailed across the country, and the machines at the Mail Processing Centers could not read the addresses that were handwritten on all those envelopes. Different colored envelopes also created problems for those mechanical readers. We would get so busy that we would have to mandate 10-hour workdays, 12 hours and I recall mandating a few 14-hour days for our employees to get all the mail processed for our Mail Processing Centers. Those mandate days were difficult for many of our employees.

Ergonomic breaks were an important part of a DCOs job. The Postal Service had done the research to determine the best way to reduce the problems that might occur with this type of work, such as carpal tunnel syndrome. After one hour of keying, the DCOs would get a 5-minute break. After the second hour, they would get a 10-minute break. After the third hour, another 5-minute break. After the fourth hour, it would be a half hour lunch. Then back to the 5, 10- and 5-minute breaks after each hour for the remainder of their day. Those breaks could be tracked, and I made it a priority for my staff to verify that they weren't being abused.

Image samples were captured and used for testing the accuracy of the DCOs. Each DCO was to be given the test sample on a regular basis, their results viewed by their Supervisor to assure that they were accurately keying the images they were receiving. The results of the tests were accumulated over time to track a composite result of their accuracy. Additional training was provided as needed, and discipline was issued if the accuracy did not improve.

The contract in effect between the Postal Service and the clerk's union mandated that RECs were staffed by 30% career employees and 70% transitional employees (TEs). Each of the RECs that were up and running did their best to maintain the proper percentages of employees. During one particular Christmas season, we had hired a large number of employees to assist in operations. When that season was over, we found that we were overstaffed, needing to get some employees off our employment rolls. Career employees were not a consideration, so my Manager, Ben and my peer Operations Manager, Max and I developed a way to make the cuts of our TEs.

We utilized a spreadsheet to sort certain criteria, such as unscheduled absences, keying speed, error rate and discipline on file. Once this was put together, we just drew a line at the number of low scoring employees that we needed to cut. Done. I was surprised that the methodology we used was not questioned or challenged by our local union representatives. I would certainly not have been able to use that criteria years later when I was a REC Manager at my own facility.

Automation was becoming an increasingly important reality in Postal Service operations. The RECs were doing their jobs getting barcodes put onto letters, and the technology improvements that were being brought to the Mail Processing facilities were ongoing and substantive. Since I had worked as a Manager in a REC prior to my first Postmaster appointment, I was very much attuned to the necessity of automation to reduce overall costs. Automation was doing the job as intended, reducing employee hours. My focus was placed on circumstances where those letters were not being automated.

While I was serving in my first official Postmaster position, I was reviewing the daily reports from the Mail Processing Center where our mail was sorted. The report I was reviewing showed the percentage of letter mail that was being automated to DPS on each carrier route. I was surprised to see that one route had a very low percentage of DPS mail. The carrier showed me letters coming to his route that had our neighboring city's name with our Zip Code on them. That meant that my clerks and the carrier on that route were having to manually sort a larger than normal percentage of the letter mail that was going to that route each day. My typical plan of action whenever I was addressing any issue was to go after the biggest bangs for the buck. In this case, it was obviously this route that would increase my DPS percentages by fixing whatever the problem happened to be there. I spoke to the regular carrier on that route and found out that an agreement had been put into place between the former Postmaster and a group of addressees who lived in newer homes in my Post Office's delivery area.

As I shared earlier, I had experienced this phenomenon in the past when new houses were springing up on the delivery borderline within a city's Post Office. I discovered that I had a reverse of the situation I had at the office where I was a Supervisor a few years earlier. The city where I was Postmaster at that point in time was considered to be inferior to the neighboring city. The value of property in that neighboring city was much higher than the value of similar properties in my delivery area. There was also the pride of those homeowners of these borderline properties that played a big part in the agreement that had been put into place. They wanted their addresses to state that they resided in the more prestigious neighboring city, not in the less prominent city that delivered their mail. My predecessor agreed to let them have their way, in part. They would receive mail that was addressed to the correct street name and number, with the Zip Code of my Post Office, but the city listed was that of the neighboring, more prestigious city. This had been going on for years, and it had not raised any flags within the Postal Service prior to my becoming aware of what was happening.

The bottom line to this situation was that unnecessary costs were being incurred due to this agreement that was in place. The intent of automation, reducing manual workhours, was being thwarted by this agreement. In the grand scheme of things, the small volume of affected letters may have seemed inconsequential to the former Postmaster. But automation, and the expected reduction of workhours that was being demanded from the top of the food chain on down, changed the paradigm of mail handling at Post Offices exponentially. It was also a matter of principle to me. As a company man, I firmly believed that automation was a good and necessary thing for our organization. I was determined to do everything I possibly could to fix this mess and get that mail automated.

As I began to research this situation, I found that the affected mail for these addresses was being processed in a few different ways. Because of the conflict of the incorrect city name with the correct Zip Code, the letters were being rejected as unresolved by the automated equipment. Those letters were then being sorted manually by clerks at the Mail Processing Center that handled my Post Office's mail. The clerks would most often send that mail to my neighboring city. They would presume that the right city was listed on the mail pieces with the wrong Zip Code. That mail being sent to the incorrect delivery office typically meant the delivery of that mail would be delayed by at least a day. The clerks who sorted the mail at our neighboring office knew that the addresses on these items were not associated with any of their routes. They were also familiar with the odd circumstances involving these addresses. They would reroute that mail to my Post Office, and it would not arrive until after the carriers had left the office for that day's delivery. It was my hope that by pointing out to the affected customers that their mail was being delayed, that they would comply by using the correct city and Zip Code on their mail. That turned out to be an unrealistic expectation on my part.

I began my attempt to fix this problem by talking to my predecessor, who had signed off on this agreement, and viewing the agreement itself. The agreement showed that my predecessor had pretty much capitulated to the desires of the affected customers. I contacted my District Office's Delivery Department to obtain an official map of the delivery areas that my neighboring office and I were responsible for. The maps showed what I expected them to show, that those affected customers were within my city's delivery zone. I then went to my Acting MPOO, Tim to discuss the matter with him. I told him my plan, and I was looking for his concurrence that it was the right thing to do under the circumstances. I had drafted an official letter to send out to the customers who lived in the affected area.

In that letter, I acknowledged that I was aware of the agreement that had been made several years earlier with the previous Postmaster. I shared that due to the dependency on automation to handle the processing of their mail, and my responsibility to most expeditiously handle the delivery of their mail, that agreement could no longer remain in effect. That was the basic gist of the official letter, and it stated that they would have six months to comply with making the necessary changes. Mail that was erroneously addressed after that date would be returned to sender. Tim agreed with me that this would be a good course of action to take.

Tim had been in his position as an Acting MPOO for more than a year at that point in time. He knew that I liked to go after problems when I found them, even if that meant going against the status quo. His titled position was that of a Postmaster in a neighboring city. He was the same titled level as I was, a level 21. As a Postmaster, he could often relate to the things that I would bring to him and the changes that I wanted to make. He did aspire to move up the food chain though. That meant he needed to be politically correct and not just look at what would achieve the best results. I knew that about him from the many conversations I had with him. To protect both of us from any potential backlash, I suggested to Tim that he share this plan with the District Manager prior to implementing it. He told me that he would do that and get back to me. A few weeks went by and I ran into Tim in the hallway of our facility. He was in a hurry, but I asked him if I should send the letter out to my customers. He gave me a hurried yes and continued on his way.

I sent the mailing that I had put together out for delivery, and the phone calls began to come in immediately. The customers who called were outraged that I was reneging on the agreement that had been officially signed off on by the previous Postmaster. A few of them threatened legal action, telling me that they were going to sue me personally. Others threatened to go to the press over the matter, and many wanted my Manager's name and phone number to voice their complaints to him. I had been through this customer outrage in the past at other locations, so I wasn't surprised when it started happening. I knew that Tim must have received at least a few calls at this time, so I went to visit him at his office. I asked him directly, "You did tell the District Manager about this situation, right?" He told me that he hadn't talked to him yet about it. That concerned me, and I told him so. He looked concerned himself but told me not to worry about it.

A few weeks later, I again experienced the shit rolling downhill process. One or more of those affected customers had taken their complaint to Headquarters, threatening the press and lawsuits. Headquarters executives do not typically respond very well to the threats of bad press or adverse legal action. The usual roll occurred from Headquarters to my Area to my District

Manager to my Acting MPOO, Tim finding ground level at me. I was too much of a lower level participant to be privy to the conversations or other messaging that takes place amidst such downhill rolls. The bottom line was all that really mattered to me anyway, since my opinion would not have any impact on decisions that were already made at higher levels. Tim gave me the basic bottom line directive to "take it back." I had to send another mailing out to all the individuals I had originally contacted, letting them know that there would be no change to the service they had been provided through the agreement they had with my predecessor. I followed my marching orders, prepared my mailing and sent it out.

Things were changing quickly within the Postal Service at that time. The stress placed on meeting service requirements for delivery of a variety of products (Regular mail, Priority Mail, Delivery Confirmation, Express Mail) was at an all-time high. Technology had advanced the processing of mail to the point where a large percentage of both letter mail and flats (magazines and larger envelopes) were being sorted down to the delivery point by machines. This meant that not as many clerks were needed to sort the residual mail, and carriers needed less time in the office to sort their mail when a large percentage was coming to them sorted automatically to delivery sequence. All the data was compiled at District and Area offices and at Headquarters, showing how many clerk and carrier hours should be reduced due to automation being implemented. The higher ups wanted those saved hours captured, and they expected to get them back through a reductions of hours worked at our offices. A reduction of hours meant employees had to go.

I was on a teleconference with my District Manager during my last Postmaster position one morning when I was confronted by him about the number of carrier hours my office had been using. These teleconferences were held daily and there were approximately 60 Managers and Postmasters in attendance on them. It could be intimidating when you were called out by the District Manager on one of them. He didn't mince words and he expected answers on the spot, or immediately following the teleconference. I was then the Postmaster of a level 24 office, one of the largest offices under his responsibility.

The latest technology advancement had been the sortation of flats to the delivery order sequence of the carrier routes in my Post Office. The numbers were crunched based on receiving an average of 60% of our flats sequenced. That meant less hours for clerks and carriers needed to sort the mail. All the figures were available to me daily showing the exact number of flats that were being processed automatically by the sortation machines outside of my office. I tracked those numbers every day, especially since they averaged only about 40 – 45% of my flats being sorted to carrier route sequence. The spreadsheet that I updated showed the variance daily, weekly and monthly between the 60% expectation and what percentage we received.

We had been tasked with adjusting all our carrier routes based on the 60% number. If that number were accurate, there would have truly been a considerable reduction in hours that the carriers would be spending sorting their mail in the office each day. Routes were adjusted reducing office hours and increasing time on the street to assure that there would be 8-hour assignments for all our full-time regular carriers. That resulted in several routes in my office being eliminated, to achieve that result of having 8-hour assignments on the remaining routes. When my District Manager called me out about the carrier hours I was using, I informed him that we were only receiving less than 45% or less of our flats automated daily. He seemed caught off guard by this and told me to send him my numbers. Before the teleconference was over, I emailed both him and my MPOO the Excel spreadsheet that showed the actual numbers I was tracking and how they fell below what we were given as a basis to adjust our routes.

Our local carrier union knew that things were not right from our route adjustments, just as my staff and I knew that things were not right. We were expected to hold carriers accountable for the times that were projected for them to complete their routes each day, and in many cases it simply couldn't be done. The union filed grievances to rectify the situation because carriers were pushed every day to complete their assignments in less time than what was needed. Eventually, the routes were adjusted again, and new routes were added back to rectify the incorrect adjustments that had been made based on inaccurate data.

When the sortation of flats to the routes began, my office was very successful in capturing the correct carrier work hours that were expected to be saved, not the bogus numbers we had been given. This took a lot of monitoring of our carriers in the office each morning. We had to make sure that the trays of letters and the trays of flats that held the DPS mail went out with the carriers directly to the street. There were occasions where carriers would attempt to bring the mail to their cases to sort it with the rest of their mail in their cases.

While several offices in my own District had started to receive flats sorted to DPS, one of our neighboring Districts had not yet gone online with having their carrier flats processed to DPS. Individuals in management within that District had become aware of the successes that my office was experiencing with the implementation of automated flats. I received a call from a Manager within that neighboring District, asking if he and several of his managers could visit my facility to see how we were doing things. We set up an early morning meeting in my conference room, and eight Delivery Managers were in attendance along with an employee of theirs with a video camera. A few of my Supervisors, my Customer Service Manager and I met with them behind closed doors to discuss implementation with them.

We answered their questions about what their expectations should be about the product they would be receiving. The accuracy of the DPS flats was very high. We shared that the biggest issues involved keeping the carriers from handling the flats. A small percentage of the carriers would do their best to get those flats and sort them in with their working mail that they were sorting into their cases. It took a lot of policing the area where the DPS flats were staged. The staging area was along the way to the parking garage where their vehicles were kept. They were supposed to pick up their trays of DPS flats and DPS letters on their way to their vehicles. Carriers who were caught taking DPS flats or letters back to their cases without authorization would be candidates for discipline.

The most common legitimate reason for bringing DPS mail to a carrier's case would be if that route was being split up for delivery by other carriers. That typically occurred when a carrier would call in sick, leaving their route to be handled by their peers on overtime. During the peak vacation times, when the largest number of carriers were scheduled for annual leave, we would often go into a workday with dark routes. Dark routes were routes that we simply did not have enough carriers to cover. The quickest sorters that knew the dark route would be scheduled in on overtime to get the route ready to be split up for delivery by other carriers on overtime. Carriers assigned to take portions of a dark route would typically be assigned to deliver between an hour to two hours of that route, depending largely on the known performance level of each carrier and how far they would have to travel to get to that route. The mail would be pulled out of the route's sorting case and left with the appropriate form identifying who was assigned to take that portion. The DPS letters and flats and the parcels for each portion would be left for the assigned carrier as well. If there was any accountable mail (Certified, Registered, Customs, Postage Due) that had to be signed for, the assigned carrier would have to retrieve that mail from our accountable cage.

The number of internal email messages that went out to management employees each day could often be quite sizable. That number was amplified even more if you were in a Postmaster or higher up Manager position. There were numerous group listings in the email system. With one tag, messages could be sent to all the Supervisors working in a District, to all the Postmasters and Managers in a specific area, to all the Mail Processing staff in a District or Area, etc. Some of these group listings were filled with management staff nationwide.

Occasionally someone would inadvertently send a message intended for a small group, or even a single individual, to a nationwide audience. The system would get seriously bogged down with responses from individuals who would click "Reply to All" instead of just messaging the original sender. There would be responses such as "Why am I receiving this?" "This was sent to me in error." "Stop sending this." I found it to be quite humorous, especially when higher up Managers in the organization from across the country would chirp in, replying to all with messages like "Stop responding to this." That would feed the beast, and sometimes it would take hours for the messaging to finally stop.

While serving in my final Postmaster position, the time came for my restlessness to spur me on to a new promotion. I had left my Operations Manager position at a REC years earlier, not wanting to be in a facility that was going to be closed down due to technology advancements. Times change and opinions change along the career path. Where there were once 55 RECs in operation at their heyday, I was now being promoted to manage one of the two that were remaining in operation. The Two RECs that remained standing each processed mail for approximately half of the country's Mail Processing Centers. The Mail Processing Centers were pretty much divided from the east coast to the west coast and split between the two RECs. In addition to hiring local employees, each of the RECs had full time regular employees who had transferred in from other RECs that had been closed across the nation. The Postal Service had an obligation to full time regular employees whose jobs were being eliminated. Attempts were always made to train and reassign those employees to other Postal jobs in their geographic areas, but there were sometimes not enough jobs available for those employees.

As groups of the 55 RECs were scheduled to be closed over the years, Postal Service Management and the clerk's union would negotiate to determine the rules that would be in effect for each successive group of employees. I don't claim to have knowledge of the various agreements that were reached over the years, but they did change considerably. At one point, full time regular employees whose seniority was not high enough to secure a Postal job in their immediate area had a choice to make. They would have to accept employment at a Postal facility within a 500-mile radius of their location or give up their employment with the Postal Service. The TEs at the RECs that closed were simply out of a job. I found that there were employees at my REC who had transferred in from several different RECs, including some who I remembered from the REC where I had served as an Operations Manager almost 15 years earlier.

Where there were once award funds in place within the REC budgets, the financial situation within the Postal Service resulted in those funds being stopped. We did give out paper awards as recognition to employees who excelled in several areas during a 3-month period (Quarter). Lists were displayed throughout the REC highlighting the accomplishments of the recipients of the paper awards. I also did have a Quarterly Pro Bowl Team that would receive recognition, with their pictures and stats posted on the walls for all to view. Those Pro Bowl members were the employees who had done better than average in several overall areas. At the end of the year, I reviewed the statistics of all the Pro Bowl members and picked the Most Valuable Player (MVP) from among them. I had a cookout to celebrate his and the other's achievements, which leads to another story about what had occurred when one of my predecessors had done cookouts.

One of the Managers who had been in place prior to my arrival was cooking food for the workers at the REC. He was moving a pot full of boiling water when it tipped and severely burned his hands. He had to go to a local urgent care facility to have the burns treated. It took some time until he was able to have normal use of his hands again. The story of what had occurred was relayed to me by one of the staff members who had been working for him at that time, now working for me. I was told that the local union representatives reported the occurrence of this accident to the Manager's higher ups. The contention was that he had failed to report an on the job injury. He was paying for the expenses incurred from the accident through his own private insurance, rather than having the Postal Service pay for those expenses as an on the job injury. That didn't matter. Failing to report an accident is considered a very serious offense by any employee. The exact details of what transpired following the accident were not known to others within the REC, but that Manager ended up retiring from the Postal Service soon after the burn event.

I often had cookouts for my employees at the REC. The Social Recreation Group that was put into place at the REC would come up with different events to make things more interesting at the facility. We would have bake sales, where employees would bring in items that they had cooked, and they would be available for other employees to purchase. Large coffee cans were in place for employees to deposit their money for the items they would buy. We had a savings account at a local Credit Union where I would bring in coffee cans full of coins. They had a coin counter that could be used by members for no charge. I enjoyed watching the digital count grow up into the hundreds while I fed the coins into the counter. On one visit, the machine broke down while I was feeding it. They were able to retrieve my coins and I had to wait a few days until it was fixed to cash in our money.

One of the items that we purchased from our funds was a large propane grill for the cookouts. It could hold up to 40 burgers or 80 hot dogs at a time. I personally handled all the cooking for those events, inviting employees to bring in side items to accompany whatever meat was being grilled. I would start cooking at about 7:00 am, with the last batch of meat typically being cooked up around midnight for the night shift. The union officials who were in place during my time at that REC were heavily involved with the Social Recreation Committee that was in place, and they were all for the cookouts and other events that we planned out. They also knew that I was aware of what had happened with the REC Manager who had been injured. To avoid anything similar happening to me, I advised them that I was not on the clock when I was doing the cookout events. No on the job injuries would be sustained by me if something were to go wrong.

In preparation for a Thanksgiving celebration, I purchased dozens of precooked turkeys with our Social Recreation funds. Some of my staff and a few union representatives worked with me to break the turkeys down, placing the pieces in bags and putting the bags in refrigerators we had at the REC. When the celebration day arrived, we loaded large crock pots with turkey pieces to heat them up. That process continued from the early morning until just after midnight, to accommodate each of the shifts of employees. Employees were encouraged to bring in side items, and there was more than enough food to go around.

Many of my employees were as supportive of our military as I am. I put a program into place for every Memorial Day and Veteran's Day. Employees would give me the names and addresses of family, friends and acquaintances who were in

201

active service in one of the branches of the military. We had a display where their pictures were posted, updated as their situations and whereabouts changed. Leading up to those holidays, we would collect items that the employees would bring in. I would have my secretary divide the items up and place them in boxes, shipping those packages off to the military personnel we had on record. I received a few letters back from recipients, thanking us for the items they received.

As I shared earlier, there were no longer funds available for awards. I did not let that stop me from putting the Christmas seeding program into place. I worked with my Social Recreation Committee to identify prizes that could be given out to employees during the 12 Days of Christmas campaign that was held. Social Recreation funds were used to purchase many of the prizes. I had a dry erase board placed by the facility entrance to show who had won prizes on each of the shifts during the 12 days. Employees were excited to see who was winning what, with the anticipation that their name might be going up on that board next.

I was able to get 2 overnight stays at local hotels, but I needed a third to have one win available for each shift. I cashed in frequent flyer miles that I had from all the traveling I had done to get that third night prize. I knew, from experience, that employees were able to donate sick leave to others in emergency situations. I had my usual topped out amount of annual leave hours that I was going to carry into the next year. I had to use some of those hours, or I would lose them. I made calls to find out if there was any way I could use some of those hours as 8-hour block prizes for our 12-day theme, ultimately finding out that couldn't be done.

We had employees turn in their favorite recipes and had a REC cookbook made. Those were sold to raise additional money for the Soc Rec fund. I bought several of them, distributing them to some of my family. We also had a contest to design the front and back artwork for a t shirt. Employees enjoyed the contest and bought many t shirts once the finished product was available. I still have one of those.

So many efforts went into keeping the morale of the employees as high as possible. My hope was that happy workers would give their best efforts on the job in the REC vs REC environment that lingered over us.

CHAPTER FIVE: TRAINING

Training was a function that was taken very seriously by the Postal Service higher ups as I moved along my career path. New employees obviously had to receive a lot of training to enable them to functionally perform the duties of their positions. Training went well beyond the initial new employee modules. It continued throughout my entire career, necessitated by changes that would take place within the company. Hours were appropriated throughout all the functions within the Postal Service, and a lot of tracking was in place to assure that those hours were being used for their intended purpose.

I had become aware of the Postal Service's Advanced Leadership Program (ALP) while I was serving in my Operations Manager position back at the REC. It was a prestigious program that was very helpful in moving employees ahead in the organization. I knew that my former REC Manager, Ben was a graduate of that training program, and I was disappointed that he had not nominated me for the program. At that time, I felt that he did not nominate me because if he did, he would have felt an obligation to nominate my peer Manager, Max as well. I was grateful that he had allowed me to go out on the OIC detail, and that he had recommended me to fill in on the Acting REC Manager detail, so I had to be satisfied with that and put the ALP consideration out of my thoughts.

It was now a few years later, and my MPOO, Stan called me to his office to talk about the ALP. Stan was an ALP graduate, and he gave me the details about how the program ran. The ALP program consisted of being assigned to a class of 48 individuals, broken down into 8 groups of six individuals. The groups would meet at the Postal Service's training location in Potomac, Maryland for four separate weeklong sessions over a year long period. There were a variety of training and situational assignments given to the groups throughout the process. When Stan asked me if I would like to participate in the ALP, I answered affirmatively without hesitation. I felt fortunate because the individuals who were sent to participate in the program were typically in a much higher level than I was. They had much more responsibilities and employees reporting to them, and I had recently dropped a level to take my new Postmaster position.

When I arrived at Potomac for my first weeklong session, I was surprised to find that some of the individuals participating really didn't want to be there. They were only there because their Manager signed them up and they had no choice. They didn't want to say no to their boss. I was among most employees who were grateful for the opportunity. I felt honored that Stan felt strongly enough about my potential as a level 21 Postmaster that he asked me about my interest in attending. That honor was magnified when I later discovered that I was the only one from his group who he had recommended for the current ALP class.

In addition to the training we received, each group was selected to work on an assigned task. The tasks assigned were things that would benefit the Postal Service in some way. At the end of the four weeks of meeting, each group was to have a presentation put together. An executive from the Postal Service would be at Potomac on our final day and each group would give their presentation to the executive. The task that my group was given was to find a way to reduce the pollution produced by Postal vehicles to be within EPA guidelines. I know that the other 5 members of my group had much greater responsibilities in their higher-level positions than I had. At the time, I was in my first Postmaster position with approximately 70 employees under my responsibility. Other members of my group were Postmasters over much larger cities in different parts of the country, with hundreds of employees and large finance operations under their responsibility. I made the decision to dedicate myself to giving our task everything that I had.

In between our 4 weeks of face to face meetings at Potomac, the members of my group and I did a lot of exchanging of information through emails and occasional telephone conferences. I presume that each of the other groups within our class handled their tasks in the same manner. We researched the pros and cons of several different fuel types and ultimately decided to use propane as our recommended alternative fuel. I don't think that it is an exaggeration to say that I did most of the work on our project. I did have the time that my teammates did not have, and I did a lot of research while at work and on my own time, outside of my work schedule.

We all knew that concerns about safety with the recommendation of propane would be an obstacle within the Postal Service. I started off by taking on the challenge of dispelling those concerns. Through my research, I was able to find that there are fleets of school busses in different parts of the country that use propane fueled vehicles to transport children. I found that a major taxi company in Las Vegas had propane powered cabs. I found out that the Schwan food delivery company uses propane powered vehicles to deliver food to their customers. Most importantly, I discovered that the Key West Post Office in Key West, Florida used a small fleet of propane powered vehicles to deliver mail to their customers. That discovery enabled me to conduct an interview with their vehicle maintenance manager. The information that he provided about the positive aspects of propane use was shared in a video recording that he had put together, and it was included as a snippet in our presentation.

Another one of the hurdles we were facing was the cost of converting gas burning engines to propane burners. The Postal Service's mail delivery fleet largely consisted of thousands of Grumman Long Life Vehicles (LLVs). The cost of converting those LLVs from gas burners to propane burners at that time would have been just under $1,000 per vehicle, and we did not want to give a presentation recommending a conversion that would necessitate a large monetary output in advance by the Postal Service. The Key West vehicle maintenance manager informed me, and included in his video presentation, that they only changed the oil in their vehicles twice per year. He said that when they did change it, the oil still looked as clean as it had gone in. The miles per gallon was just a bit lower than regular unleaded gas, but the emissions were much lower than the gas burning vehicles. The converted vehicles would be within the EPA guidelines. Making a move to propane would be a nice, responsible corporate move for the Postal Service to make. The funding would be our major obstacle for our struggling-to-make-ends-meet organization.

It was then that my ongoing research brought me to finding Jim, who was heavily involved in the propane industry. Jim ran an organization in Texas, and he knew everything there was to know about propane. I let him know early on that this was just a project I was working on for a presentation. I was obviously not in any position to do anything more than investigate and speculate about possibilities in our discussions and research. But he knew as well as I did that if the Postal Service, with the largest fleet of vehicles in the world switched to propane it would be quite a boon for that industry.

I kept the members of my team informed about my conversations with Jim, usually by just sending them email messages. As a team, we had decided to build our presentation around a proposal to convert the gas burning LLV carrier vehicles in a large city in Texas to propane burners. We had done our research, and the city that we chose was one of the worst cities on the EPA list for air pollution. Jim contacted one of the major fuel outlets in Texas to discuss some possibilities. I made a point of reminding him that this was all speculative. I was not in any position to make promises about any potential business ventures. Jim got back to me and told me that a representative of the fuel company he contacted had some positive news to share. The representative told him that his company would be willing to potentially put propane pumps at several fuel centers in the city we had chosen. The fuel company would pay for the conversion of our engines from gas burners to propane burners up front. They would then put a surcharge on the propane fuel that was purchased for our carrier vehicles, ending the surcharge once the cost of conversions was recaptured. Even with the surcharge on the propane fuel, the cost per gallon would still be less expensive than unleaded gasoline.

The members of my team were as excited as I was to hear this proposal. We put our PowerPoint presentation together, including all the data pertaining to costs for all the carrier vehicles in the designated city we had chosen. We practiced giving our demonstration until it was time to give it. There were eight presentations that were given to the assigned Postal Service executive, one from each of the teams within our Advanced Leadership Class. After all the presentations had been given, the executive told one of the members of my team that he would be contacting us about coming to Headquarters in Washington, DC, to share the presentation with a group of executives and other employees there. My team members and I were very excited at the prospect of having our efforts recognized and the possibility of our proposal being initiated.

There was a formal dinner that was traditionally held after the last week of Advanced Leadership training and after all the presentations were given. I looked very much forward to being in attendance there. Seating was not assigned, so I took a seat at a table where I saw one of my team members. She sat next to her executive Postmaster, who was there to support her and congratulate her. There were several District Managers in the group who were there to support their employees in that group. A District Manager from a Midwestern state took a seat next to me. One of his MPOOs who reported to him sat on the other side of him. The MPOO and I recognized each other because she had interviewed me for a higher-level Postmaster job that I did not get. While we were having drinks at our table, waiting for the catered dinner to be served, there was a lot of conversation going on at the tables throughout the room.

At my table, people were talking about their travel plans to go home the next day. Some were close enough to drive, but many needed to catch flights to get home. I mentioned that I had to get up early to catch a flight back home because I needed to get back to my area for an interview. The District Manager next to me asked what job I was interviewing for and I told him it was a MPOO job. I had never met the man before and I knew nothing about him. Without warning, he became very serious and started to mock interview me. He fired several questions at me in a serious tone and I reluctantly answered them. As I did my best to answer one question, he would immediately shoot another one at me. He was the one who interviewed and selected MPOOs within his own District, so he was in his element. I was extremely uncomfortable, hoping that after each question he would stop. Everyone else at our table was also noticeably uncomfortable. Finally, his MPOO leaned over to him and said "Come on Bill. Lay off with the questions. This is supposed to be a celebration." Thankfully, he did stop.

After our dinner and desserts had been served and cleared away, we were called up to a stage one by one to receive a congratulatory plaque from a high-ranking Postal Service executive. Each graduate had a picture taken with the executive, and they were mailed out to us after the event. I woke up early the next morning to get my flight back home and made it to my interview without a lot of time to spare. The interview went well, but I was not selected for the MPOO position. I found out later that the person who had been on a temporary assignment in that position was selected for it. I also found out that he had been at the Bolger Academy the night before, partaking in those same ALP festivities as a graduate from his own District. He stayed in Potomac one more night,

210

and his interview was conducted over the phone. At least someone got to sleep in.

After I had returned home from the Advanced Leadership celebration, I was contacted within a week and given a date and time to go to Headquarters to give our presentation. Four of my team's members indicated that they would not be able to attend this meeting due to schedule conflicts. Stan was proud of me for the recognition our presentation was receiving, and he had no problem authorizing payment for me to travel to Headquarters for the additional presentation. It was agreed that the remaining team member, who worked at Headquarters, would give the presentation with me. But then Murphy's law kicked in.

My propane contact, Jim contacted me and advised me that the fuel company was backing out on this speculative arrangement. They had crunched the numbers involved with our carrier vehicle's propane fuel purchases and found that this would not be an acceptably lucrative arrangement for them. Each carrier vehicle drives a limited number of miles each day in a city setting. They only needed to refuel their vehicles once a week on average. The fuel company decided that it would take much too long to recoup the conversion expense through surcharges with the limited amount of propane that would be purchased. So, it was back to the drawing board for me, with just a few weeks until I had to go to Headquarters.

I knew that the Postal Service had occasionally aligned with other companies for "brand sharing." The best example is the eBay packaging with both eBay and United States Postal Service logos on the shipping containers. I decided to pursue this speculative idea to salvage the previous presentation that was now at a loss. Jim contacted another major fuel supplier to work on the new idea. I used a photo of the back of one of our carrier route vehicles for my illustration. I superimposed the USPS logo above the proposed fuel company's logo with the terminology "The United States Postal Service and "Fuel Company", working together for a better environment."

The speculative arrangement would include the fuel company placing propane tanks at several of its locations and paying for the conversion of the gas burning vehicles to propane burning vehicles. There would be no cost to the Postal Service for the conversions due to the co-branding. I informed my fellow team members of the necessary changes that would be made to our presentation, and they were content that our project was able to move forward with the proposed changes, retaining the provision of no necessary cash output by the Postal Service.

The date finally arrived for the meeting and I had made all the necessary changes to the PowerPoint presentation. I was more than a bit nervous when I entered the room where the presentation was to be given. There were about a dozen people present, and they were all certainly much higher on the food chain than I was. Introductions were made around the room. There were representatives from the Alternative Fuel Department and other Headquarters departments and at least one lawyer was present. That's where the problem occurred.

After giving the presentation, I was grilled by the lawyer. He wanted to know what was said to the fuel company. He wanted to know specifically if any promises had been made. I did my best to assure him and the rest of them that everything was conveyed merely as speculation. The group thanked the two of us from our group for coming in, and we never heard a thing back from Headquarters about our project after that. Not one word. I heard rumor that one of the head individuals from the Alternative Fuel Department, who had been present during our presentation, had a close relative who was involved with an alternative fuel other than propane. The rumor was that the Postal Service was going to pursue that other alternative fuel. I was very disappointed.

Sometime after I graduated from my ALP class, having received the necessary number of college credits, my MPOO Stan called me to his office to advise me that he was sending me to a nearby city for an assessment of my business skills. He informed me that this was part of the process of placing me in another leadership program that he thought I could benefit from. I thanked him, and I truly did appreciate the way that he looked out for me and noted ways for me to advance my career. I reported to the agency for the assessment. The agency was not affiliated with the Postal Service. They performed similar assessments on individuals from several different companies. I spent several hours at the facility, working my way through a variety of modules that were designed to test my performance on multiple levels. I was surprised by the thoroughness of the testing, and by how closely the modules mirrored my actual job duties.

The first assessment module had me doing what I would normally do on a workday. I sat at a desk with a computer and had a variety of emails that I had to read. Some required responses, others did not. I also had an inbox of physical mail to go through and reports that were due. I had an allotted amount of time to complete these tasks, and there was not enough time to complete all of them. It was just like a typical workday. The way that I prioritized what would be done to completion, what would be started but not finished until later and what would be ignored were all part of the assessment of my skill level. Two of the modules involved meeting with two different actors that worked for the company making the assessment. One of them played an executive from the Postal Service. The other played a disgruntled customer. I was given problems to handle in each of those meetings, and those factored in for the rating I received on my assessment.

The report that was ultimately received by Stan was shared with me by him. It pointed out areas of strengths and weaknesses, but overall, I was happy with the results. Stan had me sign up for internal Postal Service training, to work on those areas of weakness that my assessment pointed out. The training that I received involved logging into a Postal Service Training website, reading through the material on each topic, being presented with different scenarios to react to and taking an online timed test for each class. I passed each of the classes I was given without difficulty.

As I moved upward in my career, I began to pay closer attention to the Voice of the Employee (VOE) survey results. The Postal Service sent surveys out to each facility every Quarter. Four times during the year, we would receive surveys for one quarter of our career employees to fill out, on the clock. A variety of questions were asked on those surveys. Many of them referenced the facility where the surveyed employee worked. Others asked overall questions about the Postal Service and their leadership. Employees and staff would be brought into a room to complete their surveys, place them in accompanying envelopes and return to their work. Local management did not know how individual employees and staff were completing those surveys. They were filled out and sealed in envelopes and anonymity was maintained. Sometimes employees would take their sealed envelopes containing their surveys with them when they left the room where they took them. They were concerned that management would somehow be able to pick their envelope out of the tub where employees were depositing them, and somehow identify the individuals who had filled them out and how they responded to the questions.

I would study the results that we would get from each Quarter, and the composite results that were given for the Fiscal Year. As I looked through the names of the individuals who were receiving the surveys each Quarter, I could often make predictions on the results I would receive based on those individuals. If there was a largely anti-management group, I knew I would be looking at lower scores. I decided to take a proactive approach to those surveys during my last few positions with the Postal Service. I think a lot of facility heads didn't pay much attention to the VOE surveys. They didn't think that much could be done to raise their scores, or they just didn't consider it be an important item to focus on in the grand scheme of things.

I dedicated display areas where I could post all the survey results. I would pick 3 – 5 items where low scores occurred, and I would focus attention and come up with a game plan for addressing those items. That plan would be shared on the display with my employees. There would also be service talks given updating progress on those game plan items. Communication, in general, was often a weak point within survey results at facilities. I went to great lengths to personally script the service talks that were given daily to my employees. There were different groups of employees at different locations, and it was important to me to be assured that they were all receiving the same information.

Training was an important medium to use for enlightening my employees. There were many processes within the Postal Service about which they simply had no knowledge. I knew that as an organization we were well versed at putting out a multitude of instructions and regulations. What we were not so good at was sharing the reasons why we wanted employees to do the things that they did. It was easy to see that employees reacted positively when those explanations were shared with them. The different methods that I employed achieved the positive results of improved VOE scores at the facilities that I managed.

During my detail as the Acting Manager of the REC that was going to be closed down after Christmas, I was concerned about what the future held for the craft employees and the staff at that facility. I was instructed to keep the closure information to myself, but I knew I had to do something. I decided to put a few things together for the employees at that facility before we started that heavy Christmas processing of mail. I wanted to be available there as much as I could to facilitate the training classes that I scheduled for the employees who worked on different tours of duty throughout the day and into the night.

I began the processes by having conversations with the Operations Manager and the Supervisors who reported to me at that facility. I asked them about their career aspirations. What were their plans and goals beyond the REC? I encouraged them to sign up for a variety of training classes that were available internally on the Postal Service training site and to look for detail opportunities to enhance their careers. For them and the employees in general, I scheduled training that I conducted for the application process and interview skills development within the Postal Service. Amidst all of this, I would slip into that poker face when I would hear that inevitable question "Have you heard anything yet?" "No, I haven't heard a thing, but it's always best to be prepared."

I would interview applicants for the variety of positions I had available at my Post Offices where I served. On one occasion, I was interviewing applicants for vacant Rural Route Carrier positions at my Post Office. Those were difficult positions to fill, because there was no guarantee of how many hours would be available for the individual to work. Rural Carriers were typically hired as Rural Carrier Associates (RCAs). RCAs would be hired to work on a regular Rural Carrier's day off, assigned to that regular's route. The RCA would work on the regular's scheduled days off, if they called in sick and during their vacations. Some regulars did not have a regular day off during the week. A Rural Route's workload was established through periodic mail counts, and with increased automation that workload was impacted. Regular carriers with a small enough evaluated route time were able to opt to work 6 days per week to get closer to a 40-hour work week, and many did.

As I was in the process of interviewing applicants, I was caught off guard when a young man approached me, accompanied by another individual. The other individual explained to me that the applicant was a deaf mute, and that he would be interpreting for him. The interview went well, and I could tell that the applicant was very excited about the prospect of being employed by the Postal Service. I was well aware of the fact that I could not do anything that could be interpreted as discriminating with the applicant. But I could not understand how this was going to work if he had to go out on a route every day, unable to hear such things as honking horns or sirens.

I called my Human Resource Department for some guidance. I was told that if there was no other reason to not hire the individual, I would have to do so. I hired the young man, then discovered I was going to be paying for someone to come in and interpret for him during his training period. The prospect of additional expenses did not amuse me, but I did what needed to be done. Time passed and I made a point of checking on this individual a few months later. When I asked his Supervisor how he was doing, she told me that he was great. He was always at work on time, doing the job at a very good pace and he was helping on other routes as well. I made a point of approaching the carrier soon after that, thanking him for the job that he was doing.

Training was also utilized in conjunction with discipline being issued. Whether the recipient of discipline was a craft employee or someone in my management team, it was often very appropriate to assign training exercises to focus on the problem area. Training classes were often scheduled at our District and Area Offices. There were also a multitude of courses that could be taken on a Postal Service website. Many of the courses were interactive, and the participating employees were required to print out a record showing that they had completed the required training.

Every week my District office would send a message out to the

Postmasters with an attachment highlighting No Record Mail for the previous week. No Record Mail was mail that was sent to the CFS Unit for forwarding but returned to that office because there was no record of a forward on file in the system. Since I managed a CFS Unit, which processed mail for several Post Offices' forwarding within my group, I felt an obligation to do whatever I could to address this problem. I visited Dan, my District's Communication Specialist at his office. It was a short trip up a flight of stairs from my office. I told him that I wanted to make a training film for our carriers to address the problem of No Record Mail. The Postal Service had recently placed the problem of No Record Mail under the responsibility of the District Consumer Affairs Managers throughout the country. Since Dan reported to the Consumer Affairs Manager just down the hall from his office, he was eager to help me.

I wrote a detailed script for the proposed training film and shared it with Dan. He knew another employee who did a lot of photography for District events. That individual also had a video camera. We met at my office, after the carriers had left for the day to go out on their routes and started filming. The carrier route cases, where the mail was sorted for delivery by the carriers each day, had a card for each row of addresses that had the forwards listed on it. The script had me pulling the forwarding cards out of a few rows, highlighting what was done correctly and incorrectly in maintaining those records. We filmed a lot of other details that would help to focus the carriers on preventing No Record Mail. I gave a narrative throughout the film, and I can recall how cheesy it looked as my eyes were focused above the camera, reading the scripted words.

The finished product was shown to all my carriers. I endured the jeers that I received from the carriers over my amateur performance, but measurable results were seen in my Post Office's No Record Mail percentages over the weeks that followed. I found out several weeks later that Dan had given a copy of the film to his Consumer Affairs Manager. She had taken the film to a meeting she attended, and several other Consumer Affairs Managers from around the country had requested copies of it for their Districts. Copies of the film were made and distributed to Post Offices throughout several Districts in the country. I read in an internal Postal Service publication that my training film won a "Cammy Award" at our Headquarters. It was a good feeling to know that the film was serving its purpose beyond my own office, and I didn't even mind that there was no mention of my name in connection with it. I was more than a little nervous when I was invited to go upstairs to attend a meeting that my District Manager had with his staff who reported directly to him. The District Manager called me up to the front of the room, where he read what he had typed up in an Award folder for my receipt. I received a $1,000 check for my contribution through the film and it was a good day for me.

The District where my Post Office was located held meetings for all the Postmasters each Quarter. There were over 100 Post Offices in the District, and these meetings were usually held in a hall at a Community College. This was back in the day when the Postal Service had money and would allow spending some of it for meetings. It was a very nice and comfortable place to meet. Coffee and snacks were available throughout the day and we had a catered lunch as well. I contacted someone from the District Manager's staff and asked if I could have 10 or 15 minutes at an upcoming meeting to give a presentation on No Record Mail to the Postmasters. I was told that I could, and I put a PowerPoint presentation together covering different ways that No Record Mail could be reduced in their Post Offices. I also had an Excel spreadsheet that I put together showing the costs associated with the handling of No Record Mail within each of the District's Zip Codes.

The costs included the handling of the mail that was unable to be forwarded by the clerks in each office and the carriers who had to handle these pieces again for proper processing. I didn't make a lot of friends with the distribution of the spreadsheets, particularly among the Postmasters whose Post Offices were incurring the greatest costs due to No Record Mail. I became even less popular when the District's Finance Department contacted me, requesting a copy of the report that I was generating highlighting those costs. The Finance Department sent out messaging to the Postmasters, letting them know that the cost of excessive No Record Mail produced at their offices would be taken out of their Post Office's budget. My Post Office was consistently under the acceptable percentage of No Record Mail, so I didn't have any worries.

Priority Mail had its own processing stream in place that started at the Post Offices. Priority Mail items that were brought in through our retail windows and pieces that were brought in from carriers on their routes had to be placed in specially marked equipment, based primarily on their size. Placards were placed on containers for the different sizes, and they had to be reviewed continually to assure compliance. When the containers left the Post Offices, they would go to a facility that was dedicated to the processing of Priority Mail in our major metropolitan area. These Priority Mail Hubs were set up in major metropolitan areas across the country. It was necessary for the Priority Mail pieces to be in the proper containers because as these containers arrived at the Hub, they would be taken to the area within the Hub where the correct processing would take place utilizing the appropriate mechanized equipment. I decided that I wanted to make another training video.

I contacted Dan, the District Communication Specialist who had helped me with the No Record filming. He gave me the contact information for Ben, an employee who worked at another nearby District Office. He told me that Ben had a lot of nice equipment for shooting videos that had been purchased for him by our Area office. Ben handled the bulk of the official photography and video filming of the major events that took place in our Area. I called Ben and introduced myself. I explained the project that I was going to need help with and asked him if he would be able to help me. I told him that I had a script written for the project, along with the filming that I wanted to accompany it, and I emailed him a copy of it. He told me that he would have to check with his Manager to see if he could free up the time to work with me. He called me the next day and told me that he was given the approval for the project, and we set up some dates to film at different locations.

We started off filming at my Post Office, focusing on the importance of placing the Priority Mail items in the correctly placarded containers. We met a few days later to film at the Mail Processing Center where our originating mail was sent. We filmed on the dock there, showing how the Priority Mail containers from all the incoming offices were offloaded to trucks that were going to the Priority Mail Hub. For our final day of filming, we went to the Priority Mail Hub, showing how the containers of different shapes and sizes of Priority Mail pieces were linked together and trucked off to different processing locations in the facility. We filmed the handling and mechanization processes for the different sized and shaped items, highlighting the delays that would take place when items were not in the proper containers. I went to Ben's office for a few different meetings for the editing of the film. He had an impressive setup with the video playing across 3 wide screens. The finished product put the No Record film I had made with Dan to shame.

I made an appointment to meet with the Mike, Manager of Delivery Operations at my Area office. I had known Mike for a few years through meetings that were held at the Area office. I brought him a DVD of the Priority training film and left it with him for his review. Mike contacted me within a week and told me that he thought it was a very good film. He had copies of it made and distributed to the different Districts in our Area to be used as training. I was gratified to hear that. My MPOO called me to come to her office several weeks later. When I arrived at her office, she had the Manager of the Mail Processing Center where some of the filming had been done with her. I was presented with an award and a check for $250 for my efforts on making the Priority film. I couldn't help but notice that the Priority effort had gotten me a $250 award, while the No Record film had been deemed worthy for a $1,000 award. Extra money was never the motivator behind my film work, so it wasn't that big of a deal for me. It satisfied my creative side to work on those types of projects and getting a good result.

My MPOO and the Mail Processing Center Manager then asked me if I would be willing to take on the task of being the Priority Guru for our District. It was not uncommon for management employees to be tasked with heading up teams to correct or improve specific operational issues. Most often in those situations, the assigned guru, or individual who was tasked to head up such an effort would be taken away from their regular responsibilities. If the individual was a Postmaster, an OIC would be placed in their office while they were away heading up the temporary concentration of efforts out of their District or Area office. I asked my MPOO if someone would be assuming my responsibilities at my Post Office while I focused on Priority Mail. She and the Mail Processing Center Manager answered no in unison. I told them that I would have to think about it, even though I already knew my answer. If I was going to have to maintain all the responsibilities associated with my Postmaster job, I had no desire for taking on other duties, other than those ones that I wanted to do. I called my MPOO a few days later and thanked her for the consideration but told her that I was not interested in the assignment. I told her that I was going to be busy working on another training film.

The Postal Service had a program available for employees called eIdeas. The program was on the intranet for any employee to submit ideas that could benefit the Postal Service. There were different categories that could be checked off by the employee submitting the idea. The primary ideas being sought were ways to reduce costs or work hours in any operation and anything that would increase revenue. With the sheer number of employees in the company, from the largest variety of ethnic, education and work experience backgrounds, there had to be a goldmine of good ideas out there. I was a believer in the program. The operative word being *was*. I had submitted an idea for generating revenue, and that idea was closed a few weeks later. The reason given by someone at my District office was that the idea I had given was decided at the Headquarters level. So, it was closed instead of moving it up the food chain.

That made no sense at all to me. There was no criticism or anything negative said about the idea itself. There was a button you could click on the eIdeas page if you wanted to submit your idea for further consideration if it had been closed. I clicked on the button and assumed that my idea was going to someone else for consideration. After a few weeks had gone by, I dug into the whereabouts of the recipient of the further consideration submission. I found that my resubmission went to someone who worked in Maintenance at a nearby Mail Processing Center. I found a contact number for him and gave him a call. I told him what was happening, and he was surprised. He said "Oh, that's why I keep getting these messages." He had no idea why he was receiving things from eIdeas, so he just deleted them.

I called Mike, the Delivery Manager at the Area, to inform him that I was going to submit my Priority film to Headquarters through the eIdea program. Even though my earlier experience with eIdeas was a negative one, I thought that the weight of having Mike involved and the film already in use within our Area would help to move it forward. After all, Mike was an Executive. He thought that was an excellent idea. The film had been distributed throughout our Area, but there was a lot more ground that could be covered. I submitted the idea and the waiting began. Email messages were sent out to the submitter when there was any change in the status of the idea submitted. I would periodically log in to the system to check the status because I didn't have 100% faith in the emails being sent. Over the course of a few months, I saw that the idea and the DVD were forwarded on to various individuals at Headquarters. Several more months passed when I received an email telling me that the idea had been closed. I logged in to see who had closed it and it was an Executive working in Delivery at Headquarters. I called Mike again and he checked into it. He called me back and told me that the DVD had been lost at Headquarters, hence the closure of the idea.

Mike told me that he had copies of the DVD and he would send one to the Executive at Headquarters. I asked him if he could send me a copy as well, since at that point I had just started at my new level 24 Postmaster job and hadn't unpacked everything yet. I thanked him for his assistance and checked in the system to see the idea was taken out of the closed status and reopened a few days later. After almost a year and a half had gone by, and I had already completed another training film, my frustration hit a peak. I composed a very professional letter, highlighting all the difficulties I had experienced with the eIdeas process, and sent it to the highest Delivery Executive at Headquarters. I copied the letter to our Area Vice President, my District Manager and my MPOO. Within a week I received what I can only describe as a chastisement call from my District Manager. Things had rolled downhill to him, and he elected to make the call to me directly, rather than pass it along to my Manager.

There was general shock amongst them that someone at such a low level (that's me) would go outside the chain of command to such a high level within the Postal Service. I attempted to intimate to my District Manager my concern that the eIdeas system was not working as it should. If this had happened to me, who knows how many good ideas were not going anywhere. I was attempting to call attention to things so they could get fixed. My concerns fell on deaf ears. My District Manager told me that I would be getting a call from someone at Headquarters about the film. I received that call days later. A lower level Executive in Delivery called to tell me that he was closing the idea out. He explained that over the time since the film had been made, some changes in the processing of Priority Mail had occurred that made the film now obsolete. I was aware of the placarding changes that he was referring to. I thanked him for his call and his time and that ended things.

I did contact Ben once again to work on another project with me. I shared my ideas and sent him a script I had written. The focus of this video was going to be on recruiting new customers for new revenue. The intended audience was Postmasters and Station Managers of Delivery Units. Ben was available, so he came out to the Post Office where I was working, and we started filming. I enlisted a Postmaster friend of mine to portray a perspective customer. All the filming was done at my Post Office over a few days, so that made the project a lot easier for all of us. I again travelled to Ben's location for the editing process. When it was finished, I gave a copy to my MPOO. He distributed the film to all his Postmasters and to those in another MPOO group. I did not receive any award for that film, but it did hopefully enlighten the intended audience and increase sales within the Postal Service.

I started to work on another training film project, for an intended audience of carriers and customers. I scripted a film that would highlight the problems that would occur involving carriers delivering mail. The script focused on a Postal Service LLV delivering curbside to mailboxes out by the street. I talked to the President of our local carrier's union about the project. I wanted to involve the local union, since there would be filming of one of their carriers delivering the mail. The local President seemed happy and interested in the project, and it was always a good thing to find ways to improve relations with the different unions and to get employees excited about participation.

I contacted my video friend, Ben and he was ready to work on yet another project with me. Then I made a mistake. I contacted my District's Safety Manager and informed him of the project. I sent him a copy of the script, and he unfortunately contacted someone up the food chain from him. A Safety Manager at our Area Office told him that this was not a good idea. The higher up said that there was too much of a potential for an accident to occur while filming. My District's Safety Manager basically told me to shut it down. I regretted that I had gone to him in the first place. I didn't follow my usual process of going ahead and doing it, asking for forgiveness later if something went wrong.

I did have yet another idea for a film I wanted to make for Postal employees and our customers. The basic idea was to follow a letter through the system. It would be dropped into a mailbox, go to the Mail Processing Center, through the automation process, shipped to its destination and sorted to the DPS in a carrier's route. I thought that would be of interest to both internal and external customers. Our own employees did not have a very good understanding of the processes that took place outside of their work areas. I did like to have things playing on a monitor where my Retail customers were waiting to be served. I thought that the "LLV Safety" and "Follow the Letter" subject matters would be enlightening for them as well. When I left the Area where I was serving in my last Postmaster position to manage the REC, I decided to end my side job of making training films.

CHAPTER SIX: THIEVES IN OUR MIDST

Think about it. Do you like getting things in the mail? I don't mean bills or bulk business (junk) mail, although some people like even getting those items. Everyone that I know loves to get things in the mail. I remember how my mom, when she was alive, loved to collect coupons and send forms to various companies for rebates. I was a carrier at that time, and I remember cautioning her about exceeding the one per family limit that most of those offers had. She would send in for rebates and have the checks sent to my house, my brothers' houses, my sister's house and other relative's houses. She would also have them sent to her neighbor's houses. It seemed like a relatively harmless stretch of the rules, but I cautioned her about potential consequences, nevertheless.

While in the position of 204B (Acting Supervisor), I was privy to some of the information that most craft employees (carriers, clerks, mailhandlers) were not clued in on. The level 22 Post Office that I worked in at that time was in a medium sized city, and it had a branch office that was located a few miles away from the Main Post Office. I didn't spend a lot of time at the branch office, whether in the position of a carrier or as an Acting Supervisor. The branch office had about twenty carrier routes that came out of it and it was in an older, posh community. The branch itself was referred to by the local Postal employees at the Main Post Office as the "Country Club". When a carrier route become available, typically due to retirement, resignation, termination, promotion or the death of an employee, that carrier route was available for bidding and was awarded based on an employee's seniority.

Most of the cushy mounted routes, those that have curbside delivery where the carrier can mostly just sit and drive through their routes, were located at the Main Office. Most of the Country Club routes were walking routes, where the carrier had to walk to make deliveries door to door in every kind of weather. Although there were many senior employees working at the Country Club, giving them the ability to be awarded a nice mounted route when one became available at the Main Office, most of the employees that worked at the Country Club usually preferred to stay there. The employees at the Main Office generally preferred to stay at their own location. There was a class distinction there. The bit of information that I found of interest related to one of the female carriers, Mary who worked at the Country Club. She had been working at that location for at least 15 years as a carrier, and she was single. This was her career, her sole source of income (so I thought), and her plan was to retire from the Postal Service (so she thought).

It seems that Mary had a penchant for the coupons and rebates, much the same as my mother did. But Mary, as a letter carrier, was able to take the rebating to heights that my mother could only have dreamed of. She was in the habit of having these rebates sent to different addresses on her postal route. She would have some sent in her name and others sent in fictitious names. Since this was her route, she was the person that saw all mail that came to those addresses five days a week. She did have a replacement carrier that did her route on the sixth delivery day each week, and I still wonder whether that person was aware of what was going on and was complicit in what she was doing. Somehow, the Postal Inspectors became aware of what she was doing. Perhaps her substitute tipped them off, or it could have been one of her customers. It could have even been the companies sending the rebate checks out, noticing that something was amiss as they sent so many checks out. At any rate, she was under suspicion and she did not know it.

Postal Inspectors showed up at the Country Club one day while I was working as a 204b there. They took Mary into an office with them after she returned from delivering the mail on her route, and that was the last I saw of her. I'm not sure if they took her off to jail somewhere or what became of her that day, but her career with the Postal Service was over. Based on what

I heard, when they took her into the office with them, they turned out the lights with a black light on, and her hands and clothing glowed from a powder that had been placed in the envelopes she was receiving from rebates on her route. It's hard for me to imagine risking a career and all its benefits over nickels and dimes in rebates.

While I never did see her again, I did receive a phone call from someone in Human Resources at one of our competitors. Mary had applied for a position at the competitor company, and apparently, she had given my name as a contact from her previous job. She may have thought that was a safe thing to do, rather than giving her titled Supervisor's name. She thought wrong. I tossed her under the bus, sharing everything that I knew with them.

Throughout my career, there were several times when I worked with the United States Postal Inspection Service on issues relating to the facility where I was working at that point in time. At times I was well informed about the Inspector-involved situations from start to finish. At other times, they worked discreetly, and I had little or no knowledge of what was happening until after their work was completed. During my first management job as a Delivery Supervisor in a large Post Office, they would contact me to inquire about the names and identification of individuals who happened to be either delivering mail to specific addresses on specified dates or collecting from specific mailboxes on specific dates. I never really thought much about why they were inquiring, even though these inquiries would come double enveloped and marked "Confidential". Very hush-hush. I did finally have an opportunity to experience the reason why they did this.

I was summoned by my Postmaster, who called me into his office to privately discuss a serious issue. He informed me that he had been contacted by the Inspection Service regarding one of our carriers. It seemed that the Inspection Service had been contacted by several individuals who reported that mail they had deposited into several boxes on one of our collection routes never made it to their destinations. They found, through their inquiries to me earlier in those envelopes marked "Confidential", that there was a common denominator to this disappearing mail. Many of the problems were occurring with one collection box. It was the jumbo collection box that was located across the street from the Post Office's downtown branch office. Customers would pull up to this box in their cars and deposit the mail through their windows.

The carrier in question had balked recently when I attempted to add work to his route. Upon inspecting his workload earlier, by sending a Supervisor along with him on his route to time his run and document how much mail he was collecting on average, I determined that he had a lot of potential free time on his route. Of course, that was because we were not aware of how he *typically* spent his day. I did end up adding work to his daily schedule, not realizing at the time what a service I was giving to our customers by doing so. By adding work to his day, it gave him less free time to do what he normally did, rifling through the mail he was collecting.

Rifling is the term used by the Postal Service to describe mail that has been violated. Apparently, this carrier was in the habit of looking through the envelopes he was collecting, opening anything that looked like it might contain a greeting card, or especially if it felt like it contained a gift card. He would then pocket any cash, checks, or gift cards or certificates he might find enclosed and trash the leftovers (some poor unfortunate customer's birthday, wedding, anniversary, get well, congratulatory, or friendship card). The vehicle that he drove was a 9-ton truck, a very large vehicle capable of transporting the large volume of mail he would collect and drop off on his route. It had a compartment in the back where one could easily stand, and it could be accessed from the driver compartment.

To gather evidence against this crooked carrier, the Inspectors planted several cards in the mail receptacles that this individual serviced daily. They placed money in with the cards and marked the bills. They then followed him around while he completed his daily assignment, noting that he seemed to spend a lot of time in the back of the vehicle, where he would place the collected mail. They checked at a local business place where they had observed him entering and making a purchase, at a stop that was not on his route. They entered the business where the carrier had stopped and informed the merchant of who they were, showing their official badges. They checked the bills of the denomination that the merchant indicated had been used by the carrier and found that one of the "marked" bills was used to make a purchase.

They continued to follow him until after he made a significant pick up from the largest collection mailbox on his route. Noting that he was doing his usual disappearing act in the back of the vehicle, the Inspectors entered through the driver's door, opened the door leading to the back compartment, and barged in on him. They found him leaning over a large hamper of mail, with several opened envelopes nearby him. When they searched him, they found that he had several of the marked bills on his person, as well as gift cards and gift certificates made out to some of those poor unfortunate customers and a large amount of cash. There was obviously no point in denying anything, and not a lot that his union representatives would be able to do for him under the circumstances. They caught him red-handed. He was taken into custody and spent the night in a local jail, until he could be bailed out by relatives the next morning.

I was not kept in the loop about all the events that happened after that. I believed at that time, learning firsthand this to be true in my own handling of problem employees, that the preferred way for things to go in cases like this was for the employee to resign. Having to terminate employees was often fraught with difficulties. A resignation was much cleaner for management, since it avoided all the grievance, arbitration and/or Merit Review Board processes that might otherwise occur. To expeditiously accomplish this, deals were sometimes offered to the affected employees, reducing the criminal charges against them and the effects of the embarrassment in exchange for their swift resignation. I'm sure that deep down the unions probably prefer this as well, although they would never openly admit it. I can't imagine any good union steward getting any pleasure out of having to defend the likes of this common criminal. This brand of carrier gave a bad name to all the decent union dues-paying members out there.

The thieving carrier gave us a call in Delivery a few days later, when it was payday. He wanted us to give his paycheck to his younger brother, who was also employed as a carrier at our facility. Not wishing to spare him *any* embarrassment, the Postmaster, Ken said to tell him no to that request. We told his younger brother that he would either need to pick it up himself, or we would mail it to his residence. He did not want to have to wait for it to arrive in the mail, since he had all the money he had on him confiscated by the Inspectors and the police as potential evidence against him, so he came in. He did wait until later in the day, when he knew that there would be less employees and none of his fellow carriers in the building for his walk of shame.

He was in Ken's office, probably discussing the few options that were available to him, when I was paged to call Ken. I was told to bring the carrier's paycheck to Ken's office. I did so, handing the envelope containing his check to the thieving carrier. What he did next has provided much entertainment to those who have heard the story since back in the day. He took the envelope, lifted it up in the air, and strained to see through it to the contents of the envelope against the background of the light on the ceiling. Old habits do indeed die hard.

Almost all Post Offices have the catwalk that extends throughout their facilities. The catwalk is in place for Postal Inspectors only. Custodians can enter the catwalk strictly for the purpose of cleaning, and only on specific dates during specific times. At the large office where I worked during my first Supervisor job, the Inspectors had a private, discreet entrance from outside the building to an office they had in our building. The office also had a door that opened to the area of our building where the administrative offices were located. Sometimes I would walk by the Inspector's door while on my way to one of the administrative offices, and I could hear activity going on in the Inspector's office. We never knew when they were in there if they did not care to advise us.

Inside their office they had a desk, chair and a door that opened to a ladder that went up to the catwalk. The catwalk was tall enough to stand in, and it wrapped around the workroom floor with windows where the Inspectors could look down on the activities going on in the office. Over the years in different management positions, I would occasionally point up to the windows, reminding the employees that they needed to keep their integrity and the trust of the public we served intact.

I received a phone call from an Inspector one morning while I was overseeing the carriers getting ready to go out to deliver on their routes. The Inspector asked me to meet him at his office in the building. I knocked on the door and he let me in to talk to me. He shared that he had received several complaints that caused him to be suspicious about one of my new carriers. Items had disappeared from mailboxes and his research seemed to point to one carrier. The research data he had was from the "Confidential" forms I had filled out advising him of who was delivering where on certain dates. He advised me that he was going to be out on the route where this carrier was assigned to deliver mail that day. He told me he was going to be placing a small parcel containing CD's marked "Return to Sender" in the mailbox at one of the addresses on the route. He asked me to keep this to myself and said that he would call me later.

I went about my business in the office and, quite frankly, forgot about this after a while. I was reminded when I received a phone call from the Inspector later in the afternoon. He asked me to get on a portable phone we had so I could walk around for him to where he needed me to go. I did what was asked of me, and he told me that the carrier in question had just returned to the office. He asked me to go to a specific door that entered the garage where our carrier vehicles were parked. I exited the office into the garage, and he directed me to a hamper that was used by carriers to place their outgoing mail when they returned from their routes. He told me to look in that hamper to see if the package he had planted was in it. I looked through the hamper and picked up one package to check it out, holding the phone to my ear with the Inspector on the other end. As I looked at the package I had picked up, he said "No. That's not it. Keep looking." I felt a chill up my spine as I realized that he was looking down from a catwalk window right behind me while we were talking. It turned out that the package in question was found by me in the hamper, and the carrier in question was cleared.

When I was in the position of Tour 1 Operations Manager at the REC, my work hours and those of many of the employees under my responsibility overlapped with the Tour 3 operation. The Tours overlapped because, unlike traditional Mail Processing operations, our work was typically finished by 4:30 a.m. each day. Tours, or shifts, were structured in roughly this fashion. Tour One was 11 pm till 7 am, Tour Two was 7 am till 3 pm and Tour Three was 3 pm till 11 pm, with lunches extending each Tour a bit into the following Tours. Many of the employees who worked for me started before my own 8:00 p.m. start time each day. Many of the employees assigned to Tour 3 worked daily beyond the Tour 3 Operations Manager and his Supervisors end of day at 11:30 p.m. We spread the number of employees and the responsibility over them as evenly as we could between the

Tours and the Supervisors on them. Communication between the Management staff on each Tour was important, to make sure that necessary information was passed along about the employees and the operations in progress.

I arrived at work one evening and the Tour 3 Operations Manager told me we needed to talk. He came to my office and told me that one of his employees had reported to him that she had seen one of my employees working at a store the night before, when he was supposed to be working at the REC. I started to look at our records and found that he was clocked in at the REC while he was working at the other location. He had either clocked in and left to go to his other job, or someone else had swiped his timecard and put him on the clock. He was a Transitional Employee (TE), not a career employee, and at that time there was not a lot that the union could do for him. I brought him to my office and asked him questions about what he had been doing. He was very flustered, but he did not admit to any wrongdoing.

As I did further research, including talking to the Tour 3 employee who had seen him at his other job, it was evident that he had been getting paid for work he had not done on more than one occasion. I wrote up a Notice of Removal and called him and a union representative to my office. When he read the notice and realized that he was going to lose his job, he started to panic. He told me he was begging me not to fire him. At one point he even got down on his knees, literally begging me not to fire him, with one of the union stewards by his side. I told him that there was nothing that I could do for him, that he had sealed his own fate by stealing from the Postal Service. The union representative told him that there was nothing they could do. He was terminated immediately.

I kept in touch with employees I knew from different locations as I moved around from job to job. I talked to a Supervisor infrequently at my old office where I had been promoted to my first management position as a Supervisor. On one such occasion he informed me of what had transpired with one of the carriers who worked there. I knew the carrier and he seemed like he was a good employee. He did have a problem being regular in attendance as I recalled, but that was the extent of the problems I had experienced with him while I was there supervising him. What I came to learn as my career in management moved along was that if an employee was being negligent in one area of their job, that negligence would sometimes expand beyond what was obvious and trackable.

In this carrier's case, he had no apparent problems completing his assignments in a timely manner. He was a Part Time Flexible employee (PTF), which meant that he was typically assigned to a variety of routes that needed to be covered. When I would return to that Post Office as the Postmaster years later, I developed an Excel tracking sheet to identify which PTFs and Overtime Desired List employees were familiar with the sorting and delivery of mail on the 100+ routes that we had. That reference tool would prove to be quite helpful towards maintaining productivity in the future, by assigning carriers to routes they knew, but at that point in time, carriers were more randomly placed on open assignments as needed. Since they were often unfamiliar with some of the routes to which they were assigned, their impact on the office's productivity was not good. It was discovered how this PTF Carrier was getting his assignments done in a timely manner when he had a fight with his wife.

His wife called the Post Office to report that there were sacks of mail in the closet at their home. Apparently, this carrier had been bringing Standard Mail (bulk mail) into his house rather than sorting it and delivering it. It was mostly advertising circulars, but it was nevertheless mailing that business customers had paid to have delivered. Postal Inspectors were dispatched to his location to retrieve the mail. He was interviewed and processed for his nefarious activity, ultimately losing his job, as well as getting a divorce from his wife.

Employees stealing from the Postal Service certainly was not restricted to the craft employees. Management had its share of employees who were looking for ways to meet their own personal needs as well. After I left my REC Operations Manager job to start the Postmaster phase of my career, I would do my customary occasional corresponding with a few of the employees back at the REC. I was told that Max, the REC Operations Manager who worked on a different shift than mine had been taken out of the building by Postal Inspectors.

Max and I had the typically competitive relationship that I had with my peers whenever I worked at a facility where I was not in charge. I didn't have such difficulties when I was the head of a facility. Imagine that. Apparently, Max had been busy at work doing his own personal business. He had started an online website where he was selling merchandise. He was regularly logging in to his website from his Postal Service computer to conduct his business, and he was observed doing this by one of his employees. That employee notified the Postal Inspection Service. An Inspector checked his computer and discovered all the activity he was involved in while he was on the clock. I hope that his online business worked out for him, because he kissed his Postal career and years of service, and probably his pension goodbye.

While serving in my level 24 Postmaster job, I called the former Postmaster, Ken who had served at that office while I was a Supervisor there. We met for lunch and discussed things about that office. I was interested in his opinions about changes that I had made and proposed upcoming changes in progress. He was now retired, and he didn't necessarily agree with some of the things that I was doing. He was certainly entitled to his own opinion, but I continued with most changes I was pursuing anyway. After all, I certainly did not agree with many of the changes he had made during my time away from that Post

Office prior to his retirement.

Ken's wife was the Postmaster of a level 15 Post Office in my District. Ken also had a son, Ken Junior who was the Postmaster of a level 18 Post Office in my District. Junior's office was close to his home and he liked it that way. I had met him previously and, as I would customarily do, I asked him about his aspirations about moving up in the organization. I knew that my MPOO, Gary utilized him for different projects and relied on him to spread the annual budgets within our group of Post Offices. Ken Junior told me that he was content to stay in his lower level Postmaster position and do special assignments for Gary. I did get an opportunity to spend time with him when Gary assigned a neighboring Postmaster and I to work with Ken on spreading the budgets for an upcoming year. We worked on the project at his small Post Office. He appeared to be a very friendly, hard-working dedicated employee. But appearances can be deceiving.

I was attending a Postmaster meeting one morning when the murmuring started within the ranks. I asked a Postmaster who was sitting next to me if he knew what was going on. He told me that he heard that Ken Junior had been taken out of his Post Office in handcuffs by Postal Inspectors. I casually gazed around the room to see if I could spot his mother. There were about 25 Postmasters in attendance at the meeting. I spotted her sitting a few rows behind me. From her outward appearances she did not seem to be troubled. If she was aware of what was happening with her son, she was doing a very good job of hiding it. Over the next few days I got the scoop on what had happened at Ken's Post Office.

Ken had apparently been having difficulties making ends meet with his personal finances. He had made the poor decision to have the Postal Service assist him with his personal bill paying. From the information I was given, Ken had begun to make a practice of paying his utilities and other personal bills with

238

Postal Service money orders. He was not paying for the money orders. The funds covering them were coming from his Post Office. I do not know how long he had been in the practice of doing this, but eventually one of his window clerks became suspicious and contacted the Postal Inspection Service. The Inspectors assigned to the case did their due diligence and discovered what he had been up to. They gave him the perp walk out of his Post Office in handcuffs, and he was arrested for his misuse of Postal funds. I do not know what the ultimate disposition of his case was, but he was a Veteran and I doubt that he ever actually did any time in jail for his crime.

Reimbursements for travel expenses are paid out routinely by the Postal Service. Travel expenses can be for airline travel, taxis, trains, car rentals, hotel stays, per diem amounts for meals and miscellaneous items while in a travel status, mileage on a personal vehicle while travelling, tolls, on and on... The expenses incurred and the reimbursements sought are always charged to a finance number. I filled out many travel reimbursement requests over the course of my career with the Postal Service. Any travel expenses incurred by an employee in the course of going to an interview for a job would be charged to the finance number of the interviewer, the Post Office or the Mail Processing Center where the vacancy existed. Those expenses would have to be approved by someone in charge associated with the finance number before payment could be made.

There are different per diem rates set for locations throughout the country, typically based on the cost of living in those areas. There were close to 400 destinations across the United States that had specific per diem rates applied to them. The highest per diem payouts were made when employees travel to or within San Francisco, New York, Boston, Washington D.C. and Los Angeles. Some of those highest rates were over $70 per day for meals and miscellaneous needs while I was still working. The lowest rates in the country were closer to $50 per day.

I appreciated going to higher per diem locations when travelling for interviews, training or meetings. I would eat at inexpensive places and get to pocket the leftover daily amounts I was entitled to receive. I know that some employees would buy a loaf of bread, a package of bologna or peanut butter and jelly for their meals while travelling, enabling them to pocket the rest of the per diem amounts.

I always preferred to take ownership of my travel arrangements. I wanted to pick the airline with dates and times, car rental and hotel locations. When doing so, I would be attentive to the GSA (Government Services Administration) rates that were published for each of those commodities. Occasionally, and inexplicably to me, the GSA rates would be higher than the "average Joe" rates that were published. As a good steward, I would choose the lower rates to save money for the company. I was chastised once for not going through the agency that was in place at that time to handle our travel arrangements.

Because of the sheer number of reimbursements that are processed within a District, there are "opportunities" for shysters to attempt to get more than their fair share of expenses paid to them. At the time of this writing, the GSA mileage rate is .58 per mile. GSA rates are what is used to compute the payouts that are made through the Postal Service. A Handbook is regularly updated with current rates for travel expenses that is used by the Postal Service. As is the case with most technological advancements, the Handbook and its contents is regularly updated for viewing online through the Postal Service intranet by employees with access.

I recall being told about a union representative who regularly turned in paperwork for travel reimbursements. His position had him traveling around to different locations within the District where he worked. He would attend meetings at facilities that addressed contract problems that were occurring within each facility. He made the bad decision to start padding the mileage he was seeking reimbursement for. The person who was signing off on his forms for reimbursement started to question some of the high mileage forms he was turning in and contacted the Postal Inspection Service. The Inspectors discovered the fraud, and his travelling days were over. Not sure if he managed to keep his job.

Prior to the suspension of awards programs, while I was in my level 24 Post Office, I had a practice in place at each of the Post Offices where I served as Postmaster to promote safety. Every Quarter (a 3-month period) I would use Postal funds to purchase 3 $50 gift cards. A drawing would be held to select the winners from the pool of employees who had been accident-free the previous Quarter. Safety was always a very important issue for me. I wanted my employees to be as healthy and as happy as possible. An on the job injury would not only adversely affect them in their personal lives, but it would also have a negative impact on the Postal Service. The suspension of awards of any kind disrupted my ability to have any meaningful incentive programs in place for my employees. That was a source of frustration to me, until a carrier unknowingly brought a solution to me.

Bob was a carrier at my office who I considered a friend. I knew him from the years I had been a Supervisor at this Post Office, and I was glad to see that he was still there when I returned as the Postmaster. He had an excellent work ethic, and he helped me out on a few different projects that may not have been successful without him. He was working at another facility within my jurisdiction, and he called me one day to ask if he could come over and talk to me. I told him to come over. When he came into my office, he looked very serious and asked if he could close the door behind him. I said that he could, and my curiosity was aroused wondering what was bothering him.

Bob asked me if I was aware that some of my carriers were

using their own rewards cards to get points when they fueled their Postal vehicles with gas purchased by the Postal Service. There was a gas station located next to our Post Office, and most of our carriers fueled their vehicles at that location. This fuel company had stations all over our area, and they typically had the cheapest prices. I thanked Bob for bringing this to my attention. I assured him I would be following up on it to correct the problem.

Before addressing the issue of carriers getting personal gain (points) from spending Postal money, I had to visit the neighboring gas station to check out their awards program. While I was at the gas station, I asked an employee to explain how the program worked. He showed me a printout of the different levels of awards that could be received based on the number of fuel points that were accumulated. When I saw the $50 gas cards, the light bulb turned on and I left with an awards card to sign up for their program. Before I could consider implementing a plan, I had to be sure there would be no ethics violations.

I called my District's Vehicle Department and asked if we received any kind of discount from the fuel companies where we made purchases. The answer was no. The only reduction in pricing that we received was that we did not pay federal taxes on any purchases from any gas station. I went online to the fuel company's website and registered my card. I looked through the details about their program and found that there was a way to set up an alias number. An alias number could be keyed in at the pump when purchasing fuel to make sure that the points went to my card. I picked a number to use that was based on our Post Office's Zip Code and would be easy to remember. I wrote a service talk that was given to all the carriers in my office. The talk started out by advising any carriers who were using their own rewards card for their personal benefit to cease and desist immediately, or there would be consequences. The carriers were then advised to only get their fuel at the gas station next to the Post Office. They were all advised of the number to key in when they purchased their fuel. It was shared that this would enable us to have the safety incentive program reinitiated at no cost to the Postal Service. I had no idea what number of points could be earned at that time. We would have to wait and see.

The carriers each had their own Postal fuel card that they used when purchasing fuel, and they would turn their receipts in when they returned from their routes on the days that they would fill up their vehicles. Up to that point in time, the carriers were not directed to where they should go to fill their vehicles when necessary. I began to look through the receipts, to make sure that all the carriers were following the new program that was in place. The first problem I found was a receipt that had a different reward number other than mine on it, the carrier putting the reward points for his purchase on his personal card. I talked to that carrier's Supervisor and he informed his carrier that if this happened again, he would be receiving discipline. Another problem I found was a few carriers who were refueling at other gas stations. It was unfortunate that there were some carriers that had such a disdain for anything put out by management, that they were hell bent on not being a contributing participant, even when they were the recipients of the inevitable rewards. It didn't take long to get all the kinks worked out and everyone participating.

I would go to the rewards program's website frequently to see how the points were adding up. I picked up a few $50 gas cards, then logged in one morning to find that some of the points had been depleted. I clicked on the history tab of my rewards account and found that enough points for $35 in merchandise had been claimed. It had not occurred to me until then that the alias number was all that was needed for anyone to redeem points. I was able to see the location where the points had been redeemed. It was at one of their fuel stations a few towns away. Based on the location of where points were redeemed, my suspicion of who did it panned out. I'll elaborate on that in a bit.

I did additional research on the rewards program website and found that points could be transferred from one card to another. Things were getting more complicated administratively, but I was determined to make this work. I picked up a second card, and I started to log in and transfer the points to that second card before they could build up to the point of being redeemed for anything of substance. I know that the Manager who worked for me and I were both putting points into the kitty with our own personal vehicle fuel purchases. Since all the employees, except for Management, were eligible to be in the drawing for a card if they were accident-free, all employees were encouraged to use the alias number when fueling their personal vehicles as well. When the program started working without any problem, I found that I was able to redeem more than 4 $50 cards per Quarter, better than the 3 I had been purchasing with Postal funds previously.

At one point while getting the fuel rewards program up to speed, the manager of the gas station next to my Post Office where we were racking up points called my Post Office. I was in the middle of a meeting with a customer when one of my Supervisors knocked on my door. I excused myself from the customer and stepped out to talk with my Supervisor. I told him that this had better be important, his reason for interrupting my meeting. He had a nervous look on his face when he told me that the gas station manager was on the phone. The manager said that it wasn't right that all our employees were getting points fueling all the Postal trucks there. I told my Supervisor to go back to the phone and ask the manager if he would like to have all our vehicles going to the gas station across the street from him instead. My Supervisor smiled and left, and I returned to my meeting. I didn't hear anything further from the gas station manager.

As I have shared elsewhere, Supervisor attrition can tend to run high at larger Post Offices where there are many Supervisors employed. At my level 24 Post Office, there were often Supervisors coming and going. Supervisors who had weak skills in dealing with problem employees did not want to work at an office where I was in charge. If they did not handle their problem employees correctly, they had me to deal with because they were now the problem. As Supervisors would transfer out to another office, get promoted, retire or get fired, the length of time it took to officially replace them would sometimes be several months.

Good Acting Supervisors (204B's) were hard to find. Most employees did not want the job of working with their co-workers as peers one day, then having to give those same employees instructions and even discipline when necessary when they served in the 204B position. I would regularly meet with the Manager who worked for me to discuss potential 204B's. My criteria of good attendance and performance would narrow down our pool of potential 204B's and we would meet with those qualifying employees to attempt to recruit them. They would receive a bump in pay while serving as a 204B, but that often was not enough of an incentive to entice them to sign on.

I always had a few good employees who would serve as 204B's when needed. Sometimes those details would last for many months, or in some cases more than a year. While the gas rewards program was starting up, I had a titled Supervisor who was out indefinitely on sick leave. Mark was one of my carriers who had been serving as a 204B for several months. He was always at work early, never called in sick and was very good at his carrier job. He also worked well with the employees he supervised. He held them accountable for doing their jobs, as expected, and was not shy about issuing discipline when necessary to those employees who were not performing as required, or who were not maintaining regular attendance. For all practical purposes, he seemed like a perfect employee. But, once again, appearances can be deceiving. I soon found out.

I was sitting in my office looking through the emails I had received when a Postal Inspector showed up at my door. He had apparently entered the building through the private entrance the inspectors had into my Post Office. They would come and go through their private entrance. Sometimes I could see them approaching their door if I happened to be looking out one certain window in my office. Other times, such as that day, I did not see them to know they were in the building. He informed me that there were several inspectors in the building and that there was a problem with one of my employees.

The Inspector told me that they had received several complaints from my customers over the past few months. Customers would receive notices to come to my office to pick up Priority, Express Mail and other accountable items for which they had received a notice from their carriers. They received a notice because they had not been home when the carrier was attempting to deliver these items. We had several shelves lined up where these items were filed away according to the address. Our window clerks would go to these shelves to get an item that the customer was coming in to pick up. The problem was that customers were coming in and their items could not be found by the window clerk serving them. I may have heard about this occurring at some point, but apparently the affected customers had not pursued the matter hard enough for it to fully come to my attention. Little did I know, since several of them had reported this problem to the Inspection Service.

The Inspectors often did not share information with me about what they were doing in my office. I'm certain that the reason for this was that I may have been a suspect as well as any other employee in a case such as this one that had been followed. The Inspector told me that they had planted a camera in my office that could view the shelving units where these items were contained. He told me that over the course of a week or two they had filmed my 204B, Mark going to these shelves and looking through the items that were on them. He would pick a few up and leave the area with them. He would not take them to the lobby area, where customers would potentially be coming to retrieve them. Instead, he would head off in a different direction towards more isolated spots in my Post Office.

The Inspectors had been in my office for a few hours already that morning, and they had made several observations from their catwalk that ran throughout my facility. I was told that they observed Mark looking through trays of First-Class Mail in an area that was isolated from other employees. If he saw an envelope that looked like it may have contained a greeting card of some sort, he would tear the envelope open. If he found cash or a gift card, he would pocket those items and throw the envelope and card into the garbage can, covering it up to avoid a custodian seeing what was in the can. If it contained nothing of value, or a check made out to an individual, he would simply throw all of it away. He was doing the same thing with Priority and Express Mail items. He would pocket things of value and throw away the rest of the envelopes or packages and their contents.

The Inspector asked me what room could be used to bring Mark to for questioning. I told him that they could use the conference room that was attached to my office. He left my office to retrieve Mark and bring him to my conference room. Two Inspectors went into the conference room with him. Two other Inspectors were busy looking through garbage cans for items that Mark had disposed of in them. It was during the morning while this was happening, and most of my carriers were still in the building getting prepared to leave on their routes. I had to call my Manager to my office and put him and the Supervisors on alert. They needed to pay close attention to all our employees as this drama was unfolding in front of them.

Life and work needed to go on, and I did not want adverse impacts on our productivity due to conversations about what was happening and pauses in work taking place.

Admittedly, my own curiosity was getting the better of me. Did I practice what I preached to my subordinates? Not always, and certainly not in this case. I tried putting my ear to the wall that separated my office from the conference room where Mark and the Inspectors were talking. I could only hear garbled speaking and did not pick up on any emotions being displayed during the talking. That got kind of boring after a while, so I gave up on it. I stayed close to the hallway entrance to the conference room, awaiting some activity or some news as to what was occurring. After a while, a female Inspector came out of the conference room. I asked her what was happening. She told me that she left the room because he was finally fessing up. He had been denying doing anything wrong up to that point, but he could no longer maintain that stance as they told him about all the observations they had made and the filming of his activities that had taken place. She left the room because he was going into his underwear to remove cash he had stuffed into them.

I spoke to one of the Inspectors who was present there who I had worked with previously on other cases. I asked him if the Inspection Service was going to pursue prosecution and/or place him in custody at a local jail. He told me that things had changed with how they handled cases such as this. He said that they would give all the information to the local county District Attorney's office. They would determine what should be done and prosecute if they felt that was appropriate. He assured me that they were usually very aggressive about these types of cases. I then contacted my District Labor Department to discuss what my appropriate action would be. I was advised to give Mark an official notice in writing that he was being placed in a Leave Without Pay (LWOP) status while this matter was being investigated.

Some of my Supervisors and other 204B's were friends of Mark's. None of them were aware of what he had been up to, but they did talk about other work and personal matters between themselves and frequently texted each other on their cell phones. All of this was happening on a Friday, and I was told that Mark was supposed to be leaving to go on vacation to Florida the next day with his family. Since he was going to be in a LWOP status, he could not be paid any vacation time he had while he was gone. I assumed he would be cancelling that vacation, under the circumstances, but was surprised when I was told by one of the other 204B's that he did go to Florida. As I gave it more thought, I realized that he had probably amassed a fair amount of cash and gift cards over the course of his thieving from our customers. The only cash and cards that had been recovered were the items he had been caught with when the Inspectors arrived. I was also informed that he did not tell his wife or his kids about anything that had happened. It was only a matter of time before he would have to tell them.

Marks' union President approached me about the situation after talking to him. She told me that his biggest concern was over whether he was going to be able to keep his job. I gave her the same answer that I always did in such egregious situations. I told her that if he resigned immediately, he would avoid being removed from the Postal Service. I could not pursue anything less than a removal under the circumstances. She told me that she would relay that information to him to let him decide what he wanted to do. And now back to those gas reward points that had been cashed in...

The location a few towns away from my Post Office where the points had been cashed in just happened to be the town where Mark lived. They were cashed in a week or two after Mark had gone on his family vacation. I asked one of the 204B's who had been communicating with him for his cell phone number. I texted Mark, telling him who I was and informing him that I was aware of the reward points having been cashed in at his town's gas station. I told him that unless the funds were returned to me by the end of that day, I would be reporting the matter to the Inspection Service. I further advised him that he did not need any more trouble than he was already in, and that cameras at those gas stations recorded all transactions such as this that occurred. I wasn't really concerned about Mark and the "trouble" he was in. He brought that on himself and deserved whatever happened to him in the court system. I just wanted the reward money back for my employees.

I never heard back from Mark, so I did contact the Inspector I knew to relay what had happened. The Inspector asked me if the gas stations did film these transactions. I told him I didn't know, but it sounded good and I wanted to put a good scare into Mark. The Inspector got back to me within a week. He told me that the gas stations did indeed film the transaction. He had gone back on their film to review the date and time that the rewards had been cashed in. He saw that it was Mark who had cashed them in and added this to his list of infractions. I never did hear what the final disposition of Mark's criminal case was. He did resign, and I moved along to a new position in another state while his criminal case was still pending. It was aggravating how long things could drag out in our internal discipline system and in the legal system. At least his resignation got him out of the Postal Service, and away from the access he had to our customers' mail.

CHAPTER SEVEN: DISCIPLINE AND DISCRIMINATION
ALLEGATIONS

My original intent was to make two separate chapters of these two issues, primarily due to the amount of information I impart on these topics. After much deliberation, I decided that it was necessary to combine them into one chapter. The reason for this is that the two topics are too inexorably linked, and it will make a lot more sense to have them together.

There are national contracts in place between the United States Postal Service and the labor organizations that represent the different groups of workers. There are numerous items covered by those contracts, with overtime, pay raises and work delineation being arguably the most important, and most argued elements within those agreements. Those contracts have expiration dates every few years and they require negotiation between Labor and Management prior to their expiration. It is not uncommon for the disagreements between Labor and Management to have to be decided by an arbitrator, someone who is neutral and listens to the arguments on both sides and renders a decision. The arbitration process can be costly, so both sides of the labor equation presumably need to feel assured that they will prevail, to justify the expenses that will be incurred.

When I started at my new Post Office, reinstated by request a few years after I had resigned, I was assigned to a Full Time Regular Carrier at that office who was a designated trainer to be trained for a few days. It all came back to me quickly, so it didn't take him long to feel comfortable enough to have me delivering the mail with him on his route. He drove his personal vehicle on his route, due to a shortage of official Postal vehicles at that office. He would park his vehicle and he would walk one block in a loop delivering the mail, and I would walk in the other direction delivering the mail to that block. We finished his route early on those few days of training that I had since we were splitting the route between the two of us.

My trainer took me to a small deli store close to his route. When we walked in the owner greeted him by name. My trainer went to a cooler and brought 2 quarts of beer back to the cashier counter. He paid for the beer and we got back in his vehicle. He drove to a spot not too far from the store and parked on a side street. Another carrier showed up a few minutes later and hopped into our car with his own quart of beer. We all sat and talked and drank our beer before returning to the Post Office. It wasn't exactly the training experience I expected. I obviously knew that what we were doing was wrong, but being the newbie, I wanted to try to fit in. I would come to find over the months ahead that drinking on the job was not that uncommon an occurrence.

I learned that there was a hot dog shop in our town where carriers would meet every day to have "lunch" at the end of their mail delivery. Their lunch included food and beer. When I became a 204B, it was my desire to put an end to this practice. I was concerned about carriers drinking while on the clock, and what might happen when they were driving back to the Post Office to finish their day. The occurrence of accidents was a distinct possibility. I was also concerned about what image of the Postal Service that conveyed to the other customers at that busy location. I drove by the hot dog shop a few times, noting that there were several Postal vehicles parked at the rear of the building. They could not be seen from the road, and I'm sure that was intended.

I approached Andy, my Supervisor, to discuss this situation with him. I was adamant about going after these carriers and getting this stopped. I was surprised at Andy's lackadaisical reaction when I brought the subject up. He told me that there wasn't really anything we could do about it. One of the culprits was the union steward at that Post Office, and the union branch that our office was part of was very powerful. They had many Post

Offices that were within their local branch, and their leadership were very aggressive about protecting their members, especially since one of their stewards would be involved. This was pretty much one of my first exposures to the politics involved with labor management, and it did not sit well with me. I would see a whole lot more of this as I moved up the management chain.

During my early years as a carrier with the Postal Service, I knew practically nothing about contracts that were in place. I was merely the recipient of all the benefits and pay raises that had been negotiated within the most current contractual agreement. When I did make the decision to pursue a career in management within the Postal Service, I picked my side in doing so. Doing the job of supervising carriers as a 204B, prior to becoming a titled Supervisor, I had my first real exposure to labor relations and contracts. I understood the Postal Service management philosophy of providing the best possible customer service, while keeping the expenses necessary to do so at a reasonable level. It made sense.

I was a dues paying member of the carrier's union, and I looked forward to being promoted to a Supervisor position. I looked forward to ending my union membership and my payment of dues to that organization. I could have chosen to end my membership earlier, because being a union member was not a requirement for having my job as a carrier. When I did receive my first promotion into management, submitting my notice to cancel my membership to the union was one of the first things that I did. I was not happy when my pay stubs showed me that the dues were still being taken out of my pay. After making a few calls, I was disappointed to find out that my membership could only be cancelled within a certain window of time around my anniversary date of joining the union. That was in the fine print at the bottom of the form I had originally signed to join. My dues paying continued, throughout what was a now adversarial relationship with the union, until I was finally able to quit.

When I started serving in that first management position, the amount of discipline being issued increased dramatically at that Post Office. It was almost entirely attendance related. Complaints were raised outside of our Post Office that the discipline that was being issued was targeting African Americans. The Postmaster who I reported to started getting calls from our District office. The District was getting pressure from different employee groups, which it seemed there was no end to, and it was agreed that a team would come in to review all our discipline records. The team came in, jointly comprised of District staff and members of different labor organizations, with too many acronyms for me to recall. They spent several days reviewing all our discipline records and the attendance records of each of our employees. At the conclusion, their findings indicated that while a larger percentage of discipline issued was to African American employees, it was warranted due to their attendance records.

The Family and Medical Leave Act (FMLA) was signed into law by President Clinton in 1993. I was promoted to that first management job as a supervisor in 1992. I can still distinctly recall the massive amount of messaging, handouts and training that we all had to go through in my Post Office as FMLA law was rolled out. It is my belief that the Postal Service and many other large organizations were bracing themselves for the abuse that was to follow. I am surprised, as I have talked to non-Postal people over the years, at how many of those people are ignorant of what their rights are under FMLA. I am even more surprised at how many companies are ignorant of what their responsibilities are under FMLA. I know that FMLA is something that benefits many people who are legitimately in need. It was never my intention to disparage them. But FMLA was, and presumably still is, a ticket to ride without facing discipline for those who know how to take advantage of it.

Although discipline was most commonly issued by me due to an employee's unscheduled absences from work, I did focus on work issues as well. As a Supervisor of City Delivery Operations, it was also my job to make sure that my carriers were following the multitude of regulations while delivering in the rain, sleet, hail, snow, etc... This was especially important where new employees were concerned. To accomplish this, I would regularly go out on the street and observe these new carriers as often as possible. I tried to avoid using my own personal car, even though there were reimbursements for mileage associated with that. I would use other Supervisors cars or occasionally borrow a car from someone. The object was to keep those street observations as covert an operation as possible.

I had a new carrier that I had personally checked on a few times. He was having problems following the rules and regulations. On at least one occasion, his vehicle was found to be unlocked while he was walking a relay delivering mail. He was sternly talked to about this and the observations were stepped up to make sure he was correcting the bad practices before they became habits. This employee was a career employee, a Part Time Flexible (PTF), and he was still within his 90-day probationary period. As I've shared earlier in detail, each career employee that is hired is given a 90-day probationary period, during which Management can train and observe the employee's work performance. Management has 90 days to evaluate new employees, to determine whether they are suitable for the position. After that, they are lifers, provided they don't start receiving progressive discipline that leads up to a Removal.

I know of several instances where the 90 days slipped by and, even though the employee wasn't performing anywhere near up to par, we bought 'em because we didn't get them off our employment rolls when we had the chance. I know of a few cases where an employee was let go, and it was then discovered that the day count was wrong. Management thought that we were within the 90 days, but it had been longer. The different unions within the Postal Service kept close track of the deadlines for new employees on probation. They would file grievances if the 90-day line was crossed. In those cases, the employee was typically brought back to work, as a lifer, once the problem was identified, resolving the grievance that was filed. Usually there was back pay involved as well.

Anyway, back to that troublesome carrier... I went out on street supervision and located his parked vehicle. I was happy to see that it was where he was supposed to be, not always the case, and he was in the middle of delivering mail down the block somewhere. I parked my car and got out to check his vehicle. It was one of our older Jeeps, something that probably should have been retired some time ago. But the budget required us to squeeze another year or two out of it, so we patched it up and kept it going. I approached the driver's door, tested the handle, and was happy to see that the door was locked. Especially since I could see a certified letter laying right on the tray next to the driver's seat.

Those old Jeeps had strange windows on them. There wasn't a crank or other device to open them. You simply pushed them up and down, with a sliding bolt to lock them. When I pushed down on the driver's window, from the outside, it opened right up. So much for security. I then got into the Jeep and discovered yet another quirk with this vehicle. As I put my hand on the ignition, on the steering column, I found that it turned and started the engine... A key was not necessary to start this particular gem. I felt that, under the circumstances, it was only fitting that I use this as a learning experience for my hapless probationer.

I started the Jeep and drove it around the corner, where it would be out of view from the carrier when he returned. I then got back into my car, drove down the street, and pulled over to the side of the road. I wanted to make sure I was close enough to see the look on his face when he returned. I really expected him to notice something missing before he completed his last delivery, but he didn't. I watched him as he finished delivering to the last house on the relay, walked out towards the street, then stood on the curb and did some crazy spins as he tried to spot his Jeep. After getting a good chuckle out my system, I drove up beside him. I could tell from the look on his face, when he finally noticed me that he was beginning to add things up. I rolled down my window, held up the certified letter I had taken from the Jeep, and said "See what can happen?" He did not ultimately make it beyond his probationary period.

While I was in that first Management position as a relatively green Supervisor, I took my responsibilities very seriously. I was a steward for the Postal Service. I maintained that frame of mind throughout my career in the Postal Service. It was my job to make sure that my employees were doing their jobs correctly, following all the training they had received and diligently applying themselves to complete their assigned duties in a timely manner each day. I did not consider that to be an unreasonable expectation, considering the good pay and all the benefits they received. To accomplish this, the first thing an employee had to do was to come to work.

One of the carriers that I supervised had obvious problems being regular in attendance. His problems went beyond attendance, and I was in the process of issuing him progressive discipline. The discipline was not having the effect of correcting his infractions. I returned home from a vacation with my family, listening to messages that had been left on my telephone answering machine. I heard the voice and I could tell that it was my problem carrier. His message told me that I needed to back off on my harassment of him, that he knew where I lived. I was aware that he lived in the same town that I did, and I suspected that he might have been a member of a local gang.

When I returned to work, I discussed the situation with some of my peer Supervisors. They were amazed that I had my phone number publicly listed. Being a new Supervisor at that point, it hadn't occurred to me that having my information available to the public could be problematic. I made the necessary changes to assure that my information would remain private. I certainly did not want to put my family at risk.

I brought the carrier into an office to have a conversation with him. I told him that I did not appreciate him leaving a threatening message on my answering machine at my house, where my family was able to hear his threats. His smirk turned into an attempted defensive posture as he told me that he didn't make any threats. An admission that he had left that message. I told him that he would have a chance to explain that to the Postal Inspector who would be coming in to talk to him. That changed his demeanor to one of extreme agitation. I sent him back to his route. I did call the Inspection Service, and an Inspector came out to talk to him. Enough fear was placed on him that he straightened up temporarily. I eventually fired him, as he returned to continuing his attendance and performance problems. Fortunately, nothing more came of that.

The aggression that I had dealing with attendance issues carried on throughout my career in Management. I did not care about the color of their skin, their religion, their age or any other factor that could be cited in a discrimination case. I only looked at the numbers, how many absences from work an employee had within a certain time period. I started to discipline employees who were not regular in attendance, whether it was calling in for a day, multiple days or multiple times being late to work. Being a new Supervisor at my Post Office, I wanted to dig right into things. Looking at the office's attendance records and discipline records, it was obvious to me that attention had not been paid to attendance by management at that Post Office for quite a long time. When I gave an employee an informal job discussion, the first step of the disciplinary process, they often immediately ceased the infractions. The ones who continued to be irregular in attendance started to receive formal discipline. Formal discipline, as outlined in the contract between the Postal Service and the various craft contracts, started with the informal job discussion. From there it progressed to an Official Letter of Warning, then a 7 Day Suspension, a 14 Day Suspension and finally a Removal.

Removal notices almost always were settled with the unions in a Last Chance Agreement settlement. Those settlements would outline specific parameters for attendance or performance situations. For attendance, if the employee had more than the number of unscheduled absences agreed to in the terms of the settlement within the specified period, that employee would be removed from the Postal Service. One of the frustrations that I had in my Supervisor position at that office was that management had made a practice of issuing an additional discipline step in the process. At that office, carriers would be issued an Official Letter of Warning, a 7 Day Suspension, *a 10 Day Suspension*, a 14 Day Suspension, then a Removal. In the grievance process, discipline would be handled by union representatives meeting with the management official who issued the discipline. In those meetings, a piece of discipline that contractually would be valid for 2 years often would be reduced to a lesser period on file in the affected employee's record. Fortunately, that additional step of a 10 Day Suspension was not spelled out in that office's Local Agreement with the Union. That enabled me to argue its existence with the local union and fall back to the 7 Day Suspension progressing to a 14 Day Suspension, as clearly outlined in their National Agreement with the Postal Service.

I can recall setting up shop in a room located close to the carrier's work location within our building. I had a stack of attendance records with me for the carriers. I started to pick up the phone and page individual carriers to come to my location. As they would come to the room, I would sit them down and talk to them about their attendance deficiencies. That process had the desired effect of shaming them as they came and went. My hope was that the shaming would get them to correct those deficiencies. As I would pick up the phone to call out a name, I could hear the other carriers on the workroom floor making noises. "Ooooooooo," was the typical sound I would hear as I called out a new name. They figured out what was happening as the carriers came and left that room, and I'm sure that some of them were hoping that their name would not be called for that walk of shame.

Of course, there were always a few employees in any office who just didn't care. They felt that their union would get them off the hook for their abuses, which they often viewed as entitlement. After all, it was their sick leave that they had earned. Why not burn it as fast as they earned it? But, ultimately, their union could only do so much for them. I had two such carriers who I issued Removal Notices to. Their union reps did their best to get those Removal Notices reduced to something lesser, to enable them to keep their jobs. I had given each of them every opportunity to correct their attendance deficiencies along the way, but they continued their infractions up to being issued Removal Notices by me, and I was not going to back down. An Arbitrator eventually came in to hear both of those cases on the same day, a double header, since the union would not back down either.

One of the employees was a white male veteran. There are other options available to veterans who are facing discipline, but this carrier did not choose another venue for his case. The other employee was an African American female. One of the methods for settling discipline cases for employees was to take a 7- or 14-Day Suspension and to reduce the time on file, as shared earlier. They could also be called a paper suspension, with no time off. That enabled the affected carrier to not have to lose any pay, but the paper suspension was supposed to have the full effect of a time off suspension.

The case against the white male veteran was upheld in favor of the Postal Service, and that individual was officially removed from the Postal Service. In the case of the African American female, she kept her job. The Arbitrator ruled that because she had more than a few paper suspensions, she never felt the full effect of a time off suspension, actually suffering the loss of pay. I found it humorous that the Arbitrator reduced her Removal Notice to a 14 Day Suspension, with 7 days off without pay and the other 7 being a paper suspension. Have to find some humor somewhere.

When I moved on to my next position as a REC Operations Manager, the African American female was still employed at that office. She managed to straighten out her attendance enough to avoid another Removal. When I returned to that office as Postmaster several years later, she was one of several employees who were no longer working there due to Removals being issued by other Supervisors.

As the Postmaster in my level 21 Post Office, my areas of responsibility were split on opposite ends of the Mail Processing Center where we were located. My delivery operation, mail sorting operation and Centralized Forwarding operation were at one end of the building. My retail window and Post Office Box section were at the opposite end of the building. I needed my clerks working at the delivery end of the building, sorting mail to the carrier routes to get them out on the street as quickly as possible. I also had an obligation to get mail sorted to the Post Office Boxes prior to the commitment time that was posted in my lobby. Every Post Office had a Post Office Box commitment time that they had to meet each day. I felt a more acute pressure on this because of the in-house District departments receiving mail at the Post Office Boxes in my office.

Ned was the individual working in my office as the Supervisor over my Retail Operations. He was the Postmaster of another Post Office who had been assigned to work overseeing the

Retail Operations at my Post Office. This was due to medical problems that prevented him from handling his responsibilities at the Post Office where he was titled as the Postmaster. This arrangement had been made some time prior to my becoming the Postmaster, and Ned had become very comfortable in this job. My problems started with Ned when I would call him at the other end of the building during the morning operations. I would tell him to pull one of our retail clerks away from the window to start sorting mail to the Post Office Boxes. More often than not, he would tell me that he couldn't do it because there were too many customers in our retail lobby. I had no way to verify the accuracy of that, since he was at the opposite end of the building from where my office was located.

As I have shared elsewhere, all Post Offices were routinely being checked for their wait time in line by mystery shoppers that were contracted throughout the country by the Postal Service. I also had the District Retail department and their staff in the same building, and they would occasionally check to see how long the wait time was for my customers. Even if I wanted to take the time to walk to the other end to see for myself, it would take me 5 minutes or more at a brisk pace. If there weren't a lot of customers when I arrived, the answer could be that the clerks did a good job reducing the number of customers. I had my suspensions about how truthful Ned was being with me based on not much more than instinct. Rather than take a chance, I would pull clerks away from my Delivery operation and send them on the long walk to sort Post Office Box mail at the other end of the building.

I contacted the Maintenance Manager of the facility and asked for an estimate of what it would cost for a camera in the lobby, a monitor in my office and a cable put in between each end of the building for me to view my retail lobby from my office. When I received the estimate, I visited my MPOO, Tim. I was able to convince him of the benefits that would be had by getting a monitor in place, and he signed off on the expense. It took about a week to get the work finished, and I could now see in real time what was happening in my retail lobby. The first morning that I called Ned to tell him to send a clerk out to sort Post Office Box mail after the monitor was in place, he told me that there were too many customers in the lobby. My only regret was that I couldn't see the look on his face when I told him "You only have 1 customer waiting in line and you have 4 clerks at the Window. Send a clerk to the Post Office Box section now."

After a short period of time, Ned gave up on resisting my focus on utilizing the clerks where they were needed and when they were needed at his end of the building. It wasn't long before I had another conflict with him. Ned's work schedule was from 7 a.m. to 3:30 p.m. daily, with a half hour lunch. My Retail Window was open from 7 a.m. to 7 p.m., with a half hour need to close out the window at the end of the day. One of the retail clerks had to be scheduled later to conduct the close out of operations. After I conducted a review of my Retail Window operations, I gave Ned an official notification that I was changing his schedule to 11 a.m. to 7:30 p.m. daily. When I gave him the notification, he was outraged and demanded to know why this was happening. I explained to him that I needed all the clerks performing their duties, not doing close out duties that a Supervisor should be doing. I also shared that the bulk of our business was being done later in the afternoon, after he was gone for the day, and I needed him there to handle any problems that came up during our busiest time of day.

A few days later, I received a doctor's note from Ned. His doctor indicated that due to physical problems he was having, he would only be able to work 4 hours each day. I walked down to the other end of the building to talk to Ned about this. I already knew where he was going with this. When we started our conversation, he told me that he could only work from 11 a.m. to 3:00 p.m. in his new schedule. I took the first bit of wind out of his sails when I told him that if he could only work four hours, it would be from 3:30 p.m. to 7:30 p.m., where I need him the most. He was momentarily deflated, but he smiled when he said, "You know that if I come to work, I have to be paid 8 hours." I did know this. There was a provision that applied to management that said there would be 8 hours of pay when they came to work. There was only one exception to the rule, which apparently Ned was not aware of. I told him that I knew about the 8-hour provision, but it did not apply to FMLA situations. He was animated once again when I told him this, and he said that he didn't want FMLA. I told him that I was obligated to give him the time off as FMLA, since he had an obvious condition that prevented him from being able to work his normal schedule. I advised him that he could use whatever leave he wanted to cover the time he was not able to work each week, including Leave Without Pay (LWOP). Ned was of age to retire, and he did so a few months later.

I was looking around in the break area that we had for my employees one day. There were a few vending machines in that room, and I would occasionally buy something from one of the machines. I also liked checking in there to see the messaging that was posted on boards to the employees from their union representatives. One day I found an official FMLA form from the clerk's union on one of the tables in the break room. It had information typed in and I struggled to figure out what it was and who it belonged to. There was a Mail Processing Center just outside of my small Post Office's doors that had several hundred clerks and a union office staffed by clerks who were union representatives on all 3 shifts. I took the form that I had found, and I asked several of my employees and staff about it.

I was told that it was a "sample" form that was left for employees by their Union. There was no name filled in, but the form indicated that the "employee" had an asthma condition. The form stated that the condition could cause the employee to be absent from work for up to 3 to 5 days per episode, and that might occur 2 to 3 times per month. It was what many of my peers in management and I referred to as the "FMLA Ticket to Ride." Under FMLA law, with that form signed by a willing accomplice, I mean Doctor, the employee could call in absent to work for 3 to 5 days up to 3 times per month and management would be unable to do anything about those absences.

Postal Service management staff deal all too often with Equal Employment Opportunity (EEO) charges being filed against them. I have talked with many people in a lot of different industries, and most of them don't even know what an EEO complaint is. Over the course of my career in Postal Service management, I would estimate that I had twenty EEO complaints filed against me. Each of these complaints of discrimination were filed after some form of discipline had been issued to the employee, and more than a few of them were filed by subordinate members of my own staff.

When their union representatives or their management representatives were not able to get discipline charges taken away or significantly reduced, an EEO complaint was the next attempt at removing discipline from an employee's record. In some cases, the employee's discipline had progressed to the point of a Removal Notice being issued. That meant the federal court system, where EEO cases were handled, might be the last chance an employee has to try to save their job. There was also the appeal to the "discriminated employee" of potentially receiving thousands of dollars either through a settlement offer or being awarded that money through a Federal Court Judge ruling due to discrimination.
I had employees file discrimination charges alleging that I was responsible for discipline being issued to them, or that I personally issued discipline to them solely because they were different from me.

Among the differences being cited were because the alleged victim was female, African American, Indian, olive skin colored and a white male who claimed I allegedly discriminated against him because he had gout. The process starts with the employee filing a complaint with the District's Human Resources office. A Human Resources Specialist then reviews the matter, contacting the alleged discriminator, and tries to find a solution that will satisfy the complainant.

The customary solution sought was to have discipline removed from the complainant's file. If I had not personally issued the discipline involved, I was aware of the discipline that was issued by one of my subordinates and I had approved it with my signature. Discipline was very rarely issued by a subordinate of mine in any office without my knowledge of the facts of the case. That being the case, I would not have issued or approved the issuance of discipline unless I felt that it was warranted. A discrimination complaint being filed almost never swayed me from standing behind discipline that I believed was warranted and justified in the first place.

If the Human Resources Specialist was unable to satisfy the complaint to the complainant's satisfaction, they would be offered the opportunity to participate in a Redress process. This process would involve having a meeting set up with the complainant, the management employee and a non-Postal facilitator, an impartial individual paid by the Postal Service who would try to get the parties to engage in conversation. The intent of those meetings was to resolve the situation. If the Redress process ended without a resolution being reached, the complainant then had the option of either withdrawing their complaint or formally filing their EEO discrimination case.

When I started my job in my first official Postmaster position, I was glad that Sara, my predecessor had taken a new job in our District office. Since the District offices were in the same building as my Post Office, she was close by to talk to about any issues that came up from the past. Sara informed me about a situation involving one of my Supervisors that had just come to light prior to my appointment as Postmaster. My new

Postmaster position had responsibility over the sorting and delivery of mail within my town, the Post Office Box section and a very busy Retail Unit. These were normal responsibilities for Postmasters. I also had a Centralized Forwarding System (CFS) under my responsibility, a bit more of a rarity. At that time, multiple Postmasters throughout the country were responsible for CFS units, handling the forwarding of mail for groups of offices in their area. Sara wanted to make sure that she had enough Supervisors who were trained to handle her CFS unit, beyond the staffing that was already in place within the unit. Redundancy has always been important because you never knew who would potentially be applying for other jobs, retiring or other attrition might take place.

Bea was the Tour 1 Post Office Supervisor who Sara had decided to train for supervision in the CFS unit. The supervision and management of the forwarding of mail was a detailed, complex process that could not be handled through on the job training alone. There were a few training facilities in different parts of the country that specialized in specific training for craft employees and for management. Bea needed to travel to the training facility where she would learn what she needed to know about how to supervise a CFS unit. Management employees are issued a Postal Service Visa card, when necessary, enabling them to charge a variety of expenses within the financial and ethical guidelines and training that they had to acknowledge and validate with their signature. Even before Bea completed her training at the facility, Postal authorities were contacted about problems.

A national hotel chain had a facility near the location where Bea had gone for her training. All the Postal Service employees from around the country who went there for multiple days of training stayed at that hotel. All the rooms at the hotel were non-smoking rooms. When the cleaning staff went to the room to clean it, they found that there was a male in the room while Bea was attending her training, and there was obviously a lot of cigarette smoking going on in the room. After Bea had completed her trip, several other problems were discovered. Bea had used her government issued Visa card to charge her male friend's flight and had received a lower government rate for her male friend. Bea was married, and the male friend was not her husband. She had also used her government issued Visa card to buy clothes and other personal items, as well as getting a cash advance on her card. Any single one of these issues would have been a good reason to issue discipline to Bea. The fact that there were several violations exacerbated the problem and reinforced the need for discipline.

I worked closely with Sara and my District's Labor department, which Sara now headed, to decide what degree of discipline should be issued to Bea. After much consideration and reviewing all the documentation related to the case, the decision was made that I should issue a Notice of Removal to Bea. I felt that was the best way to go, and we all knew that whatever discipline was issued could possibly be reduced through her appeal of the case. One facet of compiling enough information to decide involved interviewing Bea, to give her a chance to explain things to me. She was very cold during that interview, answering with one or two words when she answered at all. She did not show any remorse and appeared to not really care what happened. When the Notice of Removal was typed up and ready to go, I called Bea into my office and gave it to her to read.

Bea was emotionless as she read the Notice. It stated that she would be removed from the Postal Service in 30 days. As I expected, she refused to sign the Notice of Removal after reading it. Whenever discipline was issued, a copy of the signed piece of discipline needed to be kept on file for any future grievances or appeals. It was not uncommon that an employee would refuse to sign. A signature did not mean that the employee agreed to the action, merely that they were in receipt of it. The affected employee would keep the original document and would usually share that document with whatever group would be grieving or appealing their case. I had another Supervisor ready in waiting, and I paged her to my office to sign the Notice of Removal, indicating in writing on the document that Bea was refusing to sign it. My working relationship with Bea after issuing her the Notice of Removal was expectedly much more tense.

While all of this was going on, we were a few weeks away from Thanksgiving. I discovered that plans were being made on Bea's Tour 1 shift to have a catered meal brought in. I was told that this had been a common practice over the last few years. It was not at all uncommon for these types of food events to occur within Postal facilities all over the country. They were usually potluck events, where workers would bring in their favorite dishes to share. Occasionally, the Manager or Postmaster in charge would contribute to these events by providing something for the event. As I asked questions about this upcoming event, I found out that Bea was charging her employees $15 apiece, to pay for the food and the work that she was providing. I had no doubt that she was making a profit off her employees, and they all felt compelled to make the payment to their boss.

I called Bea into my office and informed her that she was not going to be providing any catering or charging employees for anything at any time in the future while she worked for me. This was an ethics violation. She was not at all happy to hear this news from me, and that was evident by the look of disgust on her face that I was becoming all too familiar with. The purchasing of food using Postal funds had not yet been eliminated at that point in time. I advised all the employees at my Post Office, not just Bea's employees, that I would be providing fried chicken for a Thanksgiving meal on the Wednesday preceding Thanksgiving. I invited them all to bring in dishes of their choice and it was a successful celebration. My business with Bea was not finished yet.

Craft employees working for the Postal Service received negotiated pay raises on specific dates during the life of the current contract they had in effect. They also received pay increases based on their time in service, referred to as step increases. And then there were annual cost of living allowance increases (COLA) built into their contracts as well. Years ago, much to the chagrin particularly of many in lower levels of management, the Postal Service decided to stop giving management employees COLA increases. There have been different methods used over the years for providing pay increases to management employees. They have all been performance based, unlike craft pay increases. I believe they were fair systems, and a good way to reward the best performing employees.

The system that was in place at that time was called Economic Value Added (EVA). Each of the Post Offices and Plants had several goals they were given. The better they performed at achieving those goals during the fiscal year, the greater the amount of the annual checks would be for the management staff in that Post Office or Plant for the value they added to the company. I can only presume that the same system of appropriate goals was given to the District and Area management staff. What many people did not like about this system, including myself, was that the check received was a single payment for the year. There was no increase to your salary, and the salary was all important in determining what the size of an employee's annuity would be when retiring.

As I was reviewing information about the EVA process, I found something that applied to the situation with Bea. One of the rules provided specifically for Installation Heads was that if an employee was in the process of being removed from the Postal Service, they were not to receive an EVA check. I sent Bea's information to the individual specified in the rules. When the checks arrived, Bea came to see me and ask why she didn't receive a check. I explained the rules to her, and she was very upset. She contacted our District office and her National Association of Postal Supervisors (NAPS) representative, trying to get her check. As her Removal case progressed, the decision making moved outside my office and jurisdiction through an appeal process. She ended up receiving a settlement for something less than the Removal she was issued by someone up the food chain from me. I was never informed about the details of her settlement. She transferred out of my office to a job at a Mail Processing facility and I was happy to see her go.

When Bea left the Tour 1 Supervisor position, I told one of my new Supervisors, Carol, that she would be replacing Bea in that job. Carol was not thrilled about the idea of working nights, but that is where I needed her, so she reluctantly went there. After she had been in her spot for several weeks, one of the clerks she supervised came to my office to tell me that Carol would occasionally show up an hour or two after her starting time. I took Carol into my office and asked her about what I had been told. She became very defensive and told me that she may have been late once or twice, but she was never more than a half hour late. I knew that Carol was applying for jobs at other Post Offices to be closer to home, so I had scheduled Sue, one of my ambitious CFS clerks to spend a week in on the job training with Carol.

Sue had transferred to an open job in my CFS unit from a REC in the area that had closed. She had experience working in the REC and in the CFS unit, but Sue had never worked in a Post Office. This was going to be very new to her and she had a lot to learn. She was scheduled to start her training on a very busy day. She would be reporting for her training with Carol on a Tuesday, the day after an upcoming holiday. I talked to Carol on the Friday preceding that holiday weekend. I reminded her that Sue had no experience, and I didn't want her to be alone for any period of time because of Carol being late to work. She assured me that she understood.

The drive from my home to my Post Office took me about a half hour each day. I often called ahead during that drive to see how things were going in advance. When I called that Tuesday morning, Sue answered the phone. I asked her how things were going with our operations. I could tell by the hesitance in her voice that something was wrong. I asked her if Carol was there on time. Sue told me that she did not want to get in the middle of things. I told her that we would talk when I got there. When I arrived at the office, I went about my daily morning business of checking for any urgent email messages, checking on the clerk and carrier operations to make sure they were running on time, walking to the other end of the building to check on the status of the retail window and the Post Office Box section.

I waited until the clerks were finished sorting mail for the carriers, then I brought Sue into my office. "You need to answer this question honestly," I told her. "What time did Carol get to work this morning?" She hesitantly told me that Carol arrived at around 4:00 a.m. They were both scheduled to start at 2:00 a.m. Sue again started to express a concern about being in the middle of this. I told her that I wanted her to succeed in her pursuit of becoming a Supervisor, and however high of a goal that she desired to go within the Postal Service. I explained to her that to be successful, she had to be truthful and hold the highest loyalty to her Postmaster, not to her peers.

I brought Carol into my office and asked her what time she had come into work that morning. She knew that I had already talked to Sue, so she reluctantly told me that she had arrived a few hours late. I told her I would be talking to her again about this. The next day when I arrived at the Post Office, I brought Carol in and gave her a Letter of Warning I had prepared for her. She signed for it, but she vocalized her concern that other Postmasters would see it in her Personnel Folder as she had applications out for other locations. I told her that she should have considered that before coming in to work late, especially since she had done so previously, and I specifically told her not to be late on that morning after the holiday.

A few weeks later I received a call from one of the Postmasters at an office where she had applied. He wanted to know what kind of worker she was. I told him about everything that had happened with her, and that she had a Letter of Warning on file for what she had done. Although Carol was a disappointment to me, it was a matter of integrity to me not to pass along any problem employee to someone else. The Postmaster who had called me about her did end up selecting her to fill his vacancy. I'm not sure about how she worked out as a Supervisor for him, but I was glad that I had a clear conscience about telling him how she had worked for me.

As I have shared, my Post Office was housed in a Mail Processing facility, along with all the District offices. There was also a Postal Inspection Service office with their staff in the building, serving the Postal community in the area. I was walking through my office's carrier unit one day when I overheard a few of my carriers talking about the smell of smoke. Postal facilities had been designated as non-smoking facilities years ago, so I stopped to ask some questions of the carriers. They told me that the smoke was coming from the Inspector's catwalk up above them. They said that this happened regularly.

I was outraged by this, so I marched down to the Inspector's offices, also in my building, to report it. The secretary told me that there weren't any Inspectors available to talk to me at that time. She took my phone number down and said someone would call me back. When I didn't receive a call back, I called one of the Inspectors who I personally knew the next day. He answered his phone and I told him what I had learned. I expected him to be as outraged as I was that the custodians were using the catwalk for their personal smoking lounge. I was surprised when he told me that he knew they did that and that they had been doing that for years. It was the Inspector's domain, and if they didn't care enough about it to stop it, then I just had to forget about it and focus on the issues within my responsibility. The Maintenance individuals doing the smoking worked for the Mail Processing Center, not for me.

When I was in my first carrier job, there were carrier routes that delivered in very lucrative areas comprised of mini mansions. I remember training with a carrier on one of the most lucrative routes, preparing to fill in for him on a vacation he had coming up. I was surprised when we stopped at the Country Club that was on his route for lunch. Every day he stopped there, where he was provided with a free lunch of whatever fine food they were serving that day to their customers. At Christmas time, he would return to the Post Office each day with a lot of envelopes, bottles of expensive liquor, large pieces of quality meats and an assortment of other gifts. It was estimated that he received about $5,000 of cash and gifts each year. That was a lot of money considering this was close to 40 years ago. He ended up transferring to an office in another state for personal reasons. When his route became available for carriers in the office to bid on, those carriers who had the highest seniority were eager to get that route. The Country Club is long gone now, replaced by lots of mini mansions. The free lunch may be gone, but I can only imagine what the carrier on that route now makes in tips each year.

My customers also showed their appreciation at Christmas time. Carriers all over the country look forward to the gifts they receive from their customers at Christmas time, and I was no different. I averaged receiving between $300 and $500 in gifts, and it certainly helped with my own present purchasing and bill paying. Sometimes carriers would get too aggressive about their Christmas tips. In my Postmaster position, I received a few calls from customers on one of my carrier's routes. They told me that their carrier came to their door and solicited gifts from them. She told them that they could leave their "gift" in an envelope for her in their mailbox, or they could mail it to her to the address she provided to them. I could not turn a blind eye to this blatant abuse of customer service. The carrier had over 20 years of service and was getting close to retirement.

I contacted my District's Labor Department and we agreed that I should have her issued a notice of Removal by her Supervisor. We knew up front that this would end up being reduced to a suspension in the grievance process. She had discipline on file for attendance issues but had no other serious infractions over her career. The issuance of a Removal would hopefully be a deterrent to other carriers who might otherwise be getting too aggressive about their tips. The other carriers were, of course, outraged by the harshness of the discipline she received. As was customarily the case, her peers only heard her side of the story. The point was made, as intended, and when the grievance filed over her Removal reached my desk, I reduced the Removal to a 14 day no time off suspension. It was obvious that this carrier was experiencing financial difficulties. That was the reason for her aggressive tip-seeking to begin with. A time off suspension without pay would have been catastrophic for her.

While I was willing to concede to a no time off suspension with the union representative who was handling her case, I had to stand firm on the length of time that her discipline would be on file. Union officials, at all levels, strive to get the length of time that discipline remains live in their constituent's file reduced to the smallest amount possible. The representative I was negotiating with wanted the time that her discipline would remain on file to be only six months. He argued with me that she had minimal prior discipline, and he knew that if she had any type of violation while that 14 Day Suspension was on file, she would be issued the next progressive step of discipline. That would mean another Removal Notice. I argued back that I wanted the discipline to remain on file for the full two years. There was no way that I would have been willing to allow the discipline to expire before we even hit the next Christmas season. I felt that the seriousness of what she had done necessitated having the discipline serve to remind her to do the right thing. Her representative ultimately accepted my terms for the discipline to remain on file for two years. He presumably did not want to risk an Arbitrator's decision on removing her from her job by pushing it forward without a settlement.

There was only one Supervisor who had been my peer when I worked at that office who was still in his same Supervisor position when I returned as the Postmaster at the level 24 Post Office. The union leadership had changed, and the layout of the office had changed quite a bit since I had been there as a Supervisor 10 years earlier. There was another Supervisor who I knew that was filling in as the Acting Manager, a mid-level position between myself and the Supervisors. My first chore would be to fill that vacant position with a qualified applicant. I went through the process of having the vacant Manager, Customer Service position posted.

I spent a lot of time in the morning each day out on my workroom floor, making my presence felt in an effort to make sure that all of the employees were diligently applying themselves to the work at hand, getting the carriers out of the office as quickly as possible so they could get their deliveries done and get back as quickly as possible. That was the way I had conducted business in the two smaller Post Offices where I worked previously, but I knew that I had other responsibilities that needed to be handled in this larger Post Office. I could not be spending as much time on my workroom floor as I had elsewhere.

Ben was the name of the selected individual who I picked to fill the titled Customer Service Manager at my level 24 office. He was a Supervisor from a local Post Office, and his promotion occurred soon after I was promoted to my EAS 24 Postmaster position. My MPOO knew him and thought that he would be a good selection for the job, but he warned me early on about making sure that he was spending ample time on the workroom floor overseeing carrier operations each morning. The carriers were only in the office for a few hours in the morning before heading out to deliver the mail on their routes, and it was important to make sure that they were spending their time productively. He did not share the same management style that I had, and it became obvious before long that we were not in agreement about a lot of things in operations.

I soon found that Ben was spending too much time in his office in the morning and not with the Supervisors and the carriers in their units. His office was in an administrative section of the building, near my office, somewhat removed from the workroom floor. After telling him one time too many to get out there on the workroom floor, I had his office moved to another location in the building. The new location was directly linked to the workroom floor. He was not happy about it, but I wasn't happy about him not doing as he was told, and I hoped to avoid the hassle of issuing him discipline for not doing as he was instructed. He did work well with the carrier union, but that was about the only positive thing I could say about his performance. I came to find out that even working well with the carrier union was coming at a cost.

The tracking of overtime in an office is not an easy thing to do, but it is necessary. After the end of each Quarter, the carrier union representatives would look at how much overtime each carrier had received during the previous Quarter. If there was a great disparity between the top earners and the bottom earners, payouts would be made to equalize the lower earners. Most Post Offices have varying ways with which they track overtime and the percentages of differences that will be acceptable between the lowest and highest earners. I found out that Ben was signing off on payments to carriers at the end of each Quarter, without doing much to correct the equalization problems that were causing the inequities in the first place.

Prior to the start of each Quarter, carriers could sign an Overtime Desired list. There were 3 columns on the Overtime Desired list in my office at that time. A carrier could check Route Only, which entitled them to work overtime on their own route only and only on a regular scheduled workday. If the Route Only carrier worked more than 10 hours on their route, a grievance would be filed and those hours over 10 ended up being paid to a carrier on the 12 Hour list. The Route Only carriers could not come in for overtime on their day off to work on their own route. The other two columns were the 10 Hour list and the 12 Hour list. Carriers on the 10- and 12-Hour lists were limited to that number of hours on a regular scheduled day. The overtime hours that they worked would only count towards equalization if they worked the overtime on another route. If they worked it on their own route, it didn't count.

We had carriers working on routes that needed to be adjusted, or on business routes that had much heavier volume on Mondays or days after holidays. Those carriers were working on their own routes making the overtime money, and at the end of the Quarter we were paying them because the hours that they worked didn't qualify as equalized hours. At the level 22 Post Office where I had been Postmaster previously, an agreement was made between the carrier union representatives and management that overtime was overtime. It all counted towards equalization at the end of the Quarter, even if they did work it on their own route. I tried to negotiate a similar agreement with the union representatives at my level 24 Post Office, but their local President assured me that it would never pass a vote from the union members. Of course it wouldn't. Why would they want to agree to something that would make management's job easier and reduce their payouts?

If a carrier on the 10 Hour list worked more than 10 hours, a grievance would be filed for those hours over 10 to additionally be paid to a carrier on the 12 Hour list. If any carrier worked more than 10 hours in a day, the time worked over 10 hours was paid at a rate of double time, referred to as penalty overtime. If a carrier on a 10- or 12-Hour list was called in to work on their day off, any hours worked over 8 was paid at the penalty overtime rate. If a carrier worked more than 12 hours in a day or more than 60 hours in a week, you got it. More penalties were paid. According to a local agreement that was made between the union and the presumably sleeping previous Postmaster, if a carrier was called in to work on their day off, they had the ability to pick the open route they wanted by seniority. The senior carriers would come in and pick the easiest driving routes that were available, even if they did not know them at all. A few of them would spend so much time sorting the mail in the office, because they had never sorted on that route before, that we would have to give them all sorts of assistance on the street to avoid them going into penalty overtime past their 8 hours. I often wondered how the Postal Service managed to stay in business at all with these payouts going on at locations across the country.

Back to Ben signing off on these payouts, I was determined to stop it once I became aware of it and I did. I began to personally track the overtime that the carriers worked weekly throughout the Quarter. If certain carriers started to get too many hours, they were put on a Do Not Use list that I distributed to the Supervisors. At the other end of the spectrum, if carriers were too low on hours, the Supervisors were instructed to give those carriers the available overtime. If I saw that my instructions were not being followed, I would talk to the individual Supervisors who were responsible.

I knew that I was changing a practice that had been in place for a long time with the Supervisors, and it took a few weeks to get them all in line. They had certain carriers that they relied on to get the job done, and those carriers would always accept any overtime that was available. While I could respect that, other carriers would literally hide to avoid being assigned overtime. They just wanted to see a payout for equalization at the end of the Quarter.

By the numbers, the low overtime carriers would be brought in to work overtime on their days off, and the high overtime ones would stay home. For the carriers whose routes were longer than 8 hours, they would give away the portion that was over 8 hours to another 10- or 12-Hour list carrier and they would be assigned something else for their overtime. If for whatever reason a carrier was short on hours by the end of a Quarter, I made an agreement with the local President that those hours would be made up in the next Quarter. It was certainly not the most efficient ways to do things, but once I took over the monitoring, there were no more payouts at the end of the Quarters. It wasn't long before Ben applied for a lateral assignment to another office. It was not a promotion for him, but it was closer to his home, and it got him away from his troublesome boss. Me.

Ron was a Supervisor at my office who shared the same ideals that I had. We both believed that if an employee had attendance issues, performance problems or conduct problems, they needed to receive appropriate training to help them. If the problems continued, that employee needed to start receiving corrective action, discipline, to correct their actions. If the corrective action did not solve the problem, they needed to be removed from the Postal Service. I detailed Ron into the Customer Service Manager position in my office when it was vacated by Ben. He did an excellent job for me overseeing my carrier units, and he also was able to work well with the local union President resolving grievances that were filed.

When the national contracts are being renewed, all the local contracts at Post Offices and Mail Processing facilities across the country are renewed as well. Ron was one of the members of my local Management Team that met with the carrier union at my Post Office for our local contract negotiations, when the time arrived to do so. I had several meetings with my

Management Team as we worked through the process, and the union team members were given the time that they needed to meet to prepare for negotiations. On the Management side, we agreed to allow most of the provisions in the expiring contract to remain. We wanted to remove a few of those previously mentioned overtime provisions from the local contract. Of course, the union did not want to give them up. We went back and forth on those overtime issues in a few meetings, finally deciding that we were not going to come to any agreement on those points. We agreed that we would have to send the items to an arbitrator for a decision.

I had members of my staff pull all sorts of timekeeping records to show the hardship that was being placed on our Post Office due to the overtime requirements that were specified in the previous local contract. Those records included showing the exorbitant hours needed to complete routes when allowing senior carriers to pick routes they didn't know on their days off. By the time we were finished pulling records to support our position, we had a stack of paper about a foot high. We sent all our documentation to a specific Labor Analyst at our Area office, as instructed, for follow up towards arbitration. The months started to go by, and I was busy enough to forget about the matter. After about 4 or 5 months, I asked our local union President if she had heard anything about this. She said she hadn't heard anything. I contacted our Area office to see what I could find out. I found out that the Labor Specialist at the Area office had recently retired. As I attempted to have anyone at the Area Labor department find out where our issue had left off, nobody could even locate all the documentation we had put together and sent there. Those overtime provisions remained in effect throughout the remainder of my time as Postmaster at that office. They are probably still in effect today.

While serving as Postmaster at the level 24 Post Office, I had another situation of carrier aggression at Christmas time to handle. I received a phone call from a customer I knew that lived in that city where I served. This customer informed me that her carrier was coming to her door with small items that would obviously fit inside her mailbox that was on the curb at the front of her house. Whether the customer or her husband answered the door, the carrier would spend several minutes trying to engage them in conversation about Christmas events and buying gifts for friends and family. The customer told me that she would often see the carrier similarly going up to the doors of other customers in her subdivision.

I did not even have to look at this carrier's performance records. I was familiar with the fact that she often exceeded the amount of time that it took to deliver the mail on her route daily. Up to that point, her Supervisor had been unable to catch her breaking any specific rules while delivering mail out on her route. I spoke to my Customer Service Manager and told him to coordinate the observations on this carrier with a few different Supervisors. I wanted to attempt to catch her off guard making those unnecessary trips to the doors of her customers. It didn't take long before this carrier was caught exiting her delivery vehicle to bring a small parcel to one of her customer's doors. The Supervisor who had been watching her confronted her when she returned to her vehicle. She attempted to legitimize her actions by saying that she was concerned about leaving the parcel in the mailbox for the customer. She said that she thought someone might steal it.

The Supervisor asked her for the form that the customer had to sign to receive the parcel. She told the Supervisor that there was no form needed. The parcel was not insured, certified or sent by any other method that would require a signature. She was given an Official Job Discussion, warning her that if she took any mail to a customer's door that did not require a signature and it could fit in the customer's mailbox in the future, she would receive formal discipline.

Observations of her delivery performance were continued, but my Delivery staff loosened up on them after a brief while. The carrier became more observant of the individuals monitoring her and reduced her trips to the customer's doors. She more than likely resumed that activity after she became more confident that her watchers had moved on. Over the years that I spent in management, I learned that if an employee was breaking the rules in one area, they were probably negligent in other areas as well. That same carrier who was making those unnecessary trips to customer's doors was negligent in another area with her office duties.

Sleepers were supposed to be a focus of attention in any office where carriers worked. A sleeper is a piece of mail that is inadvertently left in the carrier's case after the mail has been pulled out for delivery. Sleepers would typically be found in the first or last address separation cell in a delivery case row where the mail was sorted. They would also be found in one of the lower rows in a carrier case, where you would have to bend over to spot it in the back of the case. There were metal slats in the carrier letter cases that were used to separate the addresses for sortation. That is where pieces would often get stuck.

Carrier cases were supposed to be checked daily after the carriers left the office. The attention that was placed on getting all First-Class letter mail delivered in a timely manner daily mandated these checks. It was each Unit Supervisor's job to check their carrier cases to look for those sleepers. A piece of Standard Mail (bulk mail) would not be viewed and treated as a serious infraction. If a First-Class letter was found in a carrier case, two things had to happen.

First, it was upper management's expectation that those letters would need to be sent out for delivery. They would have to be sent out with carriers who were going out to deliver Priority or Express Mail items that arrived throughout the day, after the carriers were all out of the office delivering the mail on their routes. This was a matter of providing service to our customers, but it was also an issue of the possibility of that First-Class letter being one of the test pieces that was being tracked and would affect the office's EXFC scores. Second, the fact that the responsible carrier did not see that sleeper had to be documented for follow up. The follow up would be a minimum of an Official Job Discussion, alerting the responsible carrier to the fact that discipline would be issued to him or her if further infractions occurred.

I would occasionally walk through the Delivery Units looking for sleepers. I would wait until the afternoon to check the carrier cases, giving my Unit Supervisors their opportunity to check the cases before I did. Checking for sleepers was one of the many duties that the Supervisors had to perform daily. If I found a sleeper, that meant one of my Supervisors was not doing their job. That responsible Supervisor would then be facing potential discipline for their inaction. Trust but verify. That philosophy was followed often, and necessary to avoid trouble. The Supervisors never knew when I might decide to go around checking carrier cases. And I never knew when someone from an outside Management Team could come in to spot check my office for sleepers, or any number of things that could ultimately get me in trouble.

During one of my Unit Supervisor's checks, a sleeper was found in the case of my tip seeking carrier one day while she was out on her route. It was a piece of First-Class Mail going to one of her customers, stuck far back in the bottom row of her case. She would have had to bend over to see it when she was pulling her mail out. If it had been bulk mail, or Standard Mail, it would not have been as big an issue. She was issued a Letter of Warning for that offense, and the attention to her on her office duties increased. She did improve her performance, and no further action was necessary.

The Christmas tip chaser's husband was also a carrier at that Post Office. I remembered both from back when I was a

Supervisor there, several years earlier. The husband was a pretty quiet guy. He kept to himself, did his job well and never gave me any trouble. I did recall that he seemed to sometimes be a bit hungover in the mornings. I wondered if sometimes he might have been having a little hair of the dog before he came to work in the morning. There wasn't a whole lot I could do about my suspicions. He did have a motor vehicle accident while delivering mail on his route, but there were no injuries involved. An investigation found him to be at fault in the accident, and he was issued a suspension. At fault motor vehicle accidents resulted in an automatic suspension. Other than that, his job performance was never indicative of any imparity on his part, until one particular day.

I was sitting in my Postmaster office when I heard a lot of commotion going out on my workroom floor. One of my Supervisors came into my office to advise me that there had been an accident out in our garage. The tip seekers husband was backing his Postal vehicle out of its parking spot, when he accelerated to a fast speed before backing into the Postal vehicle parked behind him. He did not appear to be conscious, and 911 had been called. The police and an ambulance quickly arrived, and the carrier was taken to the local hospital. My Supervisor told me that he had regained consciousness prior to being taken away, and I wanted to know if alcohol was a factor in the cause of the accident. Apparently, a test had been conducted prior to the carrier leaving, and the Supervisor talked with one of the police officers, attempting to find the results. The officer he spoke with told him that he was not able to share the results of the sobriety test with him.

We did find out from one of the officers, who requested anonymity, that the carrier's blood alcohol level was over the legal limit for driving. One of the carriers who had been in the garage at the time of the accident was getting hyper in her outrage over what had happened. She shared the same opinion as many of the carriers did over the situation. If the drunken carrier had crashed into the vehicle behind him just a few minutes later, he would have hit the driver of the vehicle behind him. That carrier would have been standing at the rear of his vehicle, loading his mail into it. He would have certainly been severely injured, if not killed by the impact of the drunken carrier's vehicle. It was expected that there would be some extreme action taken against the offending carrier. I shared that same opinion.

The President of the carrier union who represented the offending carrier was concerned enough about what disciplinary action would be pursued against him that she asked to meet with me. I told her that I was expecting the carrier's Supervisor to pursue a Removal, due to the severity of the accident. She had already been hearing the outrage from her other constituents, so she was not surprised to hear that a Removal would be issued. She would, of course, have a grievance filed over that discipline, but this was an ugly situation and she wanted the path of least resistance.

She asked me if I would accept his retirement as a solution. I told her that the discipline would be issued, and he would need to make his retirement effective before the grievance ran its course. I knew, from experience, that an employee could back out of retiring pretty much up to the actual effective date of the retirement. I was not going to be caught up in a situation where this carrier's Removal would be dropped, and he ended up staying on the job. He did retire while his Removal was still in the grievance process, and he was able to draw off his pension. His wife remained on the job beyond my departure from that Post Office to my next position.

Another area of responsibility that I gave to my Supervisors and Manager involved checking the carrier cases each morning, before the carriers arrived at work. The productivity expectations for each Delivery Unit and each Post Office were unforgiving. The average acceptable productivity rating was for a carrier to sort 4 feet of mail into their cases per hour. That figure was made up of a higher expected rate for letter mail and a lower rate for flats, or magazine size items. Many carriers would consistently perform at a higher rate than 4 feet per hour, particularly if they were a regular carrier who had been on the same route for an extended period.

I wanted the carrier cases to be checked each morning to see if there was mail that had been sorted into them from the previous day. If a carrier sorted mail into their case prior to leaving the office for the day, they were responsible for filling out a form for the Supervisors. That form would detail how much mail they sorted prior to leaving for the day, and that volume would be entered into the system. If they failed to fill out that form, the associated volume was not entered and the time that they spent sorting it was not credited to them. That would reduce their productivity for the day. Multiply that by any number of carriers who may not have submitted the volume that they sorted, and the office productivity would take a hit and I would take a hit.

The Supervisors would talk to their carriers who had mail in their cases with no recorded volume each morning. They would add the missing volume to the system and the carrier would be warned about reporting that volume in a timely manner. It was, after all, in their best interest to do so. A carrier with low productivity numbers received additional attention from their Supervisor, Manager and from me, to identify what they were doing incorrectly that might contribute to their low productivity. Very few of them wanted that kind of attention. I used spreadsheets to track a lot of different operations under my responsibility, and carrier productivity was certainly worthy of that tracking attention.

I was able to pull reports for various increments of time on my carriers. I would typically look at a monthly or quarterly average of each of my carrier's productivity, sorting the spreadsheet from the lowest to the highest productivity. The lowest performing carriers were the recipients of greater attention in the office. My expectation was that a low performing individual's Unit Supervisor and my Operations Manager were doing their jobs, looking for any time-wasting practices that could be documented and corrected. I would also go out on the workroom floor, looking for any problems that might be occurring. The numbers did move in a positive direction, but they were not moving quickly enough for me. I knew that there were a certain number of experienced carriers who were capable of doing so but were simply unwilling to move at a faster pace. That was unacceptable to me.

One of the things that is nearest and dearest to many carriers is their starting time. They want to start as early as possible so they can get finished as early as possible. I distinctly recall having those same feelings when I was a carrier. I knew that I would not be able to change starting times without a valid reason. The carrier's union would be all over that in a heartbeat. I instructed my staff to give talks to all the carriers, advising them that their productivity was being reviewed. The talks further advised the carriers that if individuals were unable to meet the basic required productivity, their start times would be moved later. My rationale for this, as I advised the union and shared with the carriers, was that I had to assume that these carriers were not receiving enough mail from the clerks doing the sorting in a timely manner. Moving starting times of certain carriers would assure that they were receiving enough mail to keep busy, and hopefully enable them to achieve the required productivities. The local union was not happy, especially since they were hearing the gripes from their union members, but I had given them a valid rationale for making this move. Many of those who were not meeting the required productivities were prominent, long term dues paying members of their local union.

The carriers were advised that they would have a month to improve their productivity. I would be reviewing the data after the month had passed, and those who were not up to par would have their starting times changed. I did hear about it from the local union President when I had the productivity of all the carriers posted for all of them to see. I wanted everyone to see where they stood, particularly those who were needing to improve. I do not specifically recall if it was my intent to shame some of those low performers, but it probably was. I did agree to take the postings down, and I had the individual supervisors speak to their employees in question. When the month had passed, I had letters ready to go to the low performing carriers, advising them that their start times were moving later. I was approached by a few of the affected carriers individually, and by the union representatives as well, asking if they improved their office performance could they be moved back to the earlier start times. I told them that I would continue to review office performance, but I would need to see a sustained improvement over a period of at least a few months. I was not going to be bouncing start times back and forth, only to have the reduced performance return after a move back to an earlier start time.

The office performance numbers began to improve almost immediately, continuing to improve as carriers wanted those early start times back. I did continue to push my Operations Manager and the Delivery Supervisors to monitor the carriers for any time-wasting practices. One of those items involved carriers eating at their cases, where they sorted their mail. Apparently, not much attention had been paid to that topic by my predecessors. Early on in my Postmaster role at that level 24 Post Office, I was rather surprised to see that some carriers would bring their breakfast in with them. They would have carry out fast food items, requiring them to have to use the plastic forks and knives to eat their meals. This meant, of course, that there was no mail sorting going on while they paused to take a bite of their food. I put a stop to that in short order. Then there were other food items. Bags of chips, fruit and other items. I ended up having to basically put out instructions that any food that would require the carrier to stop sorting mail, or food that was too juicy or messy that could get on the mail had to be stopped. I sometimes felt like I was the principal in a grade school.

Talking with neighboring carriers was acceptable, if the hands were staying busy sorting the mail. Carriers who would step out of their sorting cases to talk to their neighbors were subject to warnings, leading up to official discipline if they continued to move away from their work. The greatest attention was always placed on the carriers who were not meeting those office productivity standards. I knew that many carriers who were barely making those standards were giving their best that they could. That was fine with me. If they were applying themselves as best as they were able, I could not ask for more from them. On the other end of the spectrum, there were carriers who well exceeded the minimum office productivity standards. Many of them helped to carry our good productivity numbers and assisted on other routes as well. But there are always those few bad apples who felt that they were entitled to take time away from their work, just because they had those good performance numbers. That didn't work for me, and some of them ended up being the recipients of discipline for being away from their work cases.

Another issue that caused me some grief at that Post Office was a local agreement that had been made by one of my predecessors and the carrier union. Typically, the local agreement within Post Offices stipulated that the carriers would take a 10-minute morning break during their time working in the office and their second 10-minute break out on their routes while delivering the mail. Otherwise, the local agreement would have the carriers take both of their breaks on the street, with no office break. At my Post Office, the agreement stipulated that smokers could take one break in the office and the other break on the street, and all other carriers took both breaks out on the street. It may have been a hair-splitting exercise, but I felt the necessity to dig in to find out what carriers were going out with the smokers. I found that some non-smokers were going out taking a break with their smoking friends. Some were doing it on a regular basis, while others would just go out occasionally. I had to task my supervisory staff with keeping track of which employees were going out and to warn the non-smokers who were going out. Some discipline, as usual, had to be issued to the abusers.

At that same Post Office, I was informed that one of my Supervisors was showing up late for work frequently. I had several 204Bs who had been trained to fill in where needed, and I did not need one of my titled Supervisors setting a bad example for them or for the employees they were supposed to be supervising. Technology had reached the point where the carrier's time in the office preparing to go out on their routes had reduced drastically. I had recently hired Marie for a vacant Supervisor job, and one of my 204bs let me know that she was coming in anywhere from 15 minutes to an hour late on some days. I called her up to my office to let her know that her lateness was being reported to me, but I did not share who was doing the talking. She was apologetic, telling me that she had a rough time in the mornings, but she would work harder to be on time.

There was no problem for a week or two, but then she started coming in late again. I again brought her to my office and told her that she was going to have to start using a timecard, and that if this continued, she would be disciplined. She did not like that idea, stating that the other Supervisors did not have to clock in and out. I told her that the other Supervisors were not having trouble making it to work on time.

She didn't show up for work the next day. Her starting time was 6:30 a.m. She called in sick at around 11:00 a.m. and faxed in FMLA paperwork that indicated she would need to be off work indefinitely due to stress. One of my Supervisors came to me and told me that he had overheard her talking to someone in the office about working as a bartender in the evenings close to her home. That would explain her difficulties getting to work by 6:30 a.m.

Weeks began to pass without her returning to work. I called a few bars in the area where she lived, asking for her by name. I was hoping to find her and have her take my call, to substantiate that she was working elsewhere while she was away from her Supervisor job due to stress. I was not able to reach her at any of the places I called. When her FMLA leave ran out and she still hadn't returned to work, I had disciplinary procedures started against her. She failed to show up for meetings I scheduled with her to discuss her situation and failed to call to let me know anything about what has happening with her. After the appropriate time had passed, I sent her a Removal Notice and never heard from her again. She was officially dropped from the Postal Service.

Postal employees drinking or taking any drugs while on the clock was obviously an infraction of the rules and regulations in place. Nevertheless, it did occur from time to time. At my level 24 Post Office, the Supervisor over my Retail Unit came to my office to discuss a problem she was having with one of her Window Clerks. She told me that a customer had complained to her that John, the Window Clerk who had been serving her, processed her credit card incorrectly during a purchase she had made. She went on to say that he was slurring his words and appeared to be intoxicated. His union representative was working at the time, so I called her into my office. I advised her of what was happening, then had John called into my office.

I had already learned a few things about John over the previous few weeks, so I wasn't surprised at the events that were occurring. I knew that one of my Supervisors had known John for several years, and I had asked her about him when he didn't make it in to work one day. She told me that he had been arrested and was in jail at the time, preventing him to report to work as scheduled. She also told me that he had lost his driving privileges due to being intoxicated while driving.

John had been transferred out of my Post Office several years earlier due to a reduction of workload brought about by increased automation of the mail the office was receiving. More automation meant a need for fewer employees to handle the mail. The number of parcels, flats (magazine sized pieces) and letters needing processing at Post Offices were daily being measured and reviewed. Periodic reviews would determine the number of employees needed to handle the volume. Employees who had the least amount of seniority in an office were the ones most likely to be affected by reduced volumes of mail needing to be manually processed.

Full Time Regular employees could not be terminated due to reductions in workload, so the Postal Service was responsible for finding them work within their geographic area. John and a few other clerks had been excessed out to facilities that had work available for them. Employees who were excessed out of a facility had "retreat rights." Those rights gave the affected employees the option of returning to their old facility if the workload increased or the staffing reduced through normal attrition.

John and a few other clerks who had been excessed out to other facilities opted to return to my facility due to a need for employees. The Supervisor who knew him told me that he had been in good condition prior to being transferred out of my office. He apparently picked up some bad habits while he was working at the other facility. Alcohol consumption was one of them, and I suspected there may have been drugs involved as well. From what I heard, the supervision at the location where he had been working was very lax. Perhaps the Supervisors were partaking with the employees.

John came into my office looking very shaky. He was wearing dark colored glasses and wobbling as he walked in. His union steward and my retail supervisor were already seated in my office with me. I had a pen and paper on my desk to take notes of our conversation. I told John to take a seat in a chair across from me on the other side of my desk. He did so slowly and cautiously. I confronted him about the error he had made processing the customer's credit card payment. He slurred out an incoherent answer. I asked him if he had been drinking any alcoholic beverage and he vigorously denied that. His breath did not give anything away, as he appeared to also have a habit of using mints to cover any odor.

He was obviously in no condition to continue working. The employee who gave him a ride back and forth to work from his home was working, and he was obviously in no shape to leave the facility on his own without potentially injuring himself. I would have had him taken to a medical facility in the area to have him tested for alcohol in his system, but there were rules in place that prevented me from doing this. As the head of my facility, it was my responsibility to make sure he safely made it to his home. I called a taxi and told him that I was sending him home. He talked with his union representative until his taxi arrived. I made sure that the fare was paid, again my responsibility.

I then began to dig in to find out more information about John. The first thing that I found out was that his coworkers were not going to tell me anything that might get him in trouble. By not acknowledging that they were aware that he had a problem, they were in enabling him with his obvious problem. I found out from a few individuals who were not close to him that he would often walk across the busy street in front of our Post Office to a grocery store during his lunch break. That grocery store also had a liquor department. I was also told that he would go out into our Postal vehicle parking garage during his breaks and during his lunch. I sent a few of my Supervisors out into the garage to search through it to see if they could find any stash he might have out there, but nothing was found.

He returned to work the next day and appeared to be sober. I had a meeting scheduled for him to attend an appointment with a Postal Service EAP (Employee Assistance Program) counselor on the clock. I alerted my staff and employees I could trust to keep an eye on him as much as possible during his lunch and breaks. A day or two later, one of my custodians came to my office to report an observation he had made to me. He told me that he had seen a paper bag lodged in between low branches of a tree in front of our building, near one of the entrances to the facility. He had also observed John coming and going through that entrance into the building. I advised he and my staff to pay attention to John and his use of that entrance. The custodian came to me again and advised me that he had observed John placing the paper bag up in between the branches. I told the custodian to bring me the bag and to write out a statement of his observations.

When I received the bag, I found a bottle of flavored vodka that was almost empty, a full bottle of the same vodka and a few packages of breath mints. I placed the bag at the end of a large table in my conference room and had John, his Supervisor and his union representative come to the conference room. I asked him if he had been drinking and he told me that he had not. He was nervously looking at the bag at the end of the table. I confronted him about the bag and its contents, and he denied knowing anything about it. I mentioned that the breath mints in the bag were the same kind that he always had with him, pulling the items out of the bag. He again denied that the bag and its contents belonged to him. He did not seem to be intoxicated at that point, so he was sent back to work, and his Supervisor later conducted a pre-disciplinary interview with him. He was advised that this matter was under investigation and that it could result in disciplinary action against him.

I always worked closely with a District Labor Specialist on more severe infractions such as this. John had discipline on file for attendance infractions. We were advised by a Labor Specialist to issue John a Removal Notice for this infraction. The notice was written up and issued to him within a few days. John, his coworkers and his union representative were all outraged by that, of course. His union representative and his immediate Supervisor met at Step 1 of the grievance process and there was no resolution. The grievance then came to me and I met with his local union President to discuss it. It took a few meetings to come up with an acceptable resolution. His Removal Notice would be reduced to a 14 Day Suspension with the conditions that John would follow up on regular EAP meetings, that he would not consume alcohol before or while working and that he would submit to being tested if he appeared to be under the influence of alcohol or other intoxicants. The agreement further stipulated that if John failed to cooperate and go for testing, if it was deemed necessary, he would forfeit his job with the Postal Service. John, his union President and I all signed off on that agreement. Signing off on that agreement meant that each of us would live by the terms defined in the agreement.

Within just a few days, John's Supervisor came to my office and told me that John appeared to be intoxicated. I called him into my office, along with his Supervisor and his union steward. It was easy to see that he was under the influence. His union steward requested a few minutes to talk to him alone. I allowed that, and when I returned, I was told by both that he was not going to submit to being tested for alcohol or any other intoxicant. I reminded them of the terms of our agreement that he had willingly signed his name on, but they still both declined. He was again in no shape to continue working, so I advised them that I was calling a taxi to bring him home once again. The taxi showed up, and John was nowhere to be found. Apparently, he had walked off the premises when nobody was watching him. I had to pay the driver for showing up, even though he did not have a fare waiting.

John was again issued a Notice of Removal, and I was surprised when the union filed a grievance over it. There was no resolution at Step 1 of the grievance between our local union representative and my Supervisor. The grievance again came to me and the union President. The argument given by both the local union steward and the President were the same. They indicated that only a few days had lapsed since the agreement had been signed off on, so it was unfair and punitive of Management to be insisting he get tested after such a short period of time. Sometimes I was just amazed at the arguments they would come up with.

Eventually the union had to decide whether they would be willing to incur the cost of taking John's case through the Arbitration process. Paying for an Arbitrator, a non-Postal employee, to come in and hear the case and make an unbiased decision based on the arguments raised by each side was costly to both parties. Ultimately, the union decided not to pursue arguing the case and John was removed from the Postal Service. However, things weren't quite finished yet.

I received a call a few months later from a Human Resource Specialist at my District who handled discrimination complaints. She informed me that John had filed a complaint that I had discriminated against him because of his African American heritage. The Specialist informed me that he had not filed his complaint within the authorized time limit of 45 days following the occurrence of the alleged discrimination. She told me that I would nevertheless need to schedule a Redress meeting. I begrudgingly gave her date and time options to set up the meeting. When she called me back to solidify the date and time, I told her that since he was no longer an employee, we would not be meeting at my Main Post Office. I considered him to be a potential threat and I did not want him around the bulk of my employees. I scheduled the meeting to take place at one of my small branch offices, in a basement meeting room. I also informed her that there would be an armed Postal Inspector on location during the meeting, to assure the safety of myself and others in that building. She was not happy about these conditions, but she relayed them to John and the meeting was set.

I arrived early to the appointment, greeting the mediator and the Postal Inspector. The mediator was a bit startled about the Postal Inspector being present, a handgun holstered at his side. We agreed that the Inspector would be standing outside the door of the room where we would be meeting. John showed up a few minutes late with his girlfriend. Complainants were typically allowed to bring another individual with them to Redress meetings. They would usually bring a union representative from the craft where they worked. Sometimes they would bring a fellow employee in with them. This was the first time I had been going into a meeting with the complainant and his significant other.

The meeting lasted about an hour. The gist of the meeting was listening to both John and his girlfriend trying to assure me that he was receiving help for his problem. They told me that he had joined Alcoholics Anonymous and he was regularly attending meetings. They also told me that he had not had anything to drink for several weeks. The girlfriend broke into tears a few times, telling me that he needed the job and that he would not screw things up again. At the end of the meeting, I told both that John had been given his chance and that he had not lived up to the terms of the agreement he had signed. I reminded him that he had pulled a disappearing act when I had called a taxi for him to get safely home from work. I told him that I was living up to the terms of that agreement that I had signed by removing him. The meeting ended without a resolution, and John's untimely case was dropped soon after that.

As I have shared elsewhere in this book, a lot of attention has always been placed on the processes that take place in the Post Office retail lobbies. The Postal Service has contracts with

Mystery Shop companies to regularly send in covert individuals to verify that correct procedures are being followed. Attention is given to packages that are being mailed, to assure that the window clerks are asking the appropriate security questions. "Does this parcel contain anything fragile, liquid, perishable, or potentially hazardous..." The clerks are also expected to offer additional items, such as a book of stamps, to each customer they serve. Points are assigned to each of the items that are evaluated by the Mystery Shopper, and the Postmaster or Manager who is responsible for that Retail Unit gets the praise or the punishment that accompanies the notification of the scores.

The item that received the highest number of points on a Mystery Shop was the Wait Time in Line (WTIL). The goal for customers waiting to be served was less than five minutes. I had been the recipient of unwanted, negative attention from higher ups on more than a few occasions for that issue at the different offices where I served as Postmaster. During my time at my level 24 Post Office, Postmasters who experienced WTIL failures were required to be on a telecon with both District and Area higher ups. We were verbally beaten up by the Area participants, and our jobs were literally threatened if further failures occurred.

Since my Post Office's 3 Retail Units were some of the highest revenue Units in the District, they obviously conducted a lot of business within them daily. A lot of business meant a great potential for WTIL failures. I tasked my Retail Supervisors with making observations of our clerks who worked the windows in our Retail Units, to make sure they were asking all the right questions and doing all the things that would make a Mystery Shop a successful one. The clerks, of course, would do all the right things when they knew they were being observed. I recognized that there was a need to conduct covert shops within the Retail Units, to see if the clerks were really doing what they needed to do.

A covert shop would mean that I would need an individual from Management to come in and do what a Mystery Shopper would do, bringing a package in to mail. I contacted a few of my neighboring offices to put reciprocal shops into motion. The Retail Unit clerks at our different locations within our cities would not recognize Management from another Post Office. It seemed like a good plan until I spoke with someone from our Labor Department. I was advised that discipline could not be issued for a Mystery Shop failure, even if it was not an official Mystery Shop. That was some agreement that had been made with the clerk's union. Nice. My job could be threatened, and discipline could be threatened to me for a failure, but I could not hold the workers accountable for their direct parts they played in these shops.

Automated Postal Centers (APCs, in the SALES Chapter of this book) were placed in the vicinity, if not directly within Postal Retail Units. Those machines enabled customers to use them to buy stamps, and to purchase postage for packages they were mailing. I occasionally spent time in my lobby, especially if there was a long WTIL, directing customers with packages to one of the two APCs that were in my outer lobby. As I shared earlier, I would occasionally go to my Post Office on Sundays for a few hours. There would sometimes be a line in my Retail Lobby, especially since we were the only Post Office with Sunday Retail hours for miles around. I would go into Customer Service mode, trying to move customers out to one of our APCs. Even though official Mystery Shops were not conducted on Sundays, I did not want customers getting frustrated waiting in line.

Eva was a female who I promoted to a Supervisor position at my Post Office, filling a vacancy that had been in existence for several months. I only had a few applicants to pick from, since my large Post Office was not a popular pick for applicants, due to the presumed workload and responsibilities that would come with the job. Eva had worked previously in a clerk assignment and had no experience working as a 204B. When I informed her that she would be supervising my Retail Unit after promoting her, she was noticeably upset about that.

We had not discussed exactly what she was going to be doing during her interview, and I was placing her where I needed her. She told me that she didn't know anything about Retail Units, and that she had hoped to have administrative duties assigned to her. I explained to her that she was going where I needed her, assuring her that I would provide the training she would need to do the job. I did have another individual working as my Retail Supervisor, but I needed to move her to supervising a Delivery Unit as soon as possible due to vacancies there.

I was able to arrange for someone from my District who was knowledgeable of Retail to come to my office to work with Eva. I also scheduled her for different existing training classes that involved Retail Operations. This process continued for a much longer time than I would have liked, as Eva's reluctance to take on this new responsibility was obvious. After a few months of this, with my having her gradually take away more and more of the duties from the other Supervisor working in the Retail Unit, the time finally came for me to let her go on her own there. She still had the District employee who had been helping her available to contact, if she ran into trouble or had questions. She was officially in her new position for more than a few months when the nightmare occurred. Postal Inspectors.

A team of Inspectors arrived at my Post Office unexpectedly one morning. I did not receive any advance notification of their arrival. They don't like to give any warning. As I write this, I will not recall a lot of specifics about the problems that they found while they conducted their audit. But it was bad. When they finished their audit, several days after they started, I was informed that I had to go to my District Manager's office for a meeting.

I arrived there and found that the District Manager, our District's Finance Manager, my MPOO and a few of the Postal Inspectors who had conducted the audit were there. It was fun times as they handed out copies of their findings to all of us who were in attendance. Point by point they went through the problems they found with our Money Orders, Stamp Stock on hand and other issues. I was given the responsibility of writing up an Action Plan, addressing how each of those items would be corrected, by whom and by what date.

Early the next morning, my District Manager Paul walked into my office and closed the door behind him. He had made it past my staff, who all knew they were to call me if any higher up was in the building. He pointedly told me that he had considered pulling me out of my Postmaster position there and putting me into a smaller Post Office. He said that he expected his Postmasters to thoroughly know every operation within their offices. But he was going to give me the chance to get it together and correct all the deficiencies that had been found by the Postal Inspection Team. One of the frustrating things for me was that many of the problems that had been discovered had been in place prior to my appointment as Postmaster there. My predecessor would not be held accountable for those items. The audit occurred on my watch, so tag. I was it.

Lower level Postmasters work closely with their Retail Operations. I had never served in a lower level Postmaster position. My first Postmaster position was as a level 21. In that size office, a Supervisor oversees Retail Operations. Because it was not necessary for me to run the day to day operations within my Retail Units, I did not dig too deeply into things there, especially if there were no apparent problems there. As I often told acquaintances when they asked me about any operation that I had not personally worked or had more than a rudimentary understanding of, "That's what I have peeps for." I certainly was not going to say that to Paul.

I wrote up the Action Plan in short order, sending it to the individuals on a list I was given. And just when you think the worst is over, not quite. Eva, who I had informed of all that had been found by the Inspection Team, sent an email message to my MPOO, District Manager Paul and our District's Finance Manager. She shared that she was in a supervisory position that she did not really want to be in, that she had expected to be given other responsibilities. She further went on to say that she had never worked Retail Operations, and that she had received only a small amount of training prior to being placed in that position. I can only assume that she thought that she was being blamed for the problems that had been found, fearing that she might receive discipline and wanting to cover her butt. I had no intention of disciplining her over what had occurred. I knew that the problems had been in place long before her arrival there, and I shared that with her. I only wanted them to be corrected.

Fortunately for me, the employee from the District who had spent countless hours working with her and training her backed me up. Eva's email message was dismissed as untrustworthy by my bosses. The Finance Manager did contract a retired Postmaster who I knew to come into my office and further assist Eva in her training, since she obviously still felt uncertain about her job. The payment for that contracting came out of my Post Office's budget, of course. It was worth it to me to get things on track, to where they hadn't been for several years. But the troubles with Eva were not over quite yet.

Eva's office was located directly next to all my Retail Windows at my Main Post Office. Prior to her taking over responsibility for the Retail Units, I had a counter installed on the wall directly over the Retail Supervisor's desk. The counter showed a digital display of how many customers were waiting in line at any given time. That information was obtained through tickets that were obtained by customers when they arrived in the Retail lobby. On more than a few occasions, I would walk through Eva's office and point up at the number of customers who were waiting. She liked to spend too much time on her computer, not bothering to glance up to see how many customers were waiting. It was my expectation that if the number was more than double the number of clerks who were working at the Window Units, she would go out into the lobby and try to get customers to use one of the APCs in the outer lobby.

One day when I was returning from lunch, I walked through my Retail Lobby to go to my office. The line of waiting customers was huge. Eva happened to be off that day, so I immediately began to work through the line, trying to draw customers away to the APCs. I had one of my employees page my Manager, Tom to come to the lobby. I had him assist me in trying to clear some customers out of the line and told him to continue to catch customers who were arriving to try to steer them to the APCs. Eventually, things got under control. But, unfortunately, the damage had been done. Two days later, I received a Mystery Shop report with a horrible WTIL. As I reviewed the report, I noted that the Mystery Shopper was in line that same day that I had found the long line when returning from lunch.

I ended up having to be on a nasty telecon, along with my MPOO. The Manager who was running the telecon did his usual chastisement, peppered with threats and humiliation directed at me for such an abysmal WTIL. I made a point of talking to Eva and Tom in my office about what had occurred. As my Operations Manager, Tom was directly over Eva, and I told them both that I expected much greater attention to be placed on the WTIL. I told Eva that she had better be looking at that customer count and reacting quickly when things were getting out of hand. I expected that she would follow my instructions, but she didn't.

A few days after my talk with her, Tom walked into her office and saw a much too large number of waiting customers on the display. She was sitting at her computer, as usual, oblivious to what was happening in the Retail Lobby. He instructed her to get into the lobby, then came and told me what had happened. We agreed that he was going to have to give her a Letter of Warning for Failure to Follow Instructions. Tom told Eva that he was going to need to give her a pre-disciplinary interview. She told Tom that she was going to want to have someone there from the National Association of Postal Supervisors (NAPS) to represent her at the meeting. She was entitled to make such a request, so her interview was delayed. The next day she called in sick, and I never saw her again.

Eva had her physician fax me FMLA documentation, stating that she was unable to come to work due to stress caused by her job. I had to pull another Supervisor out of another operation to fill in for her, not knowing when she would return. As time went by, I did my customary mailing of notifications to her about her FMLA entitlement running out, wanting to know when she would be returning to work. Eva ended up getting a Disability Retirement, ending her career with the Postal Service.

I did receive notice of her parting shot she took at me, filing a complaint alleging that I had discriminated against her due to her being a female and her Indian heritage. She did file her complaint late, just as her former employee, John had done. She failed to follow up on pursuing the complaint, and that was the last I heard from her.

I decided that I was not going to risk any other Supervisors ignoring that customer count over their head on the digital display. I moved the Supervisor desk and computer out of the adjoining office and placed them directly out in the retail lobby. That required moving some things around to accommodate the Supervisor's new work location, but the desired results were achieved. The Supervisor desk was positioned in a way that had the individual directly facing the line of waiting customers. Pretty hard to ignore that.

In one unique situation, George, one of my African American carriers filed a discrimination complaint against me and a Redress meeting was set up. I was caught completely off guard about the circumstances involving his complaint. His immediate Supervisor was out of the office serving in Iraq, and I had no way to contact him to hear his side of the story. While we were in our Redress meeting, I had timekeeping reports pulled to consider the accuracy of what the complainant, George was telling me in our meeting. I was able to conclude that he had not been paid for a day of work due to an error by his Supervisor. I accepted the responsibility for that error and agreed to pay George for the day that he was missing.

A few months later, George's immediate Supervisor returned to duty from his Iraq tour. Soon after, his Supervisor issued discipline to him due to his irregular attendance. Once again, a discrimination complaint was filed against me and a Redress meeting was scheduled. We all met in my conference room, as usual, to begin our Redress meeting. I had to provide coverage for George's route due to his participation in this meeting. These meetings could last up to 3 hours, to allow each side to present their side of the story. It was not uncommon for the non-Postal mediator to have one or the other side leave the room to have a private caucus with one of us. The mediators assigned to each Redress meeting were very thorough in making certain that each party had completely exhausted any and every effort towards resolving the matter on the table. I was all too familiar with how the process worked, and often would greet the mediator who would arrive at my office and found that it was someone who had previously served in a mediator capacity for a Redress meeting in a past discrimination case that had been filed against me.

I always agreed to let the complainant be the first to present their side of the story, an elaborative effort that could sometimes last a great deal of time. It was not uncommon that the hostility that an individual personally felt towards me would manifest itself as they presented their case with great gusto. I would inwardly chuckle to myself, maintaining my outward business-like, concerned composure as the complainant spoke. Almost without fail, the complainants would speak directly to the mediator, to get the mediator to side with them and agree with them that they had truly been discriminated against. They missed the whole point that the mediator was just that, a mediator. I was the decision maker who they needed to talk to for the consideration of getting what they wanted. The mediator had no role whatsoever other than remaining unbiased and facilitating the conversation between us.

In this case involving my African American carrier George, he shared with the mediator that over the years he had called in sick to work without any problem from management just one day each month on average. He was just doing what he had been doing for years, and now he was getting in trouble for it. He told the mediator that he was being discriminated against, his focus remaining on the mediator rather than me. I explained to George that I had shared with his union representatives that I was tightening the policy on unscheduled absences for all the employees, regardless of their color, sex or creed. I told him that calling in sick once a month was unacceptable. I explained to George that every time an employee calls in sick to work, it usually ends up resulting in overtime being paid to other employees to do the work that needed to be done in that employee's absence. It also meant that the service to our customers on his route was going to be delayed, because the other carriers would have to service the customers on their own routes before going to do their overtime delivering a portion of his route.

I had George's attendance records in front of me as I was talking to him in our Redress meeting. I pointed out that he had a pattern of calling in sick either before or after scheduled days off, and that looked very suspicious to me. I knew that many employees had a pattern of doing this same thing, calling in before or after scheduled days off or before or after scheduled vacation days off. They felt that it was their sick leave to use however they wished to use it. As a steward for the Postal Service, I firmly believed that one of my responsibilities was to break that mindset of sick leave being just another "entitlement" that employees could use as they liked. Attendance was a pet peeve of mine that I focused on in every position I held in management throughout my career. Thinking back on the positions I held in management, attendance control was an issue that was handled in a relatively lax manner in virtually every position I held prior to my arrival. Employees who abused their sick leave were always caught off guard after I took over the helm of a facility, and many were shocked and angry at me for expecting them to show up to work regularly and to be on time.

George interrupted me often as I explained my position to him in that Redress meeting. This was a common occurrence in such meetings. The complainants usually did not want to accept my position, and they would vehemently disagree with me as I spoke, directing their consternation at the mediator. I would sit quietly and take notes of what the complainant had to say, waiting my turn to talk when they finished with their statements. I was caught completely off guard in this meeting when George produced a copy of a check he had received for $500. It was a Postal Service check, and he claimed that he had received it as a settlement for a prior discrimination case he had filed against me. He showed it to the mediator, trying to validate that his discrimination complaints he had filed against me were legitimate. Why would he have received a settlement check if they weren't valid complaints?

The mediator was as surprised as I was since I had no knowledge of who had issued the check. I asked George if I could make a copy of the check. He agreed, and I did so. I told him that I was unaware that such a check had been issued, asking him who had informed him that he would be receiving it.

He did not give me a straight answer to that question. He simply stuck to his narrative that I should drop the current discipline against him, or he would just be getting another settlement check. The meeting ended without a resolution. As quickly as that meeting ended, I was contacting Dick, the manager I reported to, on the phone.

I explained what had happened in the Redress meeting to Dick. He was as surprised as I was that a settlement check had been issued to George. This was completely outside of normal procedures in discrimination cases. I further shared with him that I had become aware of the fact that George was sharing his story about having received a settlement check with other employees in my office. The last thing we needed was employees to be encouraged to file discrimination charges against me. Dick told me that he was going to make some calls to try to get to the heart of the matter.

Dick shared the details of this case with Paul, our District Manager who he reported to. Paul spoke to his Human Resource manager, finding out that he was as in the dark about this as the rest of us were. The settlement must have come from our Area office, since none of the District staff were aware of it. We, or at least I never did get an answer as to who had given George the $500 check. Our Area office did not provide any information about where the check had originated, or it is possible that such information simply was not shared with me. As usual, George did not pursue filing a formal EEO complaint against me following our Redress meeting.

I received a call from my District's Human Resources Manager one day. He wanted to talk to be about an anonymous tip that had been turned in to the Postal Inspection Service. One of my employees was alleging that my Acting Customer Service Manager was involved in a romantic relationship with one of my Supervisors. The Postal Service does more than frown upon romantic relationships between its Managers and their subordinates. Ron was one of the individuals referenced in the Inspection Service inquiry. The other individual was one of my Supervisors, Marie. I had hired Marie as a transfer from another large office in my District. It was not a promotion for her, but my Post Office was closer to her home and she was a single mother. I spoke with the Postmaster she was reporting to before selecting her, and I received very favorable comments about her. Marie was performing well for me and achieving good productivity numbers in her carrier unit. The only shortcoming that I observed was that she had a penchant for becoming too attached to her subordinates. In my opinion, it was always a good practice for a Supervisor to maintain a certain amount of distance between themselves and the employees who reported to them. Marie's friendship with some of her carriers sometimes tended to cloud her judgment.

Ron was the Supervisors' peer normally but, in his position as Acting Customer Services Manager, the other Supervisors reported to him. At one meeting that I was having with my staff, I was sharing my disappointment over low productivity numbers we had experienced lately. Marie's Carrier Unit had suffered the greatest productivity loss, which was more than likely due to her not being firm enough with her carriers. Ron began to verbally chastise her, and it wasn't long before she started crying. He didn't back off though. He wanted to make sure she understood the seriousness of the situation.

I recalled that event as I brought Ron and Marie both to my office separately, to investigate about the alleged romantic relationship between them. I brought them in to my office in rapid succession. I didn't want them to have a chance to talk about this with each other. They both told me that each had sons who played football. They would sit together at the games, but there was nothing going on between them. I reported back to the Human Resources Manager that the allegations were false, that both employees denied that a romantic relationship existed, and I never heard about it again from the District.

Cheryl was an African American female carrier who worked at that same Post Office. It is important to stipulate her race and sex because Cheryl filed a few different discrimination charges against me over the years. Cheryl and several other African American employees at the Post Office did not like me. Many of them were working at that office when I was a Supervisor there, and they certainly did not like the fact that I was coming back as the Postmaster. They remembered how emphatic I was about corrective action as a Supervisor, and they were correct in assuming that I hadn't changed in that regard. Skin color and the sex of an employee didn't matter to me, as I attested to in many affidavits involving discrimination charges filed against me. If the situation with an employee called for it, I recommended corrective action or issued it myself if one of my immediate subordinates was involved.

At one point, Ron told me about a situation that had occurred the previous day when he was leaving work. There was a row of marked, reserved parking spots just outside of the facility for my staff and myself. Ron was in his vehicle getting ready to back out of his spot when Cheryl pulled her personal vehicle up behind him, blocking him in. He told me that she was talking on her cell phone, acting like she didn't notice he was there. He honked his horn at her a few times, but she continued to ignore him. Another Supervisor who was walking to his car to leave for the day approached her, motioning at her to get out of Ron's way. She waited another minute or so before she finally drove away. As Ron and I discussed the situation, we agreed that Cheryl should be issued a Letter of Warning for her behavior. When she received her Letter of Warning, Cheryl said that she was sick and left the building.

A day or two later, we received a fax from Cheryl's physician. It said that Cheryl needed to be off due to stress caused by work, and there was no indication of how long she would need to be off. Later that week, I received a page in my office from Marie. She told me that Cheryl was out on the workroom floor, not in her uniform and not prepared to work, and she was insisting on seeing me. It was early enough in the morning that all the carriers were still in the building. I paged Ron and told him to escort her out of the building. I told him to let her know that if she didn't do as she was told we would call the police. She willingly went with him to the exit, and he told her that she needed to get off the property until she was cleared to come back to work by her physician.

Over the years, the Postal Service had too many violence in the workplace situations that occurred. Some of them resulted in fatalities. Primarily because of that, if an employee needed to be absent from work due any nervous or mental condition, they could not return to work without appropriate documentation from their physician. The documentation from their physician needed to specifically state that the employee would not be of any danger to themselves or others.

I was not going to take any chances with Cheryl. I did not know what she could do, and I needed to get her away from all the other employees. When Ron paged me to tell me that she had left the building, I told him to go outside and validate that she had left the premises. He called me back a few minutes later and told me that she had been standing out in the employee parking lot, talking with another carrier who was on the clock. He again instructed her to leave the premises and he watched as she got in her car and drove away.

Minutes later, I was having a meeting with Marie when she answered a phone call that was coming in. I could hear Cheryl's voice talking very loud on the other end. She was telling Marie that she wanted to talk to me. Marie told her that we were in a meeting, and she needed to leave the premises. She was practically screaming at that point, saying that she was not going to leave until she saw me. Cheryl was calling from my

Post Office Box lobby at the front of the building, and retail customers going in and out of my office were being exposed to this. I told Marie to call the local police, and I went to my office and called the Postal Inspection Service office. The police were closer, so they arrived first. I told Ron which office to send them to while we waited on an Inspector.

After the Inspector arrived, he spoke with Cheryl before coming to my office with the police officer. They both told me that she was very upset and that she said she was being targeted. The police officer asked me if I wanted to press charges against her. I said no, that I just wanted her off the property until she was cleared to come back to work. The officer told me that I could press charges later if I changed my mind. The Inspector went back to talk to Cheryl. He was able to convince her that she needed to leave and stay off the property or she would be in serious trouble. He told her that I was not going to file charges against her at that time, but I had every right to do so if I wanted.

Cheryl returned to work with the appropriate documentation from her physician soon after that. And she received the next step of discipline, a Seven Day Suspension, for her actions during her visit while she was out on stress soon after that. And not too long after that I received the notification that she was filing another EEO discrimination charge against me. I filled out the affidavit that I received, and I had Ron and Marie's statements as evidence of what had transpired on the day in question. Cheryl was very vocal about the fact that she had filed discrimination charges against me. She would often try to engage me in bantering with her about various discrimination charges she filed against me when I passed her on the workroom floor. She candidly told me that she had spent $10,000 on a lawyer for one of her charges, and she ultimately lost all her cases against me.

I needed to officially fill the vacant Manager, Customer Services job that Ron was detailed to. That vacancy was posted once District-wide, but there were only a few applicants for the job. My MPOO advised me to repost the vacancy Area-wide. That would allow employees from surrounding states and Districts to apply as well. I was content to have Ron filling in on his detail to that job, but it needed to be permanently filled, and he advised me that he was seeking a transfer or promotion to another part of the country.

Then Marie called in to report that she would not be coming to work. She faxed over documentation that stated she had a high-risk pregnancy that would require her to stay at home. I found out that her due date was several months away, so I knew she would not be returning to work for quite some time. Typically, when a Postal employee is pregnant, they attempt to work as close as they can to the due date. The new mother will then start her 12 weeks of FMLA. Marie was going to be using up her FMLA entitlement long before her child was even born. That would not be a problem for her as far as her employment was concerned. Though many might have challenged this, I did have a heart. It would mean that I would expect regular submission of documentation from her physician, to keep me apprised of her status.

I spoke with Ron about the situation with Marie. Fortunately, we had enough 204B's who were willing to step in when needed, and this would be a long-term detail for one of them. I mentioned to Ron that Marie's FMLA hours would be expiring in 12 weeks and he seemed surprised. He asked me if she had told me that she didn't want her FMLA to start until the baby was born. I told him that she hadn't talked to me about it, but that decision was not hers. The reason for her absence and inability to work qualified for FMLA, and that was how I was recording the time off. I told him to let me know if he heard any update from her.

There were only a few applications received for the job Ron was filling. I was able to conduct the interviews personally, without having to have a Review Committee put into place to conduct interviews. Unfortunately, my MPOO Gary apparently did not have enough faith in my judgement to conduct the interviews by myself. Gary was out on a detail to the District office at that time, and the MPOO he shared an office with was to conduct the interviews with me.

Greg was the level 23 MPOO who shared an office with Gary. While Gary was gone on his District detail, Greg was overseeing both his own and Gary's groups of Post Offices. On strictly an ego level, it annoyed me that a level 23 employee would be conducting interviews with me, a level 24 Postmaster, to make sure I didn't screw things up and select the wrong person. I had hoped that Gary, who had selected me for my level 24 Postmaster job, would have had more faith in me than that. As it turned out, both Greg and I were deceived about the selection that was made.

There were only two applicants for the vacant Manager, Customer Service position. One of them was a male Supervisor who lived in the next state away from my location. My MPOO did not want to incur any travel expenses for this applicant to travel to my location, so we conducted his interview over the phone. The second applicant was a female Supervisor who was relatively close to my location and worked in our neighboring District. I had worked in that same neighboring District in my previous two Postmaster jobs, but I did not know this applicant, Maureen. Recalling how my former REC Manager had told me that nobody called him to inquire about me when I had been applying for several jobs, I had made it a practice to call the Managers or Postmasters over the applicants I was interviewing. It was simply a matter of due diligence to find out as much as possible about an applicant prior to making a decision regarding a promotion.

Official Personnel Folders were also scrutinized during this process. Those files contained everything about an individual's history with the Postal Service. They included personal information about an employee, their work history and any discipline that employee had received that was still active. Because of the privacy rights of employees, those Official Personnel Folders had to be requested from a District's Human Resource office. The way the process worked, the Official Personnel Folders were sent to me by Registered Mail, the most secure mail possible, and they could only be signed for and opened by me. They were to be kept in a secure location while I had them, and they were returned to the Human Resource office by Registered Mail when I was finished reviewing them.

I called the male applicant's Postmaster to inquire about his work history, his strengths and weaknesses. The Postmaster had nothing negative to say about his employee, but he also had nothing exceptional to share about him. The interview process consisted of both Greg and I asking the applicants five questions each. Interview questions for this type of position typically centered on operational and contractual issues. Questions about overtime, discipline, delivery and collection operations and general managerial skills were most often used. Questions would also often focus on information that was available on reports that could be accessed on any finance number in the Postal Service. The myriad of information contained in those reports included how an office was performing compared to their PLAN and SPLY (same period last year). Items included were workhours, sick leave, overtime and productivity. The male applicant stumbled on a few of the questions during his interview, and we moved on to Maureen.

I made a call to Maureen's Manager prior to her interview with Greg and I, informing him about the information my inquiries had produced. Maureen worked as a Supervisor over carriers in a branch office about 20 miles from my Post Office. I knew the Manager who was responsible for that branch from meetings we had both attended while I had worked in that District. He had nothing negative to say about her, and there was nothing negative in her Official Personnel Folder. In fact, he strongly recommended her for the position she was being interviewed for at my office. Maureen portrayed herself in a very positive way during her interview, impressing both Greg and me. She had good answers for the questions each of us asked, and we agreed that she should be promoted to fill my vacant Manager Customer Service position. It is important to point out that Maureen was biracial, African American and Caucasian. It did not take long for me to start to see what a mistake it was to promote her.

Maureen started her new job at my facility letting everyone know to call her Mo. I immediately began to see things that troubled me in the way she interacted with the employees under her. She struck me as being a hard ass. There is nothing wrong with that in and of itself, but only when it is in certain circumstances that require a bit of aggression. Even then, that aggression needs to be balanced with respect for the individual or the group you are dealing with. Mo lacked that balance, and I perceived this was going to lead to trouble. At a minimum, I was going to have to watch her closely and coach her as best I could. One of the first problems I encountered with Mo was her inability to deal with the carrier union's President in my office.

My Supervisor Ron, who had been detailed as the Acting Manager Customer Service position prior to Mo's arrival, had followed our protocol of regularly meeting with the carrier union President to discuss things that were happening. These meetings were in place to attempt to deal with potential problems that might otherwise turn into grievances being filed by the union. Ron had at this point been assigned to supervise a delivery unit. Kate, the local carrier union President in my office, came to me after her first meeting with Mo. She told me that Mo was very rude to her and was not listening to points that Kate tried to make with her about problems that were occurring.

317

Kate was ready to just have her union stewards start filing grievances after that first meeting with Mo. I asked her to give me a chance to talk with Mo and try to straighten things out. When I met with Mo to discuss that meeting, she could not hide the disdain that she felt for Kate and the unions in general. I told her that she needed to put her personal feelings aside. I told her that she had to treat Kate and other union officials in our office with dignity and respect. She needed to hear them out and find ways to work with them that would ultimately save the Postal Service a lot of management time and money.

Kate came to me again after her second meeting with Mo. She told me that she could not work with Mo. She said that the second meeting was no better than the first one. Mo talked down to her and even used foul language as she spoke to Kate. I made an on the spot decision to avoid the grievances starting to fly. I told Kate that Ron would continue to meet with her, as he had before when he was the Acting Manager Customer Service. I knew that they worked well together, and order would be restored. Before telling Ron about this, I had Mo come to my office and informed her of my decision. She was angry at this decision. She said "He reports to me. I am a higher level than he is, and I should be in these meetings." I reminded her that I was the Postmaster, and that it was my decision as to who would be my designee for any meetings in my office. I told her that I was not going to risk having a union revolt in my office due to her inability to handle herself appropriately in those meetings. She clearly had a look of disgust on her face as she left my office.

Ron scheduled and held his first meeting with Kate after I informed him that he would be my designee. After that first meeting, he came to me to tell me that Mo had insisted on attending the meeting as well. He told me that she continually interrupted both he and Kate, maintaining a very negative attitude throughout the meeting. I called Mo to my office and instructed her that she was not to attend meetings between Ron and Kate. She argued that as the Manager over them she needed to know what they were discussing. I told her to follow my instruction and that Ron would meet with us after these meetings to share pertinent information with us. I again noted the look of disgust on her face as she left my office.

One morning during this time, I arrived at work to receive a call from MPOO Greg. He informed me that the reports showed that several of our collection boxes had not been collected on the previous night. There were several checks in place to avoid such an occurrence, but a new Supervisor who I had hired failed to catch the fact that one of our collection routes had not been covered. Sharise was an African American carrier from another local Post Office who I had hired to fill a vacant Supervisor position I had at my office. She had been trained in how to perform the closeout duties at my office but missed the warnings that were visible in our reports to see that missed collection. I called Mo to my office and told her that Sharise was going to need to be disciplined formally for missing the collection. I knew that things would be rolling downhill from up above over such a potentially costly mistake as this. If Sharise was not disciplined, I could be the one receiving the discipline.

While I was waiting to hear from Mo about her dealing with Sharise, another meeting was scheduled to take place with Ron and Kate. I was in my office interviewing an employee who had applied for yet another Supervisor vacancy at my office when I received an internal call from one of my Supervisors. I interrupted the interview to answer the call from that Supervisor. She told me that Mo was at it again. She said that Ron was meeting with Kate and that Mo had barged into the room and would not leave. I told her to get Mo on the phone. Mo got on the phone with me and I calmly told her that I was not happy. I told her that my interviewing was being interrupted by her and that I had given her an instruction to stay out of those meeting between Ron and Kate. I told her that I would deal with her after I finished interviewing and told her that I was instructing her to stay out of that meeting once again. When I did finish my interviewing, I came out of my office to find that the proverbial shit had hit the fan.

Ron told me that Mo blew up after my talk with her on the phone. He said that she began yelling at him and Kate, telling them that she had a right to be in on their meetings. She took her tirade out of the meeting room and onto the workroom floor. Fortunately, it was late enough in the morning that the carriers had all left to go out on their routes. Ron and Kate ended their meeting to follow Mo out of the office where they were meeting onto the workroom floor. This was going to be entertaining. Mo went off on the Supervisors who were present and continued her rant in front of Kate. She made a comment to Ron about not being able to be a part of the boy's club, referring to my directing of Ron to continue the meetings with Kate. She shouted out that she was going to "get her half black ass out of this office." The real crossing of the line occurred with the comments she made to Sharise, as Ron relayed them to me. She looked at Sharise and shouted, "You'd better hire yourself a lawyer, because that short mother fucker up there wants to fire your ass!"

I called Sharise up to my office to listen to her validation of what had been said to her by Mo. Sharise repeated what Ron had told me verbatim. I asked her if she was willing to write a statement out sharing everything that had occurred with Mo's outbreak. She said that she would do so, and she did. I commented to her that she was going to still be facing some discipline over the missed collection. She said that she understood and acknowledged that she had screwed up. I then had everyone else that was present fill out statements about what had occurred, including the union President Kate.

I contacted the Labor Department at my District to discuss what type of discipline would be appropriate for this situation. There was discussion about whether to issue her a 14 Day Suspension or go right to a Removal Notice. Ultimately the decision was made to go with a 14 Day Suspension, primarily because Mo was a veteran. The removal of a veteran was always a more complicated proposition. Veterans had layers of discipline processing protection in place to assure that they were receiving the utmost care and attention to detail. A 14 Day Suspension document was written up and signed by me, with a concurrence signature by MPOO Greg. As I shared elsewhere, any suspension or removal document that was issued needed a concurrence signature by the next highest authority to the person who was issuing it. The 14 Day Suspension notice included the exact comment that Mo had made to Sharise, about that "short mother fucker", yes me, in case you didn't get that. I assured Greg that I had several statements from individuals who had witnessed this outbreak.

Mo was, of course, shocked to be receiving this suspension when I called her into my office for her to sign off on having received it. She angrily told me that she would be contacting her management representative who would get this discipline removed from her record. Her discipline went through the Appeals process, and it was my turn to be outraged when Greg reduced her 14 Day Suspension to a 7 Day Suspension. It was the quickest way for him to get it off his desk and get him back to playing Solitaire on his computer, a regular pastime of his. Knowing Mo as I did, I didn't suspect it would be too long before she racked up another piece of discipline. She didn't disappoint me.

But back to Marie... Time was passing rapidly, and my tracking showed that Marie had exceeded her FMLA time off for her pregnancy to a degree that I had to do something. I started the long process of sending her official letters from me, letting her know that her FMLA entitlement had expired and instructing her to respond to me. Letters had to be sent by both regular mail and by Certified Mail or with Delivery Confirmation. This was a necessary process recommended by our Labor Department, to assure that every attempt had been made to reach the affected employee if charges would possibly be made in the future. I did not receive any response from Marie as I sent out several official letters.

Ron had been accepted for a transfer to a new job in another state by this point, and he had not shared anything with me prior to his departure regarding Marie. I presumed that she had not been in contact with either one of us regarding her status. I finally reached a point where I had to send out a 30-Day Notice of Removal due to her lack of response. I sent that notice out to her, by regular mail and Delivery Confirmation, and still received no response. I contacted my Labor Department after the 30 days had passed to discuss the process of officially removing Marie from the Postal Service. While the Labor Specialist I was consulting with was working on putting together information for me to remove Marie, a drawn-out process that required more than a few telephone consultations and completing the appropriate forms, Marie showed up at my office.

Unknown to me, she arrived with her baby. She made the rounds inside my Post Office to show off her new baby to the other employees there. She finally made it to my office. I had her come in and shut the door. She told me that she had just received all the letters I had sent her and that she was concerned about losing her job. Marie told me that Ron was the father of her baby and that she had been at his new job location for the past several months, unaware that her job was in jeopardy because her mail was being held. She also told me that she and Ron had gotten married.

I absorbed all the information she was telling me, calmly listening until she was finished talking. I then told her that she and Ron had both lied to me in the official investigation I had conducted in response to the inquiry about their alleged relationship. I told her that she and Ron were the witnesses to support me in the current discrimination case field against me by letter carrier Cheryl. They had both signed affidavits confirming that their statements were true and accurate over what had occurred with Cheryl. I asked her what she thought might happen when Cheryl's lawyer found out that my two star witnesses supporting me in her discrimination case had lied on an official investigation that I conducted with them. She gave me a blank stare and did not respond.

Against my better judgment, I told Marie that I would allow her to return to work and drop the Removal that was in process against her. I reduced the Removal to a suspension, feeling it necessary to have something to build on if she were to violate my trust again in the future. She told me that she would be seeking a transfer to an office by Ron so she could be with him and her son who had moved there with Ron. I assured her that I would agree to a transfer, if it was requested from a Postmaster in Ron's area. I had no desire to keep her family separated. As weeks passed, I only received one email message of inquiry about a transfer for Marie. I positively responded to that message, but the sender did not pursue any further correspondence with me to finalize a transfer. Marie would occasionally come to my office, stressing a concern about wanting to transfer. I told her that I needed a request from someone desiring her transfer there before I could do anything. It was out of my hands.

Eventually I received a call from Dick, the manager over me. He informed me that he had received a call from his boss, the District Manager about Marie. The District Manager reported to our Area Vice President, and he had received a call from his boss about Marie. I learned that Marie's father was retired from the Postal Inspection Service and he had a friendship with the Area Vice President. The message that filtered down to me from the Area Vice President was that a transfer had been arranged for Marie to a Post Office in her husband's area, and I was not to interfere with it in any way. I was given an effective date for when that transfer would occur, and it was only a week away. I attempted to relay my concerns to Dick regarding what was happening in this string of events that was not following the customary chain of command.

I relayed to him the details about how Marie and Ron had both lied to me in the official investigation I had conducted in response to the Inspection Service's official inquiry about their alleged relationship. I relayed to him the impact that could possibly have on the discrimination charge that had been field against me and the Postal Service, and how that could ultimately result in a Federal Judge's decision to give carrier Cheryl a large monetary award. My Manager Dick advised me to let it go and not to worry about it. I told him that I was concerned that the Area Vice President did not know all the details about what had happened, and that I was being inaccurately characterized as someone who was preventing her from being united with her family. Dick again told me to just let it go. I made one final attempt to get him to understand my point of view. I said "Perhaps you are content in your current position and do not aspire to move further up the corporate ladder, but I am not. I intend to continue to apply for higher positions, no matter where I may have to go in the country to obtain them. I am hoping to reach executive status in the future. Our Area Vice President having misinformation about me and my character could be an impediment to me in my future endeavors." He again told me to let it go and I did. No choice in the matter.

Marie transferred out of my office at the appointed time, and within a few weeks I was notified that she was filing discrimination charges against me. Why not? She was seeking her relocation expenses paid by the Postal Service and monetary damages due to my alleged discrimination against her due to her sex differing from mine. I had to fill out the usual affidavit in response to her charge, but I never heard anything further beyond that. She either dropped her complaint charge, or someone above me gave her a monetary settlement without my knowledge. Since several individuals in the chain of command above me had made decisions affecting her transfer, I did not consider it beyond the realm of possibility that a settlement may have been doled out without my input.

And back to Mo... One of the Rural Carriers at my Post Office had been performing his recording of the mail volume he received incorrectly. It appeared that he had been doing so intentionally. Mo had this carrier accompany her to a private office. She began to grill him about his volume recording methods in her unique, nasty way. The carrier told her that he wanted to have his union representative present during that interview. Mo told him that she was not going to allow his representative to be present. She then went on to threaten that she was going to fire him. Denying an employee union representation coupled with threatening to fire him was a severe breach of protocol. When the carrier's union steward became aware of what had occurred, she came to my office advising me that she was filing a grievance over this and told me that Mo had to go. I did obviously agree with the steward, but such things took time. I asked her to assist me in getting a statement from the carrier about what had transpired behind the closed door, and she did.

In another incident. I was approached by one of my clerks and informed about comments that Mo had made to a customer. Mo was called up to our reception desk at the request of the customer. She had been getting a passport processed, and she was unhappy about the way the African American clerk was treating her. The clerk who was also present and told me about the incident was Caucasian. According to the Caucasian clerk, the African American clerk was overheard talking to the customer in a demeaning way. The customer said that she wanted to speak with a Manager, and Mo was called up to the area. The customer told Mo that she felt the African American clerk was prejudiced by the way she was being treated. Mo managed to calm the customer down and the customer left. Mo looked at both clerks and made a few disparaging comments about the customer. She closed by matter-of-factly stating "A lot of people are prejudiced. Hell, I'm prejudiced!"

I found that I had two camps forming in my office. There were those relatively few who supported Mo, and the majority who wanted her gone. Most of the Supervisors wanted her gone. My African American male Supervisor who had recently returned from a year serving in the military in Iraq came to my office one day. He requested to have a private meeting with me. I invited him in and told him to close the door. He told me that he had been invited to go have lunch with Mo and Vanessa, another African American female Supervisor. Vanessa was clearly in the Mo camp, and I will be sharing more about her as we move further along in this story.

He met them at a local restaurant. He told me that they started tag teaming him soon after they sat down. They asked him why he was issuing discipline to African American carriers. He said that he told them he was issuing discipline to employees who deserved it, regardless of their skin color. They pressed him again about why he wasn't going after more whites and leaving the African Americans alone. He said that he told them that it wasn't his fault that the African American employees deserved more discipline than most of his white employees. I thanked him for relaying this information to me and thanked him for doing his job the way it should be done.

I had to intervene in several situations involving carriers and the way Mo was speaking to them. Her gruff way of communicating gave the carrier's union stewards enough grounds to file grievances stating that those affected carriers were being harassed by Mo. The grievances stated that those employees were not being treated with the dignity and respect that every employee was entitled to. I knew that Mo was trying to get results. She was targeting employees who were not performing up to expectations. That was her job, but she was not going about it in the correct way. She was going well beyond the fine line of giving appropriate attention and harassing. There were other instances where Mo crossed lines, but the situation with denying the Rural Carrier his right to representation was the highlight point of the 14 Day Suspension that I issued to Mo soon after that occurred. Of course, she was outraged as usual. She verbalized her opinion that I was out to fire her to me. I told her that I was just doing my job.

The next day she called in sick, telling me that a back injury she had received while working at her previous Postal job was flaring up. I called my Postal Inspection Service contact who had covertly observed allegedly injured on duty employees for me in the past. I apprised him of this situation, and he told me that he would be making his observations. He contacted me a few times, telling me what he had observed and filmed. She was taking her garbage out, carrying full bags out to her garbage container. She was going out shopping, carrying in full bags of groceries and other items into her house. He was in a van parked relatively close to her home making these observations. My Inspector friend called me one morning to advise me that he was going to have to cease his observations. He told me that Mo walked out of her house, approached his van and began to wave at the person she could not see inside. She had caught him, or at least had enough suspicion that he was watching her to render further observations useless.

The next day Mo faxed me documentation from her physician that said she would be able to return to work for only 2 hours per day. I did not want her coming back to my main office, where she could continue to stir up problems with the bulk of my employees at that facility. I called her and told her to report to a separate location under my jurisdiction. There were only a few dozen employees there, so I presumed that she could cause less damage there during her two hours of work. She was outraged by this, telling me that her job was to manage things

327

at my main office. I told her that her job was to go where I instructed her to go and work. She showed up there the next day for the schedule I gave her of 11 a.m. to 1 p.m., another point of disagreement between us. I really did not want to see her at all, but I did have to go to that location a few times to take care of business there. I asked my Supervisor at that location to let me know what she was doing. He told me that she would just sit at a desk, typing on the computer that he needed to get his work done for two hours, eating chips and drinking soda.

The matter of Mo's most recent discipline I had issued to her was still lingering. The process for dealing with that had been put on hold due to her absence from work. Mo called me to request that a date and time be set up for me to meet with her and a representative. I set the date and time and advised her that it would take place at her present work location. We met and I sat and listened to her representative lecture me about how that discipline she had been issued was punitive and unwarranted. Her representative echoed what Mo had told me, that I was out to get her fired and that was all that was motivating me. I responded in writing within the time limits defined for such responses, advising them that I was not going to withdraw the discipline. Then came the discrimination charge.

I received notification that Mo had filed a discrimination complaint against me, alleging that the disciplinary action I had taken against her was due to her being African American and a female. I had to fill out an all too familiar affidavit, swearing that the action I had taken against Mo by issuing her discipline was solely merit based, having nothing to do with her race or sex.

Mo continued to report to work in her two-hour schedule for a while, then I received a big, welcome surprise. I received notification that she had resigned from the Postal Service. I waited with bated breath to find out what was behind this maneuver. I was certain that her EEO complaint against me was still going forward, but I did not believe that she would simply throw in the towel and resign out of the blue.

I contacted my District Human Resource department to ask some questions. I found out that an employee could resign while they were in the process of seeking a disability retirement. I soon found out that this was the road she was travelling. Retirements are handled through the Office of Personnel Management (OPM) for all government and Postal employees. Since I was the Manager whom Mo reported to, the OPM sent me a packet requesting information about her. One of the main questions that caught my attention was regarding any discipline pending against the retiring employee. I had a lot to say about that one. I made copies of her discipline, time records and a host of other information and sent it off to the OPM. Soon after, the rug got pulled out from underneath me.

My District's Human Resource Manager called me, asking me questions about what I had submitted to OPM about Mo. I shared a summary with him about what I had sent under my signature. He told me to resubmit the paperwork, indicating that there was not to be any disciplinary action in my report. He told me that he wanted her disability retirement to go into effect, to get her off the Postal Service's employment rolls. I attempted to convey my disagreement with him, telling him that I had already honestly answered the questions asked of me and submitted the paperwork I had received. He insisted that I do as he asked of me in a threatening manner, and I reluctantly agreed.

Sometime after that disappointing call, I received another disappointing call from the Human Resource Manager. This time he had a Postal Service attorney on the line as well. He said that he had received a settlement offer from Mo's attorney for the EEO case she had filed against me. The Human Resource

Manager asked the attorney, who was familiar with the case, what he thought the chances were for her to win the case. The attorney gave a somber guess that the odds were 50-50. I held back my outrage when I heard the attorney's assessment.

Obviously, I felt that I had done nothing wrong. The attorney felt that a judge might see things otherwise. The cost of taking a case like this in front of a federal judge, and the potential award that might be given to Mo could be quite costly to the Postal Service.

As I reflect on that instant experience, it seemed like time literally stood still as a cascade of thoughts and considerations went through my head. I was a Postal Service employee who always put the company first. I knew that other Management individuals might put their own ambitions, their boss' desires, their office's numbers or any other number of other considerations first, but I was a true company man. The Manager who had passed Mo along to me without advising me of her major attitudes obviously was thinking of his own best interests. I thought about the interview I had in my past where I was asked by the questioner if I would do something unethical, or even illegal if they asked me to. My initial response of, with a smirk, "I know you would never do that", was not accepted. I do not actually remember what answer I gave at that time, but I think I said that I would do as asked. I wanted that job, but ultimately did not get it. I was younger and less experienced at that time in my career. I thought back to that question as my career moved along. If I were asked that question again, I would answer no to anything illegal. If it were unethical, I would have to weigh the situation against my own ethical boundaries, bearing my loyalty to the company in mind, before giving an answer.

Back to that phone call, the Human Resource Manager said that Mo's attorney would take $11,000 to make the case go away. Terms of the agreement would also stipulate that Mo would not seek employment back in the Postal Service at any point in the future. At that point, I felt compelled to chirp in and ask, "Do we offer them something less, like $5,000?" I knew that whatever money Jo received would be coming out of my finance number, charged against my office, affecting my planned expenditures. My question was summarily dismissed, and I was invited to leave the conversation. I had learned long ago that bantering didn't often occur in such matters. The path of least resistance was the one usually taken.

As the Mo saga had developed and played out, I could not help but think about her former Manager who had given me such a glowing report about her. I spoke with another Postmaster in his area and was told "You should have called me! I would have told you that she was trouble!" I told her that I had made the mistake of trusting that her former Manager was telling me the truth. He obviously had not told me the truth and saw this as an opportunity to get rid of her. He either pulled any discipline out of her OPF that I had reviewed, or he wasn't doing his job by issuing her any discipline for her seemingly habitual flaws in the first place. I had to chalk it up as a sad learning experience. I had the ethical fortitude that would prevent me from doing such a thing, but I obviously could not trust that others shared the same ideals.

Now back to Vanessa, firmly entrenched in the Mo camp. It was brought to my attention that Vanessa was soliciting carriers to file EEO complaints against me. She had already filed her own complaint against me over the work schedule I had placed her in. She had also been issued discipline for failing to check the phone messages for days when she had been working in one of the Delivery Units. Several carriers and Supervisors shared information about her solicitations with me. I had an impromptu talk with her about doing the duties of her job, and what that did and did not include. She was not as aggressive about going after the problem employees in her unit. I attributed that to the conversation she and Mo had with her fellow Supervisor about leaving the African Americans alone. I knew that Vanessa was very obviously unhappy working for me, and I would try to figure out a way to find a win-win situation for both of us, something other than continuing to issue escalating discipline to her.

I received notification that I was to appear for a deposition at Vanessa's attorney's office in a nearby city. It would basically take me away from my work for almost the entire day to do so. I hated those EEOs! A Postal attorney showed up at Vanessa's attorney's office to sit with me during the deposition. Prior to the deposition meeting, I had spoken with the Manager of our local Mail Processing Center about a possible detail there for Vanessa. I spelled the circumstances out to him, not wanting to blindside him. He told me that he would be able to help me out.

I agreed to allow Vanessa to go out on a detail assignment to our local Mail Processing Center. The detail was open ended. It lasted for more than a year, until I left my Postmaster position to start a new assignment as a Manager at another facility in another state. It did cause me difficulties in supervisory staffing at my Post Office. Because Vanessa was technically out on an open-ended detail, I could not promote anyone to replace her. That meant I had a need for 204Bs to replace her for the duration of her absence. I felt that was a fair bargain, having her out of my facility where she could potentially feed the racial tension. With her absence, the racial tensions did subside, and she ultimately withdrew the EEO complaint she had filed against me.

At that same Post Office, I had a suspicion that one of my carriers had falsely reported an on the job injury. The injury was severe enough that she was not able to perform her duties. We were paying her to stay at home while she was unable to report to work. Not an uncommon occurrence. I was sending her official notices that required a response from her to her Post

Office Box at my facility that she had listed as her mailing address. I contacted the Inspection Service and they went to work. They planted a small, unnoticeable camera inside her Post Office Box to identify who was coming in to collect her mail. The Post Office Box section was open 24 hours a day, 7 days a week all year. The Inspector wanted to see if she was the one coming in at off hours picking up the mail. That turned out not to be the case. She had someone else coming in to pick up her mail.

The Inspectors then began to covertly observe her activities at her home. The "injuries" that she had prevented her from doing any lifting or fine manipulation, two activities that were necessary for a carrier to perform their duties. From the van that they were using to make their observations, they filmed her going to a grocery store where she was picking up full bags and placing them in her car, then carrying them into her apartment. She was also filmed carrying her child around at different locations and playing roughly with her children at the swimming pool in her apartment complex. But she could not work.

My Inspector contact informed me that the next step would be to confront the doctor who had signed off that the carrier was unable to perform her duties at work, showing him the films they had taken. The Inspector called me several days later, after having met with the doctor and showing him their film. He told me that the doctor stated that there was nothing wrong. The doctor said that the things she was doing were within her capabilities, but she could not perform the duties of her carrier job. The Inspector told me that this was not good news for this case. The doctor's word and opinion were all that mattered. He said he would go ahead and schedule the carrier to come to a meeting in the conference room at my office, where he would confront her with the film to see how she would respond. She showed up on time for that meeting. She kept her composure as she was shown the films and the Inspector sent her on her way. He came to my office and informed me that there was nothing else that could be done. Once again, I ended up leaving that office for a promotion to another office, and I don't know if she ever did return to work.

Racial tensions can tend to run very high at certain Postal facilities. I worked at 10 different Postal facilities over the course of my career. The Post Office, where I started my career in management and returned as the Postmaster, was without a doubt the office where I found the highest level of racial tension. Any and every opportunity to cry "Racist!" was taken. When Civil Rights activist Rosa Parks passed away, all federal facilities were instructed to put up their American flags at half-staff. That information was not passed along to our custodial staff, whose responsibility was to take care of our flag and its placement. Carriers and other employees at my office took notice of the position of the flag as they arrived at work. It wasn't long until I had my Supervisors telling me that the employees were upset, talking about what a racist I am for not having the flag at half-staff.

I had only been in my new Postmaster position for a few months when this was happening. At that time, Jan, the Supervisor who handled the custodian staffing duties was an African American female. It was Jan's responsibility to alert the custodians when messaging was received about the placement of our flags at our various locations. I immediately had our custodians instructed to lower our flags to half-staff. I then tracked down Jan to find out why she hadn't handled this. She told me that she hadn't received the email message about lowering the flag. It is important to note that Jan and I did not see eye to eye on a lot of issues. Being new to my job, I was in the process of making across the board changes that I felt were necessary throughout our operations, including the duties that were handled by the Supervisors. Nobody likes change, but it went beyond that with this Supervisor. She was one of a few individuals who I was surprised had been promoted to a management position when I returned as the Postmaster.

Jan did not make any attempt to hide the disdain that she felt for me when I had interactions with her. She would do the things that I instructed her to do, but her demeanor told me that she was in the same camp as many of the other African American employees at my office. I suspected that she was aware of the messaging about lowering the flag to half-staff, but that she decided to ignore it. As I looked through my own email messages, I found the message that originated from Headquarters, instructing all facilities to place their flags at half-staff. I looked through the groups of employees that this message was forwarded to, and Jan was in one of the groups that it had been forwarded to. When I confronted her about this, she continued to maintain her position that she never received the message. I let the matter drop, primarily because there was no way for me to prove that she hadn't "accidentally" deleted the message instructing offices to lower the flag.

Another individual who I was surprised had been promoted to a supervisory position was a Caucasian female named Pam. Her responsibility she had been given prior to my arrival was supervising the distribution clerks who sorted mail for the carriers. Over time, I discovered that she had an ongoing romantic relationship with another white female who she supervised. That is a no no. They both worked nights and lived together, but that needed to change. I was surprised, once again, that my predecessors had allowed this to go on. I officially notified Pam that she was going to be changing her duties to supervising the Rural Carriers in our office. That meant that she would be starting later and basically working day hours. I knew that this was going to upset her personal life, working a shift different from her significant other. I explained to her that I could not have her in a position where it could even be implied that she was giving any preferential treatment to her girlfriend. Neither of them was at all happy about this change, but at least they still had jobs, at least up to that point.

Prior to moving Pam to her new assignment, I reviewed the attendance records of her employees. I was not surprised to find that some of her clerks were getting a pass on their poor attendance. Pam had worked with many of these people as their peer prior to being promoted to her supervisory position. She obviously did not want to conduct the unpleasant business of issuing discipline to her "friends." That was all too common a position I would find Supervisors taking with their employees. I told her about my findings and warned her that I would continue to follow up on how she was handling that responsibility with her new assignment. I admonished her with my customary "You can either be part of the problem or you can be the solution. I know how to deal with the problems."

While Pam was in that new position of supervising the Rural Carriers, I arrived at the Post Office one morning and became curious about what was happening in her office. The door to her office was closed, so I presumed that she had someone in there taking care of business. I saw one of my other supervisors open the door slightly, squeeze out through the door and close it behind him. He was nervous when I asked him what was going on in there, telling me I should see for myself. I knocked on the door, not knowing what to expect. Pam opened the door, smiling at me and holding a puppy she had apparently just gotten. I like a cute little puppy as much as most people do but come on. At work!?! She told me that her new puppy was lonely, so she brought him to work. I knew that she didn't live too far from the Post Office, so I told her to bring the puppy home and get back to work. I could tell by the look on her face that she thought I was being very unreasonable, but she did as she was told.

Pam's girlfriend began to call in sick with regularity, and I had the new Supervisor that I had assigned to oversee her begin the discipline process. The girlfriend's condition worsened, and she provided documentation from her doctor that stated she was unable to work at all. It wasn't long before Pam stopped coming to work as well. She provided her own documentation that stated she was unable to work due to some other medical condition. I didn't really believe any of it, but they did have their FMLA rights and protection from being disciplined or removed. Eventually, their FMLA entitlements ran out and they provided no prognosis that showed they would be able to return to work at any point in the future. I started my customary process of sending notifications to each of them, advising them that their time had run out. I did not receive any response, which took me to the point of sending Removal Notice letters. They both ended up getting disability retirements. I was surprised years later, when I became Facebook friends with someone who was a friend of Pam. Pam sent me a Facebook friend request, which I promptly deleted. My thought was, "You and your girlfriend caused me nothing but grief. Why would I want to be friends with you now?"

I received a phone call one afternoon from a cable company worker who told me that he had witnessed an accident involving one of my carriers. I took all the information he shared with me for appropriate follow up by my staff. The caller told me that he and his associates were installing cable lines in a new delivery area on my carrier's route. He told me that they both were watching as the carrier backed out of a driveway and struck a vehicle that was parked on the opposite side of the street. The carrier didn't even get out of the vehicle to check, even though there was a very audible crashing sound when the vehicle was struck. I alerted the carrier's Supervisor and waited to hear what was going to happen next. When the Supervisor approached the carrier to discuss the situation, the carrier vehemently denied that she had been in any accident.

As part of the accident investigation, the Supervisor made a note of a dent on the bumper of the vehicle that the carrier had been driving. He measured the distance of the dent from the ground, noting that there was a red paint spot in the dent. The

Supervisor went to the scene of the accident and found that the dented side door of the vehicle was red. He measured the distance of the dent from the ground and saw that it measured the same distance as the dent on the carrier's vehicle. The evidence that the Supervisor discovered, along with written statements from the witnesses, resulted in the carrier being issued a Removal Notice for her failure to report the accident. Because she was a new employee, the Removal was upheld, and she was gone.

Annual checks of carrier's driver licenses were one of the countless items that my five Delivery Supervisors had to do. While doing those checks, my Rural Route Supervisor advised me that one of his carriers had his license suspended. His license had been suspended for a few months, and he was going out in his Postal vehicle every day that he came to work delivering mail. I could only imagine the financial harm he could have caused the Postal Service if he had gotten in an accident with no license. He was issued a suspension when this was discovered, and he was obviously told that he could not deliver the mail on his route. As I dealt with his union steward over the discipline he was issued, the steward pointed out to me that the carrier had a right, according to their contract, to have someone else drive for him while he delivered his mail. I checked it out, and the steward was correct. He would come into the office and prepare his mail for delivery, then his driver would show up to go out with him on each of his workdays.

This went on for close to a month, and I lost track of the carrier and his situation while I was busy doing other things. One of his coworkers came to my office to tell me that he was back to doing his own driving of his Postal vehicle. After chastising his Supervisor for not being aware of what was happening, I had the Supervisor wait outside of the Post Office exit to observe what was happening. Later that morning, the Supervisor came to my office to tell me that the carrier was driving his Postal vehicle out of the parking lot. There was nobody with him. He flagged the carrier down and told him that he wanted to see his driver license. The carrier admitted that he still did not have his license. The carrier was instructed to leave the vehicle and walk back into the Post Office. The Supervisor drove the vehicle back into the garage, now needing to find someone to deliver the mail that it contained.

The carrier was issued a Removal Notice, which was grieved by his union, of course. When the grievance arrived at my level to meet with the appropriate union rep, I stood firm on the Removal. The steward did their best to get me to back off to something lesser than a Removal, but I argued that someone could have been injured or killed and a Removal was necessary. My union counterpart did not feel that there was enough of a chance to get the carrier off the hook by sending the case forward for Arbitration. That would be a costly venture with slim to no chance, so the Removal was upheld, and the carrier's employment was terminated.

Another situation involving a different rural carrier in my office came to my attention when that carrier did not show up for work one morning. I found out that this middle-aged Hispanic male was in jail. There were numerous charges filed against him, all revolving around his alleged sexual abuse of a minor on his route. There were several alleged instances of the abuse, which had been occurring over some period prior to his arrest and incarceration. This was a situation that I needed to talk to my Labor Department contacts about, wanting to make sure that my handling of this had all the I's dotted and the T's crossed. I sent him an official letter, advising him that he was indefinitely suspended from his job, in a Leave Without Pay status, pending the outcome of his case.

I met with the carrier's union steward to apprise her of the situation, and she filed a grievance over my action. Although the carrier was in jail, she wanted him to be able to go back to work if he was able to make bail and was released. At one point during our meeting, I attempted to explain my position as a steward for the Postal Service with her. The fact that the alleged sexual assault of a minor had occurred with someone on his carrier route reflected poorly on the Postal Service, at a minimum. There was the potential for a lawsuit and damages against the Postal Service since he was an employee and the minor lived on his route. That didn't get me anywhere with her. The peak of my frustration occurred when I attempted to appeal to her on a moral level. If he did happen to be guilty as charged, what potential danger could he bring to other minors on his route? She didn't even blink at that question.

The carrier remained in jail for the remainder of my term as the Postmaster at that Post Office. When I moved along to my next promotion, I would continue to receive update messages from the Postal Inspector who was overseeing the situation with that carrier. The messages I received repeatedly advised me that he was still incarcerated, and that his court hearings were being extended. I don't know what ultimately happened to him, since the messaging stopped when I retired. I do hope that if he was guilty as charged, he received a nice long jail sentence, and perhaps some extra attention from his jail mates.

When trays of automated presorted flats (magazine sized items) first started arriving at my Post Office for the carriers, we had containers of them set up by the garage where their vehicles were parked. They were supposed to load those trays into hampers they were taking from their sorting cases out to their vehicles. One of the problems that occurred was the discovery of carriers who were sneaking those trays of presorted flats back to their cases. They wanted to put those flats into their cases, enabling them to comingle them with the flats they were sorting into their cases. That same sort of problem occurred earlier on when carriers started receiving presorted letters. Anyone caught doing those sneaky retrievals were automatically disciplined.

It was a needful thing to monitor the carriers during their brief time in the office each morning. My Post Office was one of many that began to receive the presorted flats. The items that needed to be sorted came to the carrier routes each morning. Between the automated letters and flats that came to the carriers in delivery order each morning, the amount of mail left that needed to be sorted into delivery order was vastly reduced. One of my Supervisors came to me to report that he had followed one of his carriers out to the street. He told me that the carrier pulled over in a parking lot and was busy moving mail around from one tray to another. He approached her to find out what she was doing, and she was not happy that he had approached her. What he found was that she was moving presorted letters and flats around to align with how she had pulled her mail out of her sorting case in the office.

Apparently, she did not like how her route had been set up for delivery, so she pulled the mail out of the established delivery order to accommodate her desired delivery order. That was wrong on several levels. First, routes were set up in a specific delivery order that needed to be maintained. Automation was in place following that established delivery pattern. Her deviation from that order resulted in time being wasted while she moved mail around in her trays. It was also necessary for management to know where to find her on her route. If there was some sort of emergency where she needed to be located, it would be difficult to locate her due to her straying from the delivery order we had on record. She did receive formal discipline for her time-wasting actions and follow up showed that she did stop that behavior.

I often spent my lunch time picking up some fast food or eating what I had brought to work with me while I drove around the city where I was working. On one occasion, I observed one of my carriers driving along the same road I was. He had a cigarette in one hand and was holding his cell phone up to his ear with his other hand. Not good. I was unable to catch up with him, so I had to contact his Supervisor back at the Post Office to go out and talk to him. If a safety infraction was observed, the employee who was at fault had to be notified immediately. I did not want to risk an accident occurring after my observation. His Supervisor found him out on his route, and he was issued discipline based on my written statement of my observations.

Being arguably the largest Post Office in my District, it was not a surprise that I had the highest number of EEO complaints filed during my last fiscal year there. Our Area office sent someone out to meet with me, to discuss all the cases and attempt to find answers. I was well prepared for her arrival. As she went down the list of individuals who alleged discrimination, I sufficiently explained each situation to her satisfaction. Several of the cases had been dropped by that point in time. I made a point of wearing and sharing with her the pin that I wore on my suit. It was something I had received for being a Diversity Award Finalist from my District's HR Department.

A Hispanic male Supervisor who I had promoted recommended me for the Diversity Award. He sat in my office with me before sending that recommendation and talked about his rationale. He knew I had all sorts of discrimination charges filed against me, and he knew that they were all very much related to discipline that had been issued to those employees. One of those employees was my Operations Manager, and another was one of my supervisors. He pointed out that I had promoted him, several African American men and women, and a woman of Indian descent. How could I possibly be the racist that many professed I was when I had such a diverse staff?

It finally became time for me to relocate, once again, to the location of my next position. I began to settle into my new and final Postal Service position as the Manager of one of the last two remaining Remote Encoding Centers (RECs) in the country. As I've shared earlier, each of those RECs processed mail for half of the country's Mail Processing Centers. I did have a very knowledgeable staff of Managers and Supervisors at my new REC home, but I didn't know them all well enough to know if I could trust what I was hearing from them. As I settled into my new job, I began to see who the best members of my staff team were, and who was dragging the REC down. I did my customary pulling of records to show me where employees stood as far as attendance and performance were concerned. I then had my first staff meeting with my management crew to give them my expectations.

It is tricky trying to have a staff meeting when you have three different shifts that the staff are working on. I scheduled the staff meetings at 8:00 PM. We had 204Bs to run the operations during our meetings, and I would often bring in some type of food and soft drinks. At that first meeting, I shared my findings from the records I pulled. I admonished each of my three Operations Managers and their Supervisors that they would need to be paying much greater attention to the employees under their responsibility. That meant they were going to be needing to start issuing discipline to those employees who were not showing up regularly to work, or who were not meeting expectations when they did show up.

I was rather surprised when I reviewed a report of the productivity speed rate of all the workers on all the shifts, sorting it by fastest to slowest keyers. I thought that there must have been some kind of glitch when I looked at the incredibly slow pace of one of the DCOs. When I brought it to the attention of the Manager of the shift where this employee worked, he nonchalantly told me that she was one of the employees who fell asleep often when she was working. That was not a good answer. It bothered me all the more when I asked him what was being done about that. Nothing. I told both him and the sleeper's immediate Supervisor that I would be expecting them to make regular observations of this employee and to take appropriate action when they found her sleeping.

When things were not moving quickly enough to my liking, I chastised the Manager and Supervisor until they finally started bringing me results. As usual, the discipline started with the Official Job Discussion. The affected DCO began to work her way up the discipline ladder as her sleeping continued. I was out on the work floor at one point along the way, making my own observations. I stood behind her and watched as she sat at her console, noting that her fingers were not moving and hence, the image on her screen was not moving to completion. I moved forward enough to notice that behind her glasses she was wearing, her eyes were closed. I tapped on the back of her chair gently, enough to jostle her awake, and went on my way. I wrote up an official statement noting my observations for her Supervisor to follow up on in the discipline process. It wasn't too long before she was being issued a Removal Notice.

While her Removal Notice was pending, the sleeper filed an EEO discrimination charge against me. She claimed that her Removal Notice was given to her because of my discriminating against her due to her being a female and that she had lupus. Of course, if she had been a male with lupus, I would never have issued her a Removal Notice. Mmmmhmmm. It always amazed me that often when an employee was being issued discipline, it had to be because I was discriminating. It couldn't have been because of their own problems with rules and regulations. I didn't even know that she had lupus as her discipline moved along. Once I became aware of it, I felt it necessary to back down. We had a meeting with her representatives from the union, and I agreed to let her come back to work on a reduced schedule, something that would be more tolerable to her and recommended by her physician. Even though I did not have any advance knowledge of her condition, it muddied the waters enough that it might have caused me difficulties through an EEO process.

Contractually, we were obligated to provide remedial training in an effort to bring DCOs up to the minimally acceptable number of keystrokes per hour. This had to be done, with the tracking and logging of training hours and testing to avoid grievance trouble with the union, if and when the discipline process was to start. This was a costly process to undergo, with non-productive hours being used by the DCOs in training and by the trainers who were working with them. The numbers moved slowly in the right direction as we plodded along, with discipline being issued as some of the DCOs continued to not meet the minimally acceptable standards for their work.

Another area of attention was given to the error rate of the DCOs. They were supposed to be regularly tested with batches of images to determine whether or not they were keying the items correctly. I found this to be yet another area where my staff was behind. Some DCOs had not been tested for months. In those cases, it was largely because the DCO that they were attempting to test was not being regular enough in attendance to catch them. Union representatives would also be missed regularly because they were spending too much time taking care of union business, when they were showing up to work. There were a countless number of rules in place for how mail items were to be keyed, and the employees were responsible for knowing how to do their jobs correctly. Training, counseling and other efforts were made to correct those employees who had unacceptable error rates. When all else failed, discipline was used, up to and including Removal Notices being issued.

There were a large number of employees at that REC who had FMLA conditions, something I was always suspicious about. It was just too easy for a documented "condition" to enable an employee to randomly be able to take days off work without any repercussions. The local union president at the REC, in addition to all the union stewards, each had FMLA conditions of various kinds. A documented FMLA condition enabled an employee to be able to take up to 480 hours off work per year.

That's 12 weeks without repercussions of any kind. They could use whatever kind of leave they had available or take the time off in a Leave Without Pay (LWOP) status. Many of the employees who took time off due to FMLA conditions did not have any leave balance available. Their sick leave was used as fast as they earned it, and they often took the time off in a LWOP status. I often wondered how anyone could take so much time off without getting any pay. It was sometimes difficult getting an employee's request for time with their union steward fulfilled when the stewards were out of work due to their FMLA condition.

As I investigated the FMLA use at the REC, I incorporated a process that I had used when I was in previous positions. I tasked one of my staff to provide me with regular updates on the number of FMLA hours used by each employee throughout the year. I knew that my staff was lax on attendance to begin with, so I was not surprised to find that they were allowing employees to go well beyond the 480 hours of their entitlement. When I began to regularly review the reports, I tasked my Operations Managers with counseling their employees, some of whom would be running out of their 480 hours before half of the year was gone. Attendance discipline was being issued more frequently, and my staff was busy dealing with the grievances being filed over attendance. Attendance was one of the many things that I compared on a weekly basis between our REC and the other REC that was still open. I was determined to keep my REC open as the last one standing, no matter whose butts were kicked along the way to show more favorable results.

I was made aware of a rumor that was going around the REC that 2 of my female DCOs were working at another job when they called in to work due to their FMLA conditions. I checked the records to find that yes, when one called in the other typically did as well. I heard that they were working at a local sport stadium, where baseball games were played, and concert events took place. The rumor was that they were selling tickets there. I grabbed my camera when they next called in and headed to the stadium. My plan was to take a picture of them if I found them working there, while they were taking time away from their DCO jobs. I glanced into several windows where tickets were being sold, but I did not see either of them working there. Just rumor drama, but I did like to follow up on things that could be true.

While serving in my last managerial position, I received a fateful phone call from my boss one day. He first asked me if anyone was in my office with me. I told him that I was alone. He then asked me if we were on a secure, private line that nobody could listen in on. I told him that we were. He finally got to the point of his call, advising me to keep that secret once again. He told me that my facility was being scheduled to close down, and he instructed me to not share that information with anyone. As instructed, I met with him and our Headquarters REC liaison at a nearby hotel where they were staying. They advised me that the local union officials had been notified about the impending closure, and that meetings were being scheduled at my REC to advise all the employees about the decision.

I was present at each of the meetings that took place, and the range of emotions that were seen from my view ran the gamut of anger to tears. I knew that I would not be able to expect much from my Manager as far as my own future beyond the REC. I made the decision to retire, contacting the appropriate HR staff to get the details of what that would entail. Because I had remained a Civil Service employee, turning down the offer to switch to the Federal Employee Retirements System years earlier, I did receive some additional benefits. All my years of being attentive to sick leave use, including my own, enabled me to receive almost 2 years of service time added to my years of service. Unused sick leave was converted to years of service, a benefit of remaining under the Civil Service umbrella.

This takes us to the end of the stories, the end of this book. I will end with this tidbit. After retiring, I logged into the gas reward program website and found there were only a few employees still using the alternate ID I had set up for fuel purchases. The majority probably stopped using it because there weren't any rewards (gift cards) being given out to employees. The point balance was very high. I had to contact someone still employed with the Postal Service to get the phone number of an executive I knew at an Area Office. I called the executive who had assisted me with my Priority training film. I told him about the points that could be redeemed for a whole lot of gift cards, asking his advice on what to do. He said that he would have to check into it and call me back.

I never heard back from him. Because the number of points necessary to get a $50 gift card rises over time, I decided to start cashing the points in for cards. I wanted to redeem the points before the next increase occurred. I continue to use that alternate ID when I make purchases at that gas station. I know that those rewards don't belong to me, so I just keep those cards stashed away. Perhaps someday I will be contacted about them...